TWENTY-FIRST CENTURY INTELLIGENCE

Edited by Wesley K. Wark

Hazel,

Merry Christmas

From

Cathy & your GCHQ
colleagues.

With our appreciation.

Routledge
Taylor & Francis Group

LONDON AND NEW YORK

Christmas 2009

First published 2005 by Routledge
2 Park Square, Milton Park, Abingdon, Oxon, OX14 4RN

Simultaneously published in the USA and Canada
by Routledge
270 Madison Ave, New York NY 10016

Routledge is an imprint of the Taylor & Francis Group

Transferred to Digital Printing 2008

Typeset by Elite Typesetting Techniques Ltd,
Eastleigh, Hampshire, UK

British Library Cataloguing in Publication Data
A catalog record for this book is available from the British Library

Library of Congress Cataloging in Publication Data
A catalog record for this book has been requested

ISBN10: 0-415-46380-7 (pbk)
ISBN10: 0-415-34970-2 (hbk)

ISBN13: 978-0-415-46380-5 (pbk)
ISBN13: 978-0-415-34970-3 (hbk)

Publisher's Note
The publisher has gone to great lengths to ensure the quality of
this reprint but points out that some imperfections in the
original may be apparent

CONTENTS

STUDIES IN INTELLIGENCE SERIES

General Editors: Richard J. Aldrich and Christopher Andrew

This book collects the thinking of some of the foremost experts on the future of intelligence in this new century.

ISSN: 1368-9916

Introduction:
'Learning to Live With Intelligence'

WESLEY K. WARK

The key strategic and cultural issue of the Cold War was, as Stanley
Kubrick suggested so deliciously, 'learning to live with ("love") the
bomb'.[1] Everyone, from Pentagon planners, to spy fiction novelists, came
up with fictional cures for the atomic dilemma, ranging from MAD
(Mutual Assured Destruction) to James Bond. Fear of the bomb remains
with us, although the nightmare scenarios are under revision. It is no longer
nutters of the General Ripper variety, Frankenstein villains such as Ian
Fleming's Dr NO, or the dread possibility of accidental or uncontrollable
nuclear war between the superpowers, that preoccupies us. Since
September 11, 2001, it is the twin threats of the proliferation of weapons of
mass destruction, and the spectacle of future attempts at 'superterrorism' by
Al Qaeda and other terrorist organizations of similar, unbounded
malevolence.[2]

The events of September 11, 2001 are too recent and raw to have
allowed for the generation of fictional cures, or even of fully-fledged
strategic doctrines. But one thing seems clear. Learning to live with an
open-ended 'war on terrorism' will mean learning to live with intelligence.
We do not have a Stanley Kubrick to limn the possibilities, or tickle the dark
side, but between these pages readers will find some of the best expert
commentary on the future of intelligence.

Learning to live with intelligence means, among other things, grasping
the role that technology has played and will continue to play in shaping
intelligence practices and capabilities. Technology was a key driver in the
intelligence revolution of the twentieth century. Its most obvious impact has
been on the methods used to collect intelligence. Fundamental changes in
communications, especially the advent of radio prior to World War I,
opened up the possibility of 'real-time' intelligence.[3] The discipline of
Sigint (signals intelligence) was born and flourished during World War I and
remained the sometimes elusive jewel of intelligence for the remainder of
the century. The Wright brothers' experiments in the sand dunes of Kitty
Hawk, North Carolina eventually launched espionage into the air and gave
intelligence collection an entirely new domain – eyes in the sky. Imint

(imagery intelligence) developed historically in parallel with Sigint as a premier collection methodology.

But intelligence collection was not alone in being affected by the impact of technology. The classic intelligence cycle model identifies three essential stages in the production of finished intelligence – collection, assessment and dissemination. During World War II, experiments were undertaken with the presentation of intelligence to decision-makers, beginning with specialised maps and graphical charts for use in the 'war rooms' built for British and US leaders. This activity would spawn an on-going effort in the decades to come to fix the attention of leaders on intelligence's message through improvements to the style, visual impact, speed of delivery, and compression of reporting. In this domain, technology was an essential assist to the allure and blight of intelligence, its tight security wrapping.

The dimension of the classic intelligence cycle that was slowest to be affected by technological change was assessment. Although the concept of the interdisciplinary evaluation of raw intelligence and the use of collective expertise to provide for intelligence judgements was first articulated with the creation of the British Joint Intelligence Committee in 1936, it was not until the widespread use of desktop computers beginning in the 1980s that the analytical function of intelligence was fundamentally affected.

The computer revolution, followed by the Internet revolution, changed the ways in which intelligence data could be stored and retrieved, and altered the nature of interactions between individual analysts and analytical groups within intelligence agencies. The Internet revolution, in particular, opened up the prospect of 'open source' (unclassified, publicly accessible) intelligence as a vital tool. Fast access to a global stockpile of knowledge, assisted by increasingly sophisticated search engines, has transformed the nature of intelligence assessment and fundamentally altered its traditional reliance on secrets. The 'open source' revolution has also led to a previously unthinkable privatisation of assessment, with a plethora of private sector companies offering expertise in global risk analysis, often for a hefty fee.

Technology, as it affects the domain of intelligence as much as elsewhere, can, of course, be a double-edged weapon. Technological advances bring with them sometimes hidden costs and dangers; they can also generate inappropriate expectations. A parlour game among literary friends on a dark and stormy night in Switzerland led Mary Shelley to pen the classic tale, *Frankenstein, or the Modern Prometheus*.[4] It is always needful to be on the lookout for the Frankensteinian impulse and the monstrous birth in the application of technology to intelligence. But talk of

Frankenstein might seem fanciful in the context of technology's seeming role as a beneficent deliverer of solutions to knowledge problems. Technology has delivered 'real time intelligence', a historical breakthrough; it has vastly broadened the conceptual lens through which information is collected and assessed; it has facilitated the processing and delivery of knowledge to decision-makers. Where be monsters?

They lie in wait in various corners of our experience and imagination. One is that technology's contemporary bounty has come to threaten the integrity and quality of the intelligence process itself. For much of its modern existence, intelligence services trafficked in scarcity. Secrets were hard to acquire; truly valuable secrets were a rare commodity. Certainly there were historic periods during which technology helped unleash a flood of intelligence. The most notable example was during the glory days of Ultra in 1943 and 1944, when Allied Sigint played a vital role in military victory on multiple fronts, on land in Normandy, at sea in the culmination of the vicious Battle of the Atlantic, and in the air in the prosecution of the bomber offensive and the blunting of Hitler's secret weapons offensives.[5]

But at some undefined point during the Cold War, the technological tide turned, once and for all, and the normal conditions of intelligence scarcity were replaced by the opposite problem of an increasing surfeit of intelligence, often generated through high-tech collection systems.

'Information overload' is now a common problem for all major intelligence systems. What Roberta Wohlstetter observed as a central problem explaining intelligence failure at Pearl Harbor in 1941, namely the difficulty of distinguishing true 'signals' from the ambient 'noise' in which they are embedded, now truly defines the twenty-first century intelligence challenge.[6]

What has changed since Pearl Harbor is the sheer volume of both signals and noise. As the mass of raw intelligence grows, it spawns worrisome problems for intelligence warning, analytical failures, and politicisation and manipulation of data and assessments by decision-makers. If 'cherry picking' has to be the norm inside intelligence communities, because of informational plenty, what resistance can there be to cherry picking of the intelligence product by political decision-makers intent on confirming pre-conceptions and finding support for policies determined on grounds other than that of intelligence judgements?

A second dilemma created by the stunning advances in technological intelligence collection has been its tendency to distort and channel the overall intelligence effort. The advent of Sigint and Imint, and their increasing sophistication, introduced an inevitable, if not necessarily examined, hierarchy of intelligence products, with the high-tech and most expensive systems valued at a premium and more 'old fashioned' methods of intelligence collection discounted. There remains good reason to value the Sigint product and the imagery that modern satellite, spy plane and drone systems can produce. The future of these systems may well be impressive. But to the extent that their allure has led to a devaluing of traditional agent reporting, or even a failure to fully appreciate the value of open source material, then intelligence communities have lost their balance.

The events of September 11 and the war on terrorism have led to much public speculation about the decline of operational capabilities in the field of agent penetration and reporting and a call for the re-invention of a key intelligence collection discipline, human intelligence or Humint. Humint is, by nature low-tech; its tools are human beings and their capacities. Humint lacks the 'real time' potentiality of other collection methods; its product frequently lacks the apparent clarity of information drawn through the technological spectrum. Yet it is an indisputable part of the intelligence function and there may be many future questions, especially in the realm of counter-terrorism operations, which cannot be answered without a highly capable system for agent reporting.

In this regard, technology's strengths have reminded us of technology's weaknesses. There are secrets into which the aerial spy, the sensor, or the technological listener cannot fully penetrate.

Technology has also profoundly shaped intelligence power.[7] The cost and sophistication required to sustain technological advances in intelligence collection have led to a great concentration of intelligence power, which became manifest in the second half of the twentieth century. At the beginning of the modern intelligence revolution, just before 1914, intelligence capabilities were the preserve of a handful of European Great Powers. Thereafter, the idea of intelligence as a tool of statecraft was slowly exported until the practice became globalised and more or less universal, at least in the form of domestic security agencies. Paradoxically, the globalisation of intelligence did not create the conditions for the diffusion of intelligence power, but rather the reverse.

This was thanks to a growing technology gap between have and have-not states. Those that could afford some or all of the high-tech intelligence systems were the haves; those that could not, were the have-nots. In contemporary terms, the technology gap, combined with post-Cold War geopolitical realities, has created an unprecedented situation in which a single nation state, the United States, has emerged as an intelligence super, or hyper, power. The rest of the world struggles to avoid relegation to the status of intelligence have-not.

There may be an 'imperial' condition to deal with in the emergence of such a terrific concentration of intelligence power. Imperial intelligence, if that is what the United States suffers, or may suffer from in future, is a condition in which arrogance and insularity of judgement can easily flourish. The informal checks and balances built into traditional intelligence alliances, in which participating states had the capacity to challenge the intelligence judgements of an ally, could easily be lost in a new imperial system.

Equally, the shared sense of political objectives and the shared vision of threats that can be an outcome of intelligence alliances, the by-product of the intimate sharing of secrets and the reliance on burden-sharing in the global accumulation of intelligence, could be at risk. The most remarkable of all intelligence alliances is that which links the Anglo-Saxon powers, the United States, Britain, Canada, Australia and New Zealand. This alliance was first fashioned during World War II and was sustained throughout the Cold War and post-Cold War eras. It has reason to be concerned about its future. A certain imbalance of power always existed within this secret alliance, at least since 1945; now the imbalance is huge, casting the various rationales for the alliance into doubt.

The high cost of true intelligence power, especially imposed by technological collection systems, has also had the effect of forcing choices and distorting the intelligence capabilities of many states below the first-rank powers. Canada is a prime example of a state with global interests and a need for wide-ranging intelligence that felt compelled, because of limited resource allocations, to make historic choices about its intelligence capacities. These choices have proved hard and deterministic. At the onset of the Cold War period, the Canadian authorities decided to put their technological eggs in one basket, by creating a Sigint agency to function within an alliance setting.[8]

This decision, in turn, shaped both future resource allocation (heavily favouring collection at the expense of assessment and other intelligence functions) and the fundamental structure of the overall Canadian system. Struggling to create a functioning Sigint capacity, and favouring it, the Canadian authorities decided to eschew the creation of any foreign intelligence service along CIA or SIS lines.

A fourth technological 'monster', lurking alongside those of information overload, structural distortions within intelligence systems, and the imposition of concentrated power, is the shapeless phantom of expectation. Technological systems seem to hold out the promise of the perfectibility of intelligence. Multi-spectral intelligence delivered in real-time offers a vision of the transparency not just of the 'battlespace', but ultimately of conflicts and threats in general. Much of this thinking has been driven by speculation regarding the so-called 'revolution in military affairs' (RMA) and the impact that new sensor systems, new 'smart' weapons, and new methods of command and control will have on the future of war.

Several commentators in this collection reflect on the expectations delivered by RMA futurists. Perhaps no-one is closer to the mark than Nick Cullather, who is scathing about the 'infantilism' of many of these technological visions of the future of war.[9] The pursuit of 'perfect' intelligence is just another manifestation, though no less dangerous, of the general faith in technological progress to solve the world's problems. In the specific case of intelligence, technology is seen as a powerful tool to overcome secrets and penetrate what is hidden. In reality, technology is of strictly finite utility in tackling the classic intelligence dilemma of the complexity and unpredictability of events.

Indeed, technology has contributed to the problem by increasing the scope of complexity and helping fuel unpredictability. To create a powerful, technologically-driven intelligence system in the hope of solving complexity and resolving unpredictability has a Frankensteinian edge. The solutions, partial ones, lie elsewhere. They are to be found, especially, in the quality of intelligence assessment, which calls on very human capacities for local knowledge, wise judgement, imagination, intuition, and the courage of conviction.

In thinking about the future of intelligence, all the evidence before our eyes suggests that technology will continue to be a driver of change. In this case, predicting future developments as a form of continuity with the past seems a safe bet. The prediction also means that technological change will continue to be a double-edged weapon, with some Frankensteinian possibilities. The detailed ways in which new technological systems will contribute to the power of intelligence collection is beyond our capacity to imagine. But intelligence perfectibility will be forever elusive. The power of technologically driven change to corrupt systems and practices will remain.

Learning to live with intelligence means more than just grappling with the genie of technology. It also means learning to live with 'Orwell', more precisely with the infiltration of a nightmare vision of the national security state into popular consciousness.[10] George Orwell's dystopian novel, *Nineteen Eighty-Four* is rightly celebrated for warning us about many things, including the dangers of a debased collective mentality, the tenuousness of our grasp on history and private memory, the shaping influence of propaganda, the appetite for power for its own sake, the threat of a world plunged into eternal conflict between warring blocs. But the warning that Orwell, perhaps unintentionally, planted most deeply in the popular imagination, was a warning about the powers of state surveillance. 'Orwellian' conveys above all a picture of telescreens, thought police, the Ministry of Truth, and the 'really frightening one,' the Ministry of Love. 'BIG BROTHER', Orwell, eternally reminds us, 'IS WATCHING YOU.'[11]

Orwell, writing in 1949, fixed a fear in our minds about what intelligence could become.

It is both a salutary fear and an exaggerated one. Salutary to the extent that Orwell reminds us of the potential abuses that a too-powerful intelligence system could inflict on civil society – abuses against truth and against civil liberties. But the Orwellian vision is exaggerated (as it must be to fulfill the demands of dystopian creation) in that few intelligence services have ever come appreciably close to possessing the capabilities of Orwell's Oceania troopers (perhaps the East German Stasi was a partial exception). More importantly the Orwellian vision lent itself to misunderstanding. It was not the Thought Police and the apparatus of surveillance that created the totalitarian political system of *Nineteen Eighty-Four*. Rather the system created the surveillance.

This is an important but little understood lesson about the place of intelligence in society. Intelligence services need their potential power held in check by cultural mores, traditions, laws, and systems of accountability and review. Yet intelligence services have to be seen as products of the society in which they function, not as exotic 'rogues'. Learning to live with Orwell means appreciating the Orwellian warning for what it is, essentially a dark signal about what can go wrong when a society loses its hold on history and memory and falls into the hands of a doctrine of absolute power for its own sake.

Learning to live with Orwell means having a healthy fear of the abuse of power, but not succumbing to an automatic distrust, or any kind of fearful caricature, of the role of intelligence services in the state. Learning to live with Orwell, means the need for citizens to recognize intelligence as a critical component of international statecraft and an important foundation of the night watchman state.

Orwell's *Nineteen Eighty-Four* was not, of course, an argument for the Thought Police. But neither was it an argument against intelligence services. Orwell himself recognized the need for vigilance against fanaticism and enemies of the state.[12] He had seen such things at work firsthand during the Spanish Civil War, and feared their coming to Britain under fire during World War II, and under pressure during the Cold War.[13] But thanks in part to the penetration of an Orwellian vision, as well as to other popular culture manifestations, we have inherited an automatic distrust of the intelligence function. The future of intelligence depends in part on 'Orwell' loosening his grip on our imagination.

The diminution of 'Orwell', a codeword for the fear of intelligence, will be a necessary condition for the success of a revolutionary change now unfolding in the practice of intelligence. Looking back, the twentieth century may be seen as the age of 'secret intelligence.' This age was born at the intersection of two needs – the need to uncover, in a rapidly destabilising Europe prior to 1914, the secret military plans, equipment and deployments of the enemy; and the need to protect one's own military secrets from discovery by foreigners.

Intelligence practice, for most of the remainder of the twentieth century was focused on penetrating secrets and protecting secrets. There were, to be sure, some conscious and famous lapses, such as the public use of British Sigint decrypts to denounce Bolshevik perfidy on several occasions in the 1920s, and the presentation to the United Nations of classified U-2 photographs revealing the Soviet deployment of long-range ballistic missiles to Cuba in October 1962. But for the most part, secrecy ruled.

The twenty-first century may prove, by contrast, the age of 'public intelligence'. Events and doctrine both give weight to this possibility.[14] In the aftermath of the terrorist attacks of September 11, governments in Britain and the United States in particular, have felt compelled to make public their intelligence in support of decisions on war and peace. The trend began with the release of a British government dossier linking Al Qaeda and its bases in Afghanistan to the September 11 assault. The trend accelerated in the Fall and Winter of 2002/3 as the governments of Tony Blair and George Bush prepared themselves for a controversial war on Iraq. In September 2002, the British government led the way by releasing a Joint Intelligence Committee assessment of the threat posed by Iraq's weapons of mass destruction programmes. The document carried a preface by the British Prime Minister that stated:

'It is unprecedented for the government to publish this kind of document. But in the light of the debate about Iraq and Weapons of Mass Destruction, I want to share with the British public the reasons why I believe this issue to be a current and serious threat to the UK national interest.'[15]

The UK Parliamentary Intelligence and Security Committee, drawn from all parties, approved the concept of the release of the dossier. Its annual report for 2002–3 noted 'The Committee supports the responsible use of intelligence and material collected by the Agencies to inform the public on matters such as these.'[16] The Parliamentary committee did not alter its judgement about the principle of releasing intelligence into the public domain, even after finding some fault with the contents of the dossier itself.

These British straws in the wind were matched by public statements based on US intelligence. In October 2002, the US government released a declassified version of the CIA's National Intelligence Estimate (NIE) on Iraq's weapons of mass destruction (WMD). This estimate had been drawn up at the express request of the Senate Select Committee on Intelligence, suggesting an uneasy alliance of motives between the Congressional and Executive branches of government. The US NIE was later supplemented by the televised presentation made to the UN Security Council by Secretary of State Colin Powell in February 2003, surely the most dramatic public use of intelligence for the purposes of swaying domestic and global public opinion since the Cuban Missile Crisis, over 40 years earlier.

Underpinning at least the American use of 'public intelligence' in the run-up to the war against Iraq was a newly declared, and radical, statement of US strategy. In September 2002, the Bush White House released a document called the National Security Strategy.[17] Previous iterations of this strategy paper had been pro-forma exercises to meet an executive branch reporting requirement. The September 2002 document was something different. Its most controversial feature was its advocacy of a doctrine of pre-emption, designed to legitimate the exercise of military force against emerging threats to US security. It was billed as the proactive answer to September 11, in a new environment in which a fusion might occur between the new age's worst nightmares – terrorism, rogue states, and the proliferation of weapons of mass destruction.[18]

One feature that went generally unnoticed in commentary about the National Security Strategy was the onus placed on intelligence, and indeed on public intelligence. The document laid down three conditions for successful pre-emption, all of which had implications for the future performance of intelligence. The conditions included:

1. the requirement for good intelligence on, and early warning of, emerging threats

2. the need to build international coalitions on the basis of a shared conviction about emerging threats

3. the capacity to win pre-emptive wars quickly and with minimal casualties to friendly forces or civilian populations.

Cumulatively, these three conditions place an extremely heavy burden on intelligence, suggesting a degree of expectation about intelligence capabilities never before levied. The National Security Strategy paper concluded its discussion with a statement that when the pre-emption option is exercised, 'the reasons for our actions will be clear, the force measured, and the cause just'.[19]

Providing clarity, and proclaiming a just war, inescapably require the use of intelligence in the public domain. So, in a different way, does international coalition-building, especially when the intended partners and the arena for such activities exist outside the framework of traditional intelligence alliances, with their established circuitry for the passage of secret intelligence.

The Iraq War was the first test case for the strategy of pre-emption. Its long term outcome, impossible to foretell, and the growing evidence of badly flawed trans-Atlantic intelligence assessment about Iraq's WMD, may yet call the strategy into question. But at the time of writing there is no sign that the current US administration of George W. Bush intends to abandon it. Quite the contrary. Amid a worsening security situation in post-war Iraq, President Bush delivered a speech on 16 October 2003, in San Bernadino, California, on his way to an Asian summit. In that speech, Bush reiterated American determination to pursue a strategy of pre-emption, when circumstance demanded. The challenge for America, as Bush put it, was to 'show our motives are pure'. A display of 'pure motives' requires, of course, public intelligence.

If an age of public intelligence is upon us, it will demand a revolutionary change in the practice of intelligence and in the doctrine of secrecy. New attention will have to be paid to devising intelligence assessments designed for public consumption, as opposed to products shaped for intelligence's traditional government 'consumers'. While such forms of intelligence assessment are devised, great care will have to be given to protecting the role that intelligence traditionally plays in informing government decision-making on national and international security issues. Great care will also be required in protecting intelligence sources and methods – the lifeblood of intelligence work. New restraints will have to be devised to ensure that the intelligence product does not become completely politicised in its transit to the public audience, both domestic and foreign. As US scholar John Prados put it, 'what is there to prevent public intelligence from becoming public relations?'[20]

Integrity of intelligence reporting will be a huge issue. The quality and persuasiveness of intelligence judgements will face an enormous test, in the open and fractious marketplace of public debate. To persuade its new, and much more diverse audience, intelligence assessments will have to be very good indeed.

Finally, there will be a reciprocal onus on public consumers of intelligence to understand the nature of the intelligence product, both its strengths and its limitations.

If public intelligence is the radical future, its emergence will build on the technological enhancement and delivery of intelligence. Public intelligence requires display, precisely of the sort delivered by Colin Powell's address to the Security Council in February 2003, with its Sigint soundtrack, and its satellite imagery. Public intelligence is unthinkable without the technological infrastructure that supports a global media and global Internet.

Public intelligence has emerged in the context of an unprecedented and open-ended war on terrorism, with its attendant doctrine of pre-emption. Perhaps the political and strategic conditions that have given rise to it will disappear, and intelligence will return to the relative safety of its traditional doctrine of secrecy and its traditional role as a discrete provider of special information to government decision-makers. Such a reversal seems unlikely. More pertinent may be the issue of whether public intelligence will be restricted to the hopefully rare case of pre-emptive war, or whether it might, with time, become the norm.

Whether rare, or the norm, public intelligence will require a new public outlook on intelligence, one beyond, as suggested above, the habit of 'Orwell'. To achieve this, the future of intelligence requires a discovery of the past. For much of the twentieth century, intelligence had no usable past. Its failures were sometimes visible, but its general operations and practices were not. The evolution of intelligence 'power' remained obscure. A substantial literature on intelligence did not begin to emerge until the last quarter of the twentieth century. Writing on intelligence began from a relatively narrow base. It was sparked in the beginning by a historical fascination with newly released documentation on the impact of signals intelligence during World War II, the famous story of Ultra, and contemporary concerns about intelligence abuses, particularly in the conduct of covert operations.[21]

Since the mid-1970s, the literature on intelligence has grown exponentially and moved well beyond its original interests. Intelligence now has at least the outlines of a usable past, with a library of case studies, national histories, and synoptic studies waiting the reader. Two pioneering essay collections, both published 20 years ago, in 1984, helped point the way forward.

Christopher Andrew and David Dilks reminded us that intelligence was the 'missing dimension' in our understanding of critical policy-making decisions in the realm of international relations. The concept of the 'missing dimension' was both a rallying cry for new research and writing and a manifesto suggesting the overlooked significance of the intelligence process and input.[22]

Ernest May, in the same year, called our attention to two realities. In the opening essay of *Knowing One's Enemies*, May explored the decision-making process of three European great powers in the crisis-filled years before 1914. His examination of how these states used their nascent intelligence capabilities suggested the significance both of political structures and of the phenomenon of bureaucratic feuding and competition.[23]

The message of both books was simple, but needful. Intelligence was important, pace Andrew and Dilks; intelligence practices were idiosyncratic and rooted in national political structures and cultural norms, pace May. The future of intelligence may well depend on a true digesting of such messages.

But intelligence's usable past remains under-exploited and unrealized, thanks to two phenomena.

One is the contrary motion of popular culture representation, which disinclines us from taking intelligence seriously, with its polarities of conspiracy theories and civilisation-saving, heroic adventure.[24]

The other is the curious unwillingness to learn lessons from history. Learning lessons from history is a different exercise from the practice of post-mortems, and after-action reports, which have been a part of the landscape since the British government set out to learn what went wrong during the South African War (1899–1902) and discovered that a good part of the difficulty resulted from poor intelligence.[25] In such studies, the focus is on the short term and on the case in hand. The business of learning lessons from history has to take a longer view, and look for the deeper patterns, not least in the mentality of intelligence practice, its unexamined inner 'culture'.[26]

There are various possible explanation for this failure of learning, ranging from the notion that the pace of change in intelligence has been so rapid, that historical lessons have no purchase, to the lack of interest on the part of intelligence communities themselves, steeped as they are in present concerns, to the failure of the literature itself to offer usable lessons, beyond the bleak one that intelligence failures are inevitable.[27] None of these explanations is fully plausible.

The failure to draw on a usable past may simply be a product of the lack of any sense of urgency about connecting intelligence's past to intelligence's future. But the elements of the future of intelligence suggested in this essay, whether in the realm of technological change, the adjustment of cultural vision, or the redrawing of a definition of the purpose of intelligence, cannot be appreciated without a sense of the past. That sense of the past must call attention both to things that must be overcome, and aspects of established intelligence practice that must be preserved or acknowledged as essential elements of continuity.

The essays to follow all hold visions of the future of intelligence that are disciplined by expert knowledge of intelligence's past. All prediction about the future of intelligence is, in this sense, a prediction about what mattered in the recent and more distant past. Certainly prediction, even through a historical rear-view mirror, is not easy. The history of this collection is proof of this. Many of the essays contained here were first envisaged as contributions to a conference organized by the Canadian Association for Security and Intelligence Studies on the theme of 'The Future of Intelligence'. The conference was held in Ottawa in the Fall of 2000. None of us predicted the near-term future of September 11. All of the essay writers returned to their subjects afresh in the aftermath of September 11. Still, it is hard to keep up with the future. Yet unless students and practitioners of intelligence can find a way to link past and future, we risk the fate of John Hollander's fictional agent, 'Cupcake'. Hollander's 'poetical, ineffective, meditative spy' ultimately found no way to live with intelligence.[28] His last message before going off the air conveys a paralysing fear of unintelligibility:

This transmission sent out on all frequencies,
Encoded uncommonly; the superflux
Here is no dross, though, and I have sat watching
Key numbers in their serial dance growing
Further apart, outdistancing their touching,
Outstretched arms.[29]

NOTES

1. 'Dr. Strangelove or: How I Learned to Stop Worrying and Love the Bomb,' dir. Stanley Kubrick. Columbia Pictures, 1963.
2. Useful reflections on the new reality of superterrorism include Lawrence Freedman (ed.), *Superterrorism: Policy Responses* (Oxford: Blackwell Publishing 2002) and Walter Laqueur, *No End to War: Terrorism in the Twenty-First Century* (New York: Continuum 2003).
3. A point well made by Sir John Keegan in his *Intelligence in War: Knowledge of the Enemy from Napoleon to Al Qaeda* (Toronto: Key Porter Books 2003), Chapter 1.
4. Mary Shelley, *Frankenstein, or the Modern Prometheus* (Oxford UP/Oxford World's Classics, 1998 edition), introduction by M.K. Joseph. The novel was first published in 1817.
5. The best general survey of Sigint in World War II is, in my view, Stephen Budiansky's *Battle of Wits: The Complete Story of Codebreaking in World War II* (NY: The Free Press 2000). F.H. Hinsley's multi-volume official history, *British Intelligence in the Second World War* (London: HMSO 1979–90) remains indispensable for a full understanding of the development and application of Sigint.
6. Roberta Wohlstetter, *Pearl Harbor: Warning and Decision* (Stanford UP 1962). Wohlstetter's remarkable book remains the classic study.
7. For a broad ranging study, see Michael Herman's magisterial *Intelligence Power in Peace and War* (Cambridge: CUP/Royal Inst. for International Affairs 1996).
8. The Canadian Sigint agency was formally established in 1946, based on the remnants of its wartime efforts. It was first named the Communications Branch of the National Research Council (CBNRC). Following a media exposé, the name was changed to Communications Security Establishment (CSE) and it was transferred to the administrative control of the Department of National Defence. There is no full study of Canadian Sigint, but see the useful survey by Martin Rudner, 'Canada's Communication Security Establishment from Cold War to Globalisation', *Intelligence and National Security* 16/1 (Spring 2001) pp.97–128. For the early history of Canadian Sigint, see Wesley K. Wark, 'Cryptographic Innocence: The Origins of Signals Intelligence in Canada in the Second World War', *Journal of Contemporary History* 22/4 (Oct. 1987), pp.639–65.
9. See Nick Cullather, 'Bombing at the Speed of Thought: Intelligence in the Coming Age of Cyber War', in this collection.
10. There is much interesting work on the elevation of George Orwell to the status of prophet. See, in particular, John Rodden, *The Politics of Literary Reputation: The Making and Claiming of 'St. George' Orwell* (NY: OUP 1989).

11. George Orwell, *Nineteen Eighty-Four* [1949] (Penguin paperback edition, 1990) p.1.
12. In 1949, Orwell provided a list of 'crypto-communists' to the Foreign Office's Information Research Department. See Timothy Garton Ash, 'Orwell's List', *New York Review of Books* 50/14, 25 Sept. 2003, pp. 6–12. The original of Orwell's controversial list has now been released as FO 1110/189 in the British National Archives.
13. Recent work on Orwell includes a jaunty polemic by Christopher Hitchens, *Why Orwell Matters* (NY: Basic Books 2002) and two new biographies, Gordon Bowker, *George Orwell* (Boston: Little Brown 2003) and D.J. Taylor, *Orwell: The Life* (NY: Henry Holt 2003)
14. Greg Treverton has tentatively raised the prospect of intelligence serving a wider audience. See Gregory F. Treverton, *Reshaping National Intelligence for an Age of Information* (Cambridge: CUP/RAND 2001). For example, Treverton writes, on p.15 'Should intelligence primarily support military planning and operations? Or should it also serve the entire U.S. government – and, perhaps, the broader American society as well ...?' My remarks push the argument further.
15. 'Iraq's Weapons of Mass Destruction: The Assessment of the British Government', 24 Sept. 2002, available online at <www.pm.gov.uk>.
16. Cm 5837, quoted in Cm 5972, Intelligence and Security Committee, 'Iraqi Weapons of Mass Destruction – Intelligence and Assessments', Sept. 2003, p.4. Available online at <www.cabinet-office.gov.uk/reports/isc>.
17. Available online at the White House website, <www.whitehouse.gov>.
18. For one assessment see John Lewis Gaddis, 'A Global Strategy of Transformation', *Foreign Policy*, Nov./Dec. 2002. The article is available online at <www.foreignpolicy.com/ issue_novdec_2002/gaddis.html>.
19. National Security Strategy, Chapter V, 'Preventing Our Enemies from Threatening Us, Our Allies, and Our Friends with Weapons of Mass Destruction', quote at p.16.
20. Remarks by John Prados during a session of the annual conference of the Canadian Association for Security and Intelligence Studies, Vancouver, British Columbia, 17 Oct. 2003.
21. Critical to the development of the literature on intelligence was the publication of the British official history of intelligence in World War II, written by a team of historians headed by the Cambridge don and Bletchley Park veteran, F.H. Hinsley. The more contemporary orientation of intelligence studies was sparked by the investigations and published reports of the US Congressional committees, especially the Frank Church committee, in the mid-1970s.
22. Christopher Andrew and David Dilks (eds.), *The Missing Dimension: Governments and Intelligence Communities in the Twentieth Century* (London: Macmillan 1984)
23. Ernest R. May (ed.), *Knowing One's Enemies: Intelligence Assessment before the Two World Wars* (Princeton UP 1984).
24. For some reflection on these polarities, see the introduction by Wesley K. Wark in idem (ed.), *Spy Fiction, Spy Films and Real Intelligence* (London: Frank Cass 1991).
25. For this story, see Thomas G. Fergusson, *British Military Intelligence 1870–1914: The Development of a Modern Intelligence Organization* (London: Arms & Armour Press 1984).
26. For a fine study of how historical lessons can influence thinking on foreign policy, see Ernest R. May, *'Lessons' of the Past: The Use and Misuse of History in American Foreign Policy* (London: OUP 1975).
27. The most powerful statement on the inevitability of intelligence failure is to be found in Richard Betts, 'Analysis, War and Decision-Making: Why Intelligence Failures are Inevitable', *World Politics* 31 (1978) pp.61–89. Betts reformulated his argument to focus on the events of Sept. 11, 2001, in an essay entitled 'Intelligence Test: The Limits of Prevention', in James F. Hoge and Gideon Rose (eds.), *How Did This Happen: Terrorism and the New War* (NY: Public Affairs/Council on Foreign Relations 2001), pp.145–61.
28. The description of 'Cupcake' is from a letter by Hollander to Noel Annan, undated, in my possession.
29. John Hollander, *Reflections on Espionage* (NY: Atheneum 1976), p.71. Hollander's long poem is a unique and wonderful reflection on intelligence, stimulated by the reading of Sir John Masterman's 1972 book on World War II deception operations, *The Double Cross System*. For an interview that I conducted with Hollander about his poem, see the special issue of *Queen's Quarterly*, 'The Future of Espionage' (Summer 1993) pp.351–4.

Intelligence for the Twenty-First Century

ALAN DUPONT

Strategic discourse over the past decade has been dominated by a debate over the nature of future warfare and whether or not there is a 'revolution in military affairs' (RMA). Supporters contend that developments in military technology, especially precision guidance and high-speed data processing, in conjunction with advances in doctrine and strategy, will fundamentally transform the way in which future wars will be fought and privilege RMA-capable forces in the contest to achieve battlefield dominance.[1] Sceptics, on the other hand, regard the RMA as being more evolutionary than revolutionary, and argue that many of the technical advances associated with the RMA do not necessarily presage a paradigm shift in warfare.[2] However, all agree that timely, accurate and useable intelligence will be critical to the successful conduct of war in the twenty-first century, perhaps more so than in any previous era.

It is surprising, therefore, how little academic attention has been devoted to the changes that are taking place in the technology, management and integration of the intelligence systems that will underpin any RMA. It is the contention of this article that the transformation of intelligence architectures, particularly in the West, is no less profound than that of the weapons, platforms and warfighting systems they are designed to support and enhance. Moreover, the cumulative weight of the changes in prospect will redefine the way in which intelligence is used and conceived. The old demarcation lines between strategic and operational intelligence and between operations and intelligence, once starkly differentiated, will become more amorphous and blurred. Decision-makers will have better access to intelligence as a result of advances in electronic 'pull' technology which have made possible intelligence on demand. Open source intelligence (Osint), while unlikely to supplant traditional intelligence gathering, will enrich and add value to national intelligence databases. There is, however, a downside. Information overload, already a serious problem for intelligence analysts and managers, threatens to diminish the gains from technical improvements in intelligence collection and dissemination. Contemporary manifestations of long-standing policy and doctrinal issues may further erode the promise of an intelligence-driven 'knowledge edge' for those states and military forces able to harness the new intelligence technologies.

In order to articulate and cast light on some of these important trends, this essay focuses on recent and anticipated developments in US intelligence and draws out some of the lessons from the September 11, 2001 terrorist attacks on the World Trade Center and the Pentagon. There are two main reasons for drawing on the US experience and vision.

First, the US is at the cutting edge of modern intelligence technology and management. The emerging national intelligence architecture will be the exemplar for the next generation of intelligence systems operated by the US, as well as its allies and coalition partners.

Second, the ongoing debate in the US over the capabilities, role and management of intelligence has significant ramifications for other nations, both friend and foe alike. Not only is the US the pre-eminent state in the contemporary international system, it also sits at the centre of a web of bilateral and multilateral intelligence relationships that span the globe.

Definitions of intelligence abound, all too often obfuscating rather than clarifying.[3] A useful starting point is to define what intelligence is not. It is not merely information or data. Intelligence is information or data which has been processed, evaluated and distilled into a form which fulfils some useful purpose, either to inform policy or, in the case of military conflict, to support operations. For the purposes of this analysis the intelligence process or cycle will be disaggregated into five elements – intelligence collection, assessment, dissemination, use and management.[4]

COLLECTION – EYES AND EARS IN THE SKY

Intelligence collection is increasingly the function of automated systems mounted on dedicated and multi-purpose platforms which include a variety of ground-based facilities, as well as ships, aircraft and submarines. When US and coalition forces deployed to Afghanistan in search of Osama bin Laden at the end of 2001, they were supported by an impressive array of airborne intelligence collection platforms. They included the E-3 Airborne Warning and Control System (AWACS); upgraded U-2 surveillance aircraft; RC-135 Rivet Joint Sigint aircraft; E-8C Joint-STARS radar surveillance aircraft; Navy EP-3E Aries Sigint aircraft and Navy EA-6B Prowler aircraft. But the US also positioned nearly 50 satellites to support Operation 'Enduring Freedom', many of them specifically designed for intelligence gathering, illustrating how critical satellites have become to the collection and dissemination of intelligence.[5] Their unique vantage point in the sky makes satellites particularly well-suited to gathering intelligence in a world ever more reliant on global information networks, smart machines and man-made nuclear, biological and chemical processes all of which display tell-tale signatures that are capable of being recorded or 'imaged' from space.

To understand the role that satellites will play in future intelligence collection, it is instructive to look at a representative sample of the satellites currently employed by the US which continues to lead the world in space-based intelligence systems.[6] The US deploys four broad categories of intelligence satellites.

First, there are satellites equipped to produce imagery from visible light photographs, radar or reflected infrared emissions. An example of the former is the highly successful KH-11 series of imagery or Imint satellites first launched in 1976 which combine a wide-area, high-resolution photographic capability with real-time transmission of the images produced. The resolution of the cameras in the KH-11 and the follow-on Advanced KH-11/*Ikon* is so good that intelligence analysts are reputedly able to see, although not read, the licence plates of cars from an altitude of 100 miles.[7] *Lacrosse* satellites use synthetic aperture radars to produce images in all weather conditions.[8] Unlike satellites which rely on visible light for their images, radar satellites can see through cloud and at night, but their resolution is generally not as good.

A second constellation of early warning satellites is designed to detect ballistic missile launches. They include the Defense Support Program (DSP) satellites and the replacement Space-Based Infra-red System (SBIRS), which will greatly enhance US ability to detect and intercept ballistic missiles while adding technical intelligence collection and battle space characterisation to the DSP satellite's early warning function.[9] SBIRS High, consisting of four satellites in geosynchronous earth orbit and two sensors in elliptical high Earth orbit is designed to give early warning of ballistic missile launches and track them until the booster rockets burn out. The SBIRS Low system of about 24 satellites in low Earth orbit will then take over tracking the warheads from their point of separation until powerful, X-band ground radars lock on.[10]

A third category of satellites produces Signals Intelligence (Sigint) and Electronic Intelligence (Elint) by monitoring radio and electronic signals. Throughout the Cold War the US deployed a range of satellites for Sigint and Elint collection which grew steadily in capability, sophistication, weight and cost with each succeeding generation. The most important Sigint satellites over the past three decades have been the *Rhyolite/Aquacade, Chalet/Vortex* and *Magnum/Orion* series, stationed in geo-stationary orbit at strategic locations around the globe and capable of monitoring an extensive range of signals, from missile telemetry to micro-wave communications. The follow on to the *Magnum/Orion*, nicknamed *Jeroboam* by one observer, is over six times heavier than the early *Rhyolite/Aquacade* satellites and is estimated to cost in the order of US $2bn.[11]

A fourth class of satellites is equipped with sensors that measure seismic, acoustic, chemical and biological signatures. Known as measurement and signature intelligence, or Masint, these satellites can detect evidence of chemical and biological warfare agents or clandestine nuclear tests. With the proliferation of weapons of mass destruction, and fears that rogue states and terrorists might acquire nuclear, biological and chemical weapons, Masint is almost certain to receive higher priority in resources and funding. The US has launched at least one experimental Masint satellite, code-named *Cobra Brass*, to measure signatures associated with nuclear proliferation. A lightweight satellite known as *Forte*, for Fast On-Orbit Recording of Transient Events, has been developed for the same purpose. *Forte* will be equipped with advanced optical and radio-frequency sensors to monitor the flash and emissions from covert atmospheric tests of the kind thought to have been carried out by Israel and South Africa in 1979.[12] Much effort is going into creating an integrated Masint architecture and to improving the timeliness, accuracy and volume of Masint data.[13]

Prior to the 1991 Gulf War, US Imint satellites were considered to be strategic assets and their product was seldom made available for tactical or theatre-level operations. Exceptions were made, but even then satellite imagery was often days old and highly sanitised.[14] Delays in disseminating vital satellite intelligence to coalition commanders during Operation 'Desert Storm' and security restrictions on its use fuelled calls for space-based intelligence systems to be reconfigured to better serve the operational and tactical needs of combat commanders and precipitated a major rethink of the structure and priorities of US intelligence.[15] Since the Gulf War the US intelligence community has come to accept that intelligence derived from satellites and other national technical means must become more affordable and relevant to the needs of the warfighter and the security challenges of the twenty-first century. This has forced a reassessment of the number and mix of satellites in the US inventory and consideration of alternative collection platforms.

Dedicated intelligence satellites are extremely expensive to build and operate. A KH-11 is estimated to cost around US$800m plus another $300m for the launch vehicle. Even a nation as technologically and financially well-endowed as the US cannot afford to invest in too many billion-dollar intelligence satellites.[16] As a consequence, the US is moving towards the deployment of a range of smaller, cheaper and more robust satellites to augment its highly capable but expensive and less flexible KH-11 and *Lacrosse* satellites.[17]

Plans are well advanced to develop a constellation of space-based radar (SBR) satellites that will move the US closer to the holy grail of intelligence – around the clock, all-weather surveillance of the globe. SBR will operate as part of an integrated intelligence 'system-of-systems' that will link satellites with manned and unmanned airborne intelligence, surveillance and reconnaissance platforms. Each of the 24 to 48 satellites will cost about $100m. When fully operational, SBR will be able to detect moving and camouflaged ground targets in all weather and terrain and instantaneously transmit the images to friendly forces in the field. Later, improved satellites will be able to identify moving air targets, including possibly stealth aircraft.[18] The object is to provide the US and its allies with real-time global surveillance for both strategic and tactical purposes. Importantly, and contrary to past practice, it is envisaged that operational commanders will be able to directly task and in some cases control these space-based intelligence assets.[19]

Central to the new collection strategy is the deployment of diverse imaging sensors aboard single platforms. In the past secondary Sigint and Elint systems were sometimes carried on board Imint satellites, but in general intelligence satellites had one primary function. Satellites of the future are much more likely to be multi-functional, combining visible-light, electro-optical, hyper-spectral and radar sensors, thereby improving the utility and value of each platform.[20] Including radar sensors on an Imint satellite, for example, would benefit an operational commander by ensuring that if the satellite's pass is obscured by cloud, radar images would still be available. Hyper-spectral sensors break reflected light into different spectral bands which help to penetrate camouflage and to identify the location and composition of objects that would otherwise be hidden from even the most advanced visible light cameras and conventional colour sensors.

Improvements in the collection capabilities of the more expensive satellites through enhanced wide-area imaging and hyper-spectral systems are also being vigorously pursued. The successor to the advanced KH-11 is expected to be able to cover eight times the area of its frame with the same degree of resolution. Current wide-area surveillance by intelligence satellites image only about 500 kilometres either side of the satellite track, which is often insufficient to overlay the full battlefield area.[21] Making sense of the Imint collected will eventually be made easier by holograms and lenticular displays that present the data in scaled, three-dimensional images.[22] Imint is now expected to do more than count numbers or identify military platforms and the whereabouts of command centres. Contemporary Imint must answer when and how, rather than just how many.

The intelligence collection capabilities of satellites will be supplemented in the coming decades by a range of highly capable, land-, air- and sea-based systems. In the opening sequence of the film *The Empire Strikes Back*, the second of the well-known 'Stars Wars' trilogy, an imperial intelligence unit dispatches an advanced, all-weather reconnaissance drone to seek out the well-hidden rebel forces on the ice planet of Hoth. Although destroyed by the film's hero, the drone does its job, alerting Darth Vader's imperial storm troopers to the rebel's presence. Such leaps of imagination are no longer just the product of the fertile minds of novelists and screen-writers but are today's reality. Unmanned aerial vehicles (UAVs), military drones and robots will in future play a major role in providing real-time battlefield intelligence in all terrain and climatic conditions. Equipped with sensors that can see through smoke, cloud and bad weather, they will provide critical intelligence and targeting information, monitor troop and vehicular movements and allow post-strike analyses for a fraction of the cost of satellites and expensive aircraft.

Among the current generation of UAVs in the US inventory, the *Predator* has already proved extremely valuable as an intelligence collector and hunter-killer in Kosovo and Afghanistan.[23] Costing around $10m, the *Predator* can remain over the target area for around 20 hours, relaying data, Sigint and Imint via satellites directly to the field.[24] It has seen extensive service in Afghanistan and was directly responsible for a strike against Al-Qaeda leaders that led to the death of bin Laden's key lieutenant, Muhammad Atef. Pinpointing a hotel in a remote part of Afghanistan with a *Predator*'s night vision camera on a moonlight evening in September 2001, US commanders, located in faraway Florida, monitored a meeting of senior Al-Qaeda figures in real time and then used the *Predator* to direct three incoming F-15 Eagle strike aircraft onto their target. As the F-15 bombs slammed into the hotel, killing Atef, the *Predator* demonstrated its versatility by destroying several Al-Qaeda vehicles in the hotel car park with its two Hellfire anti-tank missiles.[25]

Newer generations of UAVs are even more capable than the *Predator*. The much larger *Global Hawk* has a 3,000-nautical mile range, can reach altitudes of over 65,000 feet and carry payloads of up to 3,000 lb.[26] Comparable in size to the venerable U-2 spy-plane it can be equipped with multiple sensors, including electro-optical, synthetic aperture radar and infrared.[27] While *Predator* searches only for a few signals of interest, *Global Hawk* is designed to be 'an electronic vacuum cleaner', sucking up a variety of signals and emissions.[28] The US will probably deploy its first dedicated Sigint *Global Hawk* in 2004 while some UAVs have already been fitted with Elint suites.[29] *Global Hawk* was rushed into service in Afghanistan and has played a central role in intelligence collection. If the 1991 Gulf War demonstrated the potential of precision-guided munitions, Operation 'Enduring Freedom' in Afghanistan marks the first operational demonstration of the US ability to conduct real time, net-centric warfare featuring UAVs as a core enabler.

HUMAN SPIES

Old-fashioned human spies, producing so called Human Intelligence or Humint, are still crucial to intelligence-gathering notwithstanding the impressive advances in technical collection by unmanned systems. September 11 was a salutary reminder to the US that no amount of technological superiority can compensate for quality Humint. In the aftermath of the successful strikes against the World Trade Center and the Pentagon, the Central Intelligence Agency (CIA) came under sustained criticism for neglecting covert operations and presiding over a decade-long decline in its ability to gather Humint. When the US decided to deploy forces to Afghanistan the CIA had only a single Afghan analyst and a handful of agents fluent in the country's many dialects. Unsurprisingly, its ability to penetrate Al-Qaeda was virtually non-existent. The CIA has since begun the lengthy task of re-building its clandestine networks, re-learning the value of people and language skills, and recruiting individuals with 'the savvy to take risks'.[30] But these efforts are unlikely to yield results for several more years.

A great deal of the intelligence from agents in the field is derived from, or communicated by, technical systems and devices which can rival satellites and UAVs in their sophistication and stealth. They include state-of-the-art audio and visual eavesdropping equipment, frequency-hopping communications and the use of randomly generated computer encryption. Humint has traditionally been considered a potentially high-value but low-volume contributor to the overall product of Western intelligence communities. However, like other collectors, the tasks and modus operandi of human agents are being transformed by technology and changing priorities.

Clandestine services will increasingly be directed towards support for military operations and the penetration of hard targets, and less for turning out political and economic reports which may add only marginally to information already available from diplomatic and informed public sources. In wars of the future, whether against conventional forces or in low-intensity conflicts, Humint will be vital to the successful conduct of military operations. Even in areas where intelligence-gathering is largely the province of automated collection, humans will play significant roles in deploying and monitoring small intelligence-gathering robots known as microbots or insectoids. Insectoids are essentially miniature robots which can look like insects – or anything else for that matter – and can be configured with a variety of sophisticated sensors. Their low signatures and small size making them extremely difficult to find. In a typical deep penetration operation a special force unit might deploy a mix of intelligence insectoids and walk them forward to positions where they could monitor a critical command facility and provide warning of entry and egress by enemy commanders and leaders.[31] Alternatively, insectoids or other tiny microbots could be used to determine if an ostensibly commercial building is actually a front for a clandestine chemical or biological weapons programme.[32]

INTELLIGENCE ASSESSMENT, DISSEMINATION AND THE POLICY PROCESS

If intelligence collection in the twenty-first century is likely to be dominated by smart machines, intelligence assessments will still reflect the perspicacity of human minds. No amount of raw data can substitute for an insightful human analyst able to discern the critical policy or operational significance of an event, action or trend which may be hidden within a mass of confusing and contradictory information. In attempting to quantify the value of high-quality, finished intelligence former US Secretary of Defense, James Schlesinger, once remarked: 'when you have good analysis, it's more valuable than the facts on a ratio of ten to one'.[33]

While one might quibble with Schlesinger's arithmetic it is difficult to dispute his basic contention. Major intelligence failures are seldom rooted in lack of information. They are generally failures of analysis and sometimes also of dissemination.[34] In the future, they may also result from information overload. The CIA has admitted that the delay in recognising that the Iraqis were storing chemical weapons at Khamisiyah in 1997 was largely due to problems in managing the vast amount of data available to the US intelligence community. And the problem is likely to grow as the volume of raw intelligence multiplies. The US Future Imagery Architecture, for example, is expected to result in a tenfold increase in imagery.[35]

With the world awash in a sea of information the task of the intelligence analyst is growing daily more difficult and mastery of the art of assessment will be an even more indispensable component of tomorrow's knowledge edge. To sift through, organise and evaluate the vast amount of classified and unclassified raw information now available will be a major challenge for even the most informed and agile of human minds.[36] In the future there will be an even higher premium on analytical skills, particularly at the strategic or national level, where relatively few are sufficiently well-trained or equipped intellectually to deal with higher levels of analysis and the aggregation of information.[37] Analysts who are able to make quick, accurate and informed judgements on fast-moving events and to articulate them in policy relevant assessments will be highly sought after. But the analysts of the future, no matter how gifted or well-trained, are unlikely to realise their full potential unless they can be accommodated in an organisational environment which encourages innovative thinking and allows for genuine debate on issues and problems which may be contentious, ambiguous and sometimes inherently unknowable.

Even here technology is having a significant impact reshaping, in quite fundamental ways, the whole intelligence assessment and dissemination process and redefining the relationship between intelligence producers and consumers. Consider the traditional intelligence cycle which typically begins with a set of broad requirements purportedly representing the collective intelligence needs of customers ranked in priority order. Collectors, both human and technical, work to these requirements, producing raw intelligence reports and data. These are fashioned by analysts into assessments of various kinds and at different levels of classification which are distributed to diverse customers. Economic policy-makers receive forecasts of oil and energy trends, ministers their briefings on the character and peccadilloes of their foreign counterparts and military consumers receive critical data on the capabilities of a potential adversary's weapons systems or order of battle.

The 'push' architecture which supports this edifice requires the analyst, not the user, to select from the available information what he or she believes the consumer wants to know. Further up the line intelligence managers and coordinators determine which assessments will be produced and when. Frequently, however, the product does not meet the consumer's needs, either because users are ignorant of what is available or the producer is unable to determine precisely what it is that the user really wants. The value of the finished product can be further diminished by delays in dissemination, especially of national estimates and assessments that may take weeks, and sometimes months, to prepare and endorse.

Since the late 1980s these deficiencies have been magnified by revolutionary changes in information and communication technology, especially the advent of commercially available, real-time information services on television, cable news networks and the Internet. When the Gulf War exploded in 1991, military and civilian officials alike were compelled to watch television images of terrain-hugging cruise missiles meandering down Baghdad streets while the equivalent satellite imagery was not available to decision-makers for hours and frequently days. This same revolution, however, now enables consumers to access the intelligence they want on demand, through what has been dubbed 'pull' architecture, so called because users electronically pull down or download intelligence from a networked database through a dedicated terminal.[38]

Furthermore, it is now possible to access 'all-source intelligence' from a computer terminal that integrates classified and unclassified information. Thus policy-makers with the appropriate security clearances have the considerable advantage of being able to select and download material from the same raw and finished intelligence product that is available to the professional intelligence analyst. And they can do so at a time of their own choosing. This clearly has major implications for the producer–consumer relationship.

On the positive side, the value and relevance of intelligence to policy-makers is likely to be significantly enhanced by the new pull architecture which, in theory at least, should stimulate more informed discussion of issues and allow consumers to quickly differentiate useful, high-quality analysis from pedestrian, low-value-added assessments or largely descriptive summaries of raw material. In a process known as 'disintermediation', top-level decision-makers will tend to bypass middle-level managers and coordinators in favour of downloading their own data or speaking directly to the geographical or functional specialists.[39] Disintermediation will reinforce the trend towards flatter management structures. In the longer term a more discriminating and informed customer community will demand higher product standards forcing producers of intelligence to become more responsive and to subject their assessments to the marketplace of competitive analysis.

If national intelligence communities fail to meet these higher standards they risk marginalisation. One major risk of the new pull architecture is that policy-makers with direct access to a comprehensive intelligence database may take it upon themselves to act as their own intelligence analysts, either through hubris, dissatisfaction with the existing service or because of time constraints. The temptation to do so will be even more acute if the professionals are demonstrably unable or unwilling to deliver a satisfactory product. Over 25 years ago, the Church Report of the US Senate highlighted the danger of do-it-yourself intelligence analysis. The report warned that not only may consumers of intelligence 'be depriving themselves of the skills of intelligence professionals; they may also be sacrificing necessary time and useful objectivity'.[40]

Technological change has sharpened another long-standing and related debate over the desirable degree of separation between the policy and intelligence communities. Managers of intelligence tend to argue that the two processes ought to be separate and even compartmentalised. The reason? 'Analytic intelligence provides a reality check on policy-driven hopes and aspirations. It fosters objectivity... Policy-makers, optimists by nature, are apt to clutch at straws and tiny crevices as they scale impossible heights to reach desired goals.'[41] Policy-makers respond that such distinctions are over-drawn. While they agree that intelligence officials should refrain from offering policy advice, they dispute the claims of intelligence officials to a monopoly on objectivity and impartiality and their attribution of automatic policy bias to the policy-maker. US Deputy Secretary of Defense Paul Wolfowitz is one who believes that neither side can completely avoid policy bias when it comes to dealing with uncertainty.[42]

Both views clearly have merit. Those intelligence officials who cross the policy line do so at their own peril, risking their objectivity and credibility. At the same time intelligence analysts must accept that their assessments and judgements are not completely free from intellectual and policy bias. But this dichotomy obscures the more important question of how producers and consumers can better understand each other and work more closely together in the interests of constructing an effective system of intelligence support for policy and operations.[43]

Decision-makers ought to recognise that a competent intelligence analyst is uniquely equipped to provide meaning, clarity and order to the rising tide of information which confronts and informs them. The intelligence community, on the other hand, must customise and render more user-friendly the material and support which it provides, particularly to politicians and senior officials whose culture is primarily an oral not a written one.[44] Intelligence analysts must also be more accessible to decision-makers and prepared to dialogue regularly and freely with experts and thinkers outside their own somewhat cloistered environment. Excessive secrecy and insularity, as Gregory Treverton observes, is the enemy of timely and insightful intelligence.[45]

NEW INTELLIGENCE TARGETS AND PRIORITIES

Intelligence planners will be compelled to broaden and diversify the scope of their collection and assessment activities in response to a range of new security threats such as terrorism, transnational organised crime, illegal migration and environmental degradation.[46] These non-traditional security threats have intruded onto the international security agenda with growing frequency over the past decade and they are beginning to be reflected in national intelligence priorities.[47] In 1995, the then US Vice President Al Gore instructed the CIA to evaluate for the first time the degree to which environmental factors influence global and national security.[48] Counter-terrorism, long a priority for police forces and domestic security agencies is a task which is increasingly likely to fall within the purview of the military and to warrant the allocation of strategic and operational intelligence assets.

Much of the existing apparatus of intelligence can be readily adapted to new targets and purposes while intelligence analysis and collation is one of the most immediately transferable of skills. There is also political advantage in making intelligence more available and relevant to the community at large. Domestic political considerations were important in the decision by the Clinton administration to de-classify and release some 800,000 satellite images in response to requests from the scientific community for help in monitoring the environment.[49] In the longer term, however, the allocation of scarce intelligence resources to such tasks will have to be carefully weighed against the needs of other users and be consonant with the future role and objectives of national intelligence communities.[50] For defence forces judgements will have to be made about the priority to be given to Operations Other Than War (OOTW) and the extent to which new capabilities are needed to counter transnational threats such as drug trafficking, terrorism and people smuggling.[51] In an era of holistic intelligence these issues need to be carefully considered when developing national intelligence collection and assessment priorities.

OPEN SOURCE INTELLIGENCE (OSINT)

Another important trend with potentially far-reaching implications for intelligence professionals and their diverse constituencies are the qualitative improvements and volume growth in Osint. Estimates of the proportion of US intelligence derived from non-classified, publicly available sources ranges from 40 to 95 per cent, although a commonly accepted figure is 80 per cent.[52] While the balance between classified and non-classified material is difficult to quantify precisely, for many subjects there is little doubt that Osint is at least as important as classified intelligence. Most intelligence professionals accept that Osint should be better integrated into the national intelligence process but some want to go much further. One well-known advocate, Robert Steele, believes that Osint 'can serve as a foundation for reinventing and reorienting the clandestine and technical disciplines'.[53]

While such claims may overstate the role that Osint can play in the intelligence architecture of the twenty-first century Osint clearly has much to offer. It is a relatively cost-effective way of tapping into the expertise that exists in the community at large thereby multiplying the pool of available intelligence and freeing up scarce resources for tasks where Osint is less able to contribute. Osint is often useful to policy-makers precisely because it is unencumbered by security caveats and restrictions on dissemination. Osint can also be tailored to the tastes and interests of individual consumers at minimal cost which intelligence agencies find difficult to emulate. There are already in existence a significant number of reputable private organisations capable of providing timely, high-quality political, economic, strategic and technical analyses on a subscription basis. Some well-known examples in the strategic domain are the various reports and assessments produced by the UK-based Oxford Analytica, Jane's Information Group, the International Institute for Strategic Studies and Stratfor.

Osint is also set to challenge the major powers' dominance of space-based intelligence systems. By 2015, most small and medium-sized states will be able to acquire intelligence from a diverse range of commercial satellites that are steadily closing the once considerable technological gap with dedicated intelligence satellites.[54] The proliferation of commercial satellite technology, especially the order of magnitude improvements in high-speed data transmission and imagery resolution, are making it feasible for virtually all states to integrate commercial systems into their national intelligence network. Although currently lacking the resolution for precise targeting information, off-the-shelf images from Landsat and SPOT satellites have provided useful area coverage and hyper-spectral imagery for over a decade freeing up military satellites for high value tasks. SPOT images were used by coalition commanders for planning air raids on Baghdad during Operation 'Desert Storm'.

The next generation of commercial satellites will be far more useful for targeting and intelligence purposes because they are capable of producing relatively high-quality images of less than one metre, width panchromatic (black and white) resolution. A resolution of one metre is sufficient to identify aircraft and ships, and to classify vehicles, making it more difficult to conceal military capabilities and preparations for war. In October 2001, the QuickBird observation satellite operated by DigitalGlobe was launched, further narrowing the gap with US spy satellites. QuickBird is capable of panchromatic resolutions of 61 centimetres and 2.5-metre multi-spectral images.[55] Data collected by scientific spacecraft and satellites can also yield valuable intelligence. Radiometer data from NASA's Modis and Sea WiFS spacecraft have helped coalition special forces operating in Afghanistan to determine the specific characteristics of snow, sand and dust thereby aiding them with tactics and targeting.[56]

However, Osint has its dangers and limitations. By definition commercial imagery is available to anyone who is prepared to pay, including rogue states and terrorist groups. That is why the US has developed contingency plans to deny potential enemies access to high-resolution commercial imagery. Immediately after the September 11 terrorist attacks, for example, the US National Imagery Mapping Agency (NIMA) banned the release of 3D terrain elevation measurements made over the US by the NASA/NIMA shuttle radar topography mission.[57] More generally, Osint varies tremendously in quality and reliability. Because it is driven primarily by commercial considerations Osint tends to focus on topical issues which may be ephemeral rather than fundamental. Underlying trends or subjects that are considered to be too technical or arcane are less likely to merit commercial attention and investment when in fact they may be vital to national security planning.[58]

Ironically, the phenomenal growth in Osint over the past decade is a major reason for the information overload which intelligence assessment agencies are struggling to overcome. The CIA estimates that the amount of open source information grew by a factor of ten in the five years between 1992 and 1996, a rate that shows no signs of slowing.[59] The key question for intelligence communities is not whether Osint has an important role to play but how can it best be integrated into national intelligence systems.

HOLISTIC INTELLIGENCE

Fusing and integrating previously unlinked platforms, technologies and resources into holistic intelligence systems will be a defining trend of the next decade, and effective management of holistic intelligence may be the key to unlocking the promise of the still nascent RMA. Managing the vast amount of information gathered, analysed and disseminated by the military will be the critical force multiplier of the future, equivalent in its impact to stealth technology. The shape of tomorrow's intelligence architecture is already discernible. Secure intranets, adapted to commercially available software and Web-systems, which find, organise, filter and analyse information are now in common use. Classified and unclassified material, including imagery, Sigint, Elint and Masint, are available literally at the touch of a key. Small, hand-held personal digital assistants that give soldiers in the field access to huge databases using web-enabled, wireless communications, are transforming the use of intelligence at the operational level of war. Advanced search engines and text analysis tools like Pathfinder are having a similar effect in the strategic domain, allowing analysts to swiftly extract useable intelligence from large amounts of data.[60]

The US Defense Intelligence Agency plans to operate a virtual intelligence network, known as the Joint Intelligence Virtual Architecture (JIVA) which is intended to establish a single 'knowledge' database for commanders, policy-makers and those responsible for acquisition. JIVA will link geographically separated users and producers of intelligence in a global electronic network featuring full motion video and graphics displays, interactive data manipulation and search and retrieval from mass storage.[61] The US military has made steady progress towards its aim of integrating the capabilities of multiple intelligence collection platforms to produce a comprehensive picture of the battlefield in all its complexity regardless of weather, terrain or time. For example, the Joint Forces Air Component Commander Situational Awareness System (JSAS) feeds intelligence from satellites, aircraft and UAVs onto a single screen showing friendly and enemy forces in unprecedented detail and clarity.[62]

Established on 1 October 1996, the National Imagery and Mapping Agency (NIMA) provides a 'one-stop shop' for imagery, mapping and dissemination services for commanders and decision-makers, subsuming the functions previously carried out by four separate agencies.[63] Senior Air Force commanders now talk about 'predictive battlefield awareness' where superior intelligence and profiling will provide the capability to actually anticipate an enemy's actions and respond accordingly. In a typical pre-planned attack based on predictive intelligence, a loitering stealth fighter armed with a new generation of small, precise stand-off weapons waits for the tell-tale glint of metal under camouflage that tells the pilot his quarry is moving out of an underground bunker. As anticipated, the target emerges only to be destroyed within seconds by a missile launched from the waiting fighter.[64]

What is often not appreciated is the massive amount of data modern weapons need for maximum performance. Smart weapons such as cruise missiles and precision-guided munitions require high-resolution imagery and accurate positional data to be effective.[65] Some Cold War strategic intelligence systems have been adapted to meet these needs but a new generation of purpose-built intelligence and targeting systems designed to support operational commanders is beginning to emerge. In early 1998, the US Air Force deployed an initial version of the Rapid Targeting System (RTS) to Kuwait. Its ground-based computer system has been designed to provide real time imagery from a range of photographic and radar satellites for strike aircraft. These images are correlated with archived intelligence obtained from airborne reconnaissance platforms and matched against a map to give the highly precise GPS coordinates essential for accurate targeting.[66] A complementary system is the Moving Target Indicator (MTI) used by Joint Surveillance Target Attack Radar System (JSTARS) aircraft. MTI has a unique capacity to track and target moving vehicles through its synthetic aperture radar which is able to see in all weather conditions including through obscurants like smoke.[67]

The fusion of intelligence with command, control, communications, computers, surveillance and reconnaissance (C4ISR) will blur the distinction between each of these functions and compel commanders and planners to treat them as an integrated whole with the end goal being the creation of 'seamlessness' across all elements of a fighting force.[68] The Command and Control (C2) Augmentation System that was deployed to

Bosnia indicates the potential of the integrated C4ISR architecture of the future. The C2 Augmentation System handled a thousand times more communication traffic than was possible during the 1991 Gulf War and merged data from many different sources, routing the information electronically to wherever it was needed. It also allowed other nations to share the same intelligence as US forces, or a sanitised version, depending on their status within the hierarchy of US allies and coalition partners.[69] By 2015, the new C4ISR architecture will give the US and its allies an unmatched ability to identify, target and destroy hostile forces and war-fighting infrastructure.

The wider dissemination of fused intelligence will not only force intelligence communities to become more user-friendly and less production-oriented, it will also lead to new divisions of labour and the decentralisation of decision-making, particularly in the military realm. Traditionally, sensors and shooters have belonged to the one organisation. Ground attack aircraft were directed to their targets by military forward air controllers or by self-contained, highly specific sensors attached to the aircraft or ordnance being delivered. However, today's generic intelligence platforms and sensors feed their data into a wide variety of weapons systems and the controllers of the sensors are often from different bureaucracies to the shooter's. Holistic intelligence will empower users at all levels, further blurring the boundaries between tactical and strategic level intelligence and creating more decentralised intelligence systems that are agile, network-based and highly responsive to the needs of its users.[70]

WILL THE 'FOG' OF WAR BE LIFTED?

However, for all the undoubted improvements in the collection, integration and management of intelligence, either extant or in prospect, there are serious reasons to doubt whether the fog of war can be sufficiently penetrated or lifted to permit the 'dominant battlespace knowledge' which RMA enthusiasts proclaim.[71] Intelligence, especially in war, will remain a less than perfect approximation of an adversary's intentions and capabilities. Good intelligence can reduce uncertainty and inform decision-making. It can help distinguish vital signals from background noise, but it is subject to the same foibles and fallibilities as its human producers and users. More information does not equate to better intelligence. It may, in fact, diminish the capacity of users to perceive, know and predict. The Jeremiah Report into the failure of the US intelligence community to provide warning of the Indian nuclear test on 11 May 1998 found that US intelligence satellites produced far too much information for overworked and under-trained analysts to handle.[72]

There is also the problem of what John Ferris and Michael Handel call the 'Schwarzkopf syndrome' – 'the desire to wait just one more moment in order to read just one more report, the reluctance to act on imperfect knowledge because it is known to be imperfect and that at any point another report might well produce perfection'.[73] While this is not just a contemporary failing, the centrality of intelligence to decision-making at both the strategic and tactical level and the sheer volume of information now available can induce a form of intelligence dependence which hinders decisive action. It is not only the volume and detail of information which threatens to overwhelm analytical capability. The rapidity with which information can be collected and disseminated to decision-makers in the modern era poses problems of its own. There is simply less time for reflection and considered judgements.

In future crisis situations strategic analysts will not only have to compete with the near real time images of CNN and other global news services. Their monopoly over the flow of assessed and raw intelligence is also under internal challenge – by collection agencies which make available to key policy-makers raw material which is judged to be of particular importance or time sensitivity; and by individual collectors in the field who use email, the Internet and cellular telephones to disseminate information on fast moving events directly to users. By their very nature such informal intelligence reports circumvent the established checks and balances within the intelligence system and raise issues of control, accountability and authenticity. Thus, qualitative technical improvements in collection and dissemination can actually undermine the efficacy of the overall system.

On the other hand, the development of ad hoc and informal intelligence networks is not intrinsically undesirable or necessarily a bad thing. In some circumstances the fluidity and flexibility of such networks may be preferable to the relatively unresponsive and de-personalised 'coordinated' intelligence that is still the stock trade of assessment agencies.[74] Much depends on the balance struck between the two. Clearly, users will continue to demand more timely and tailored intelligence. But without a mechanism to ensure quality control, informal reporting from the field or unevaluated raw intelligence may prove to be more risky than beneficial.

Militarily weak states and non-state actors such as terrorists and transnational criminal organisations will almost certainly make use of asymmetric strategies designed to combat, neutralise and disrupt the intelligence systems upon which the US and its allies depend for their knowledge edge and combat superiority. Osama bin Laden knew that his satellite phone could easily be monitored and limited its use to non-sensitive matters. Important operational directives were usually sent by courier or trusted personal messengers.[75] Asian terrorists and criminals make extensive use of the traditional underground banking system (UBS) or 'hawalla', as it is known in South Asia. The UBS is a highly personalised, family-based network of gold shops, trading companies and money exchanges which maintains minimal records and relies on mutual trust between brokers for its efficiency and internal discipline. Financial exchanges typically rely on coded messages, telephone calls, handwritten chits or symbols which guarantee a high degree of personal security and virtual anonymity.[76] Thus, large sums of money can be moved expeditiously all over the world with very little chance of detection by the authorities because they are outside the regulated banking system.

At the technical level there remain many problems to overcome. The exponential increase in high-speed communications and data transfer, particularly of images, has raised concerns about existing bandwidth capacity, the power demands of sustaining the supporting architecture for modern C4ISR systems and the vulnerability of these systems to power failures and hostile action.[77] While communications advances such as cell phones and email have opened up new avenues for exploitation, other developments have had the opposite effect. Fibre optic cables do not give off electronic emanations and commercially available high-grade encryption technology and radio frequency hopping has impeded intelligence gathering by severely reducing or complicating technical collection to the point where some potential adversaries may be on the verge of denying access.[78]

The more reliant military forces become on satellites and electronic data for intelligence and targeting, the more likely it is that potential adversaries will seek to exploit their vulnerabilities. Concealing high value facilities from the prying electronic eyes of airborne and space-based intelligence collection platforms, suppressing electronic emissions or moving potential targets around prior to an anticipated strike are some obvious defensive counter-measures. Offensive measures might include physically attacking critical intelligence nodes, or else rendering them dysfunctional through computer viruses and other forms of information warfare (IW).[79]

INTELLIGENCE AND INFORMATION WARFARE (IW)

As a result, national intelligence communities will inevitably become more directly involved in planning and executing IW strategies. Intelligence collection agencies will work closely with operational planners to develop and implement IW doctrine and information operations (IO) while assessment agencies will be more actively tasked to report on the intelligence vulnerabilities of potential adversaries and to identify IW targets. Intelligence assets and platforms which are currently used for monitoring the C4ISR systems of hostile states can also be used more aggressively to help disrupt and corrupt these systems or to assess the results of an IW strike. Rather than shooting down a commercial satellite, which is being used by an adversary for reconnaissance and intelligence purposes, it might be considered preferable to commandeer the satellite by sending a strong over-ride signal ordering the satellite to shut down or change its orbit.[80] In IW, operations and intelligence may become so interconnected and entwined that the distinction between the two becomes largely academic.[81]

IW poses important policy and doctrinal issues for intelligence communities. For example, during a conflict is it better to monitor or destroy an enemy's C4ISR systems? If the latter, should the task be accomplished with iron bombs or electronic bullets? Of course, this is not an entirely new conundrum. On one side of this long-standing debate are intelligence officials who for bureaucratic, security and cultural reasons are disinclined to actively interfere with systems that have been penetrated and are providing rich seams of intelligence. Military commanders, on the other hand, are more disposed to disrupt or destroy intelligence systems especially if they are causing significant casualties and problems for friendly forces. This dilemma has become progressively more acute as the salience of computers and information systems to modern warfighting has grown, forcing military planners to contemplate a range of aggressive IW options for corrupting, manipulating, deceiving and destroying an adversary's intelligence systems.[82]

FUTURE TRENDS

In the decades ahead, the forces of change will continue to play out their dialectic, reshaping and transforming the art of intelligence in a myriad of ways. While information will become more plentiful and less of a privileged source in the 'global information environment' of the twenty-first century, paradoxically the demand for timely, high quality strategic and operational intelligence will intensify rather than diminish.[83] The ever-increasing volume of information will be a test of a different order for the analysts, warfighters and policy-makers of the future. Yet the core of the intelligence dilemma will remain – how best to reduce the element of risk for decision-makers and cast light on what might otherwise be unknown?

Dedicated intelligence collection platforms will of necessity become multi-functional and the chariots of war will see, hear and sense as well as kill. In the drive to reduce costs, and to extract more return from expensive intelligence assets, commercial off-the-shelf technology and Osint will supplement, strengthen and sometimes replace the classified systems that dominated intelligence collection during the Cold War. However, although classified material will make up a smaller proportion of the overall intelligence available to users it will still provide critical pieces of the intelligence puzzle. Just how critical will depend in large measure on the particular puzzle and the urgency of the required response. Classified collection methods are generally more useful for current assessments and for sensitive and difficult to obtain military or technical intelligence rather than long-term forecasts and economic analysis.

Non-state actors will pose challenges of a different order. Operating in the shadows, and steeped in the arts of deception and disguise, terrorists and criminals may be much more difficult to identify, locate and eliminate than the political leadership or military forces of hostile states. Costly, high-tech intelligence systems designed for conventional warfare or monitoring the electronic environment may be ineffective against organisations employing simpler methods of clandestine communications as Osama bin Laden demonstrated in his well-coordinated, devastatingly effective attack against the US that some have labelled this century's 'Pearl Harbor'.[84] Despite impressive advances in sensors, automation, technical collection and code-breaking, it remains the case that humans provide the critical intelligence edge. There is simply no substitute for effective managers, prescient analysts, gifted linguists and dedicated spies.

The traditional intelligence cycle clearly has less explanatory and organisational utility in the post-Cold War world. The discrete functionality implied in the separation of the intelligence process into collection, collation, analysis and dissemination reflects the concepts, practice and organisational dynamics of an earlier era. What will distinguish the successful practitioners of twenty-first-century intelligence is the ability to fuse and integrate all elements of the process to provide seamless support for policy-makers and operational commanders. As has already been argued, the bureaucratic walls which once separated the providers and users of intelligence are coming down at a rapid rate, removing the artificial and dysfunctional distinctions between strategic, operational and tactical intelligence assets. The imperatives of modern warfare, particularly IW, will reinforce the need for holistic intelligence and erode the distinction between operations and intelligence.

On balance, these developments are likely to enhance the contribution which intelligence makes to national security although they are not without their risks and liabilities. Prudence and historical experience suggest that wise leaders and commanders will retain a healthy degree of Clausewitzean scepticism about the capacity of intelligence to completely eliminate the difficulties and uncertainties involved in attempting to divine the intentions and capabilities of others, especially in the heat of battle. Asymmetric warfare, human fallibility, technological failure and the development of effective countermeasures will ensure that no intelligence system, no matter how efficacious, will ever be able to completely dispel the fog of war.

NOTES

1. Typical of the 'true believers' in the revolutionary nature of the latest generation of military technology is the former vice chairman of the US Joint Chiefs of Staff, Admiral Bill Owens. See, e.g., Admiral William Owens, 'The Emerging System of Systems', *US Naval Institute Proceedings* 121/5 (May 1995).
2. Lawrence Freedman, *The Revolution in Strategic Affairs*, Adelphi Paper 318 (London: OUP for IISS April 1998) p.8; and Colin Gray, *The American Revolution in Military Affairs: An Interim Assessment*, Occasional Paper No. 28 (Hull: Strategic and Combat Studies Inst., Univ. of Hull 1997).
3. For a comprehensive discussion of definitional questions and issues, see Angelo Codevilla, *Informing Statecraft: Intelligence For A New Century* (NY: The Free Press 1992) pp.3–47.
4. There is much debate in the literature about the relevance and adequacy of the traditional intelligence cycle. Among the more insightful works dealing with this issue are Bruce Berkowitz, 'Information Technology and Intelligence Reform', *Orbis* 41/1 (Winter 1997) pp.109–11; and Amos Kovacs, 'The Uses and Nonuses of Intelligence', *Center for International Security and Arms Control Report* (Inst. for Int. Studies, Stanford Univ. Oct. 1996), p.1.
5. Just how important is detailed in Jeffrey Richelson's pathbreaking book, *America's Secret Eyes in Space: The U.S. Keyhole Spy Satellite Program* (NY: Harper & Row 1990). See also Desmond Ball, 'Desperately Seeking bin Laden: The Intelligence Dimension of the War Against Terrorism', in Ken Booth and Tim Dunne (eds.), *Worlds in Collision: Terror and the Future of Global Order* (London: Palgrave Macmillan 2002) pp.66–7, for an analysis of the airborne and satellite intelligence collection systems deployed to Afghanistan in Sept. and Oct. 2001.
6. Indeed, in many areas, the US has extended its lead in space-based systems. Barbara Starr, 'USA Sees Vital Role for Commercial Satellites', *Jane's Defence Weekly*, 30 July 1997, p.21.
7. Jeffrey T. Richelson, 'High Flying Spies', *The Bulletin of the Atomic Scientists*, Sept./Oct. 1996, p.53; and Alan Dupont, 'The US and Verification of SALT II', *Pacific Defence Reporter*, Oct. 1979, p.26.
8. Desmond Ball, *The Intelligence War in the Gulf*, Canberra Papers on Strategy and Defence 78 (Canberra: Strategic and Defence Studies Centre, Australian National Univ. 1991) p.15.
9. Statement by Paul G. Kaminsky, Undersecretary of Defense for Aquisition and Technology, to the National Security Subcommittee, House Appropriations Committee, 23 March 1995, <www.defenselink.mil/speeches/index.html>.
10. SBIRS and its functions are described in Richard J. Newman, 'Space Watch, High and Low', *Air Force Magazine*, July 2001, pp.35–8. Satellites launched into geosynchronous orbit 35,000 kms above the equator are able to hover over a single spot because their orbit speed matches that of the earth's rotation.
11. Desmond Ball, *Signals Intelligence in the Post-Cold War Era: Developments in the Asia-Pacific Region* (Singapore: Regional Strategic Studies Programme, Inst. of Southeast Asian Studies 1993) pp.15–19.
12. Richelson, 'High Flying Spies' (note 7) p.53.
13. 'Streamlining MASINT', *Aviation Week & Space Technology*, 7 Sept. 1998, p.55.
14. During Operation 'Desert Storm', frustrated by his inability to locally access vital imagery which he needed for operational planning, one US Marine Corps General in the Persian Gulf dispatched a personal aide to Washington to pick up photographic intelligence and bring it back by safe-hand.

15. Photographic imagery took up to four days to reach operational commanders during 'Desert Storm' according to the deputy director of the Defense Intelligence Agency, Admiral Ted Shaefer. Shaun Gregory, *Command, Control, Communications and Intelligence in the Gulf War*, Working Paper No. 238 (Canberra: Strategic and Defence Studies Centre, Australian National Univ. 1991) p.8. Various programmes were already underway in the US well before the Gulf War to make intelligence derived from satellites and other 'national technical means' available to operational commanders. There is little doubt, however, that the Gulf War experience accelerated the trend.

16. Bill Sweetman, 'Spy Satellites: the Next Leap Forward', *Jane's International Defence Review*, Jan. 1997, p.27.

17. Each kilogram of weight adds about US$5,000 to the cost of a commercial launch. Initial enthusiasm for small satellites in the commercial sector was dampened in the 1990s because of a series of high profile failures but they are back on the agenda. Small satellites generally weigh less than 100 kilograms and may in future be launched for as little as $1m. 'Incredible Shrinking Satellites', *The Australian (Cutting Edge)*, 16 Oct. 2001, pp.1, 4.

18. Robert Wall, 'New Space-Based Radar Shaped by SBIRS Snags', *Aviation Week & Space Technology*, 18 Feb. 2002, p.30; and Michael Sirak, *Jane's Defence Weekly*, 22 Aug. 2001, p.8.

19. Warren Ferster, 'U.S. Wants Radar Satellite', *Defense News*, 16–22 March 1998, p.20. On small satellites, see Pat Cooper, 'U.S. Intelligence Reshapes Techniques, Goals', *Defense News*, 12–18 Aug. 1996, pp.8, 18.

20. For example, an advanced KH-11 satellite launched on 28 Feb. 1990 also carried a Sigint package for intercepting video transmissions and monitoring radio and microwave transmissions. Ball, *Signals Intelligence In the Post-Cold War Era* (note 11) p.15. In general, however, senior US policy-makers have been wary about placing too many valuable intelligence assets on the one platform in case the platform malfunctioned or was destroyed during launch. Richelson, *America's Secret Eyes in Space* (note 5) p.220.

21. Sweetman, 'Spy Satellites: the Next Leap Forward' (note 16) p.27.

22. A lenticular display shows images in alternating perspectives that allow the human brain to fuse them into a three-dimensional picture. Mark Hewish, 'Panning for Gold', *Jane's International Defense Review*, Dec. 2001, p.24.

23. In Kosovo, a US *Predator* became the first UAV to designate a target in combat. 'Prospects for Unmanned Aerial Vehicles', *Strategic Comments* 6/7 (Sept. 2000); John Tirpak, 'Complications Overhead', *Air Force Magazine*, April 1998, p.25.

24. Richelson, 'High Flying Spies' (note 7) p.52.

25. Stephen Grey, 'Iron Fist Reaches out from the Other Side of the Globe', *The Australian*, 19 Sept. 2001, p.1; John G. Roos, 'Hunter-Killer UAVs', *Armed Forces Journal International*, Jan. 2002, p.58.

26. These are the capabilities of the second generation Global Hawk II. 'The Global Super Hawk', *Heads Up* 230, 5 Dec. 2001, p.5.

27. John Tirpak, 'The Robotic Air Force', *Air Force Magazine*, Sept. 1997, <www.afa.org/magazine/1997robot.html>.

28. David A. Fulghum, 'Computer Warfare Offense Takes Wing', *Aviation Week & Space Technology*, 19 Jan. 1998, p.56.

29. Robert Wall, 'Global Hawk In Australia Auditions For New Role', *Aviation Week & Space Technology*, 30 April 2001, pp.32–3.

30. CIA Director, George J. Tenet, quoted in Robert K. Ackerman, 'Intelligence at a Crossroads', *Signal*, Oct. 2001, p.19. See also Mickey Galeotti, 'Boom or Bust for the CIA', *Jane's Intelligence Review*, May 2002, p.51. Jeffrey Richelson canvasses the option of using clandestine operatives to conduct assassinations against especially egregious leaders and scientists involved in weapons programmes. Jeffrey T. Richelson, 'When Kindness Fails: Assassination as a National Security Option', *International Journal of Intelligence and Counterintelligence* 15/2 (Summer 2002) pp.243–79.

31. Artur Knoth, 'March of the Insectoids', *Jane's International Defence Review*, Nov. 1994, pp.55–8.

32. Pat Cooper, 'Microbots Will Help U.S. Combat Bio-Chem Weapons', *Defense News*, 11–17 Nov. 1996, p.22.
33. Cited in US Senate, 'Foreign and Military Intelligence', *Final Report of the Select Committee to Study Governmental Operations with Respect to Intelligence Activities, 26 April 1976* (Washington, DC: US Government Printing Office 1976) p.351. Also known as the Church Report after its senior member, Senator Frank Church.
34. On this point, see Kovacs, 'The Uses and Nonuses of Intelligence'(note 4) p.6; Richard Betts, 'Analysis, War and Decision: Why Intelligence Failures Are Inevitable', *World Politics* 31/1 (Oct. 1978) pp.61–89.
35. Hewish, 'Panning for Gold' (note 22) p.23; Barbara Starr, 'CIA Looks to Web to Solve Data Overload', *Jane's Defence Weekly*, 23 July 1997, p.29.
36. This problem is not confined to the US and other states with advanced intelligence capabilities. South Korea's Agency for National Security Planning has identified information management and the ability to organise and sort the massive raw material received from its agents as one of its highest priorities in the reform process initiated in early 1998 by its newly-installed head, Lee Jong Chan. Shim Jae Hoon, 'Secrets and Lies: Reform of Spy Agency Aims to End its Political Meddling', *Far Eastern Economic Review,* 9 April 1998, p.26.
37. Michael Handel (ed.), *Intelligence and Military Operations* (London: Frank Cass 1990) p.12.
38. For a useful discussion of the changing nature of intelligence analysis and the implications of pull architecture, see Peter Sharfman, 'Intelligence Analysis in an Age of Electronic Dissemination', *Intelligence and National Security* 10/4 (Oct. 1995) pp.201–11.
39. Ibid., p.210.
40. US Senate, 'Foreign and Military Intelligence' (note 33) p.267; Michael Handel, *War, Strategy and Intelligence* (London: Frank Cass 1989) pp.196 and 259.
41. A.D. McLennan, 'National Intelligence Assessment: Australia's Experience', *Intelligence and National Security* 10/4 (Oct. 1995) p.72.
42. Remarks made by Paul Wolfowitz in a short essay on intelligence which appears as a commentary in Douglas MacEachin, 'The Tradecraft of Analysis: Challenge and Change in the CIA' (Washington DC: Working Group on Intelligence Reform Papers 1994).
43. This issue is addressed by a number of recent studies on intelligence, including *Preparing for the 21st Century: An Appraisal of U.S. Intelligence*, Commission on the Roles and Capabilities of the United States Intelligence Community (Washington, DC: U.S. Government Printing Office 1996), <www.access.gpo.gov/su docs/dpos/epubs/int/index.html>. Otherwise known as the Brown Commission named after former US secretary of defense, Harold Brown.
44. On this point, see Gregory F. Treverton, 'The Intelligence Agenda', *RAND Paper P-7941* (Santa Monica, CA: RAND 1995) p. 15.
45. Gregory F. Treverton, *Reshaping National Intelligence for an Age of Information,* (Cambridge: CUP 2001) pp.253–5.
46. These emerging threats, and their implications for security, are discussed in Alan Dupont, *East Asia Imperilled: Transnational Challenges to Security* (Cambridge: CUP 2001).
47. Barbara Starr, 'Intelligence Community Coaxes its Analysts off the Fence', *Jane's Defence Weekly,* 29 Oct. 1994, p.20.
48. Mark Sommer, 'Non-military Factors Bring New Meaning to Art of Spying', *The Jakarta Post,* 15 Jan. 1996, p.5.
49. *Strategic Assessment 1996: Instruments of U.S. Power* (Washington DC: Institute for National Strategic Studies, National Defense Univ. 1996) p. 65.
50. Scott Pace, Kevin M. O'Connell and Beth E. Lachman, *Using Intelligence Data for Environmental Needs: Balancing National Interests* (Washington DC: Acquisition and Technology Policy Center, National Security Research Division, RAND 1997), <www.rand.org/publications/MR/MR799>.
51. Jim-Holden Rhodes and Peter A. Lupsha, 'Gray Area Phenomena: New Threats and Policy Dilemmas', *Criminal Justice International* 9/1 (Jan.–Feb. 1993) p.24.

52. See, for example, Robert David Steele, 'Open Source Intelligence: What Is It? Why Is It Important to the Military', <www.oss.net/MILITARY/>; *Strategic Assessment 1996: Instruments of U.S. Power* (note 49) p.66.
53. Robert David Steele, 'Private Enterprise Intelligence: Its Potential Contribution to National Security', *Intelligence and National Security* 10/4 (Oct. 1995) p. 215.
54. Primarily due to the rapid reduction in the cost of microwave integrated circuits and digital processing. Starr, 'USA Sees Vital Role for Commercial Satellites' (note 6) p.21.
55. 'High-resolution Commercial Satellite Imagery Available', *Jane's International Defense Review,* Feb. 2002, p.4.
56. Craig Covault, 'Navy Enlists NASA In the War on Terror', *Aviation Week & Space Technology,* 8 April 2002, p.31.
57. 'Afghanistan in 3D', *Aviation Week & Space Technology,* 7 Jan. 2002, p.17. On the other hand, the US was quick to reserve exclusive rights for commercial satellite imagery of Afghanistan useful for targeting and assessing battle damage. An additional benefit was that this material could be made available to coalition partners who did not have access to classified imagery. 'US Renews Rights to Afghan Satellite Images', *The Times of India,* 8 Nov. 2001, <www.timesofindia.com>.
58. On this point, see Bruce Berkowitz and Allan E. Goodman, 'Why Spy – and How – in the 1990s?', *Orbis* 36/2 (Spring 1992) p.270.
59. *Preparing for the 21st Century: An Appraisal of U.S. Intelligence* (note 43).
60. Hewish, 'Panning for Gold' (note 22) pp.25, 27.
61. 'DIA Plans Virtual Intelligence Network', *Jane's Defence Weekly,* 2 Oct. 1996, p.11.
62. Steven Watkins, 'USAF System Links Battlefield Intelligence Data', *Defense News,* 12–18 Aug. 1996, p.12.
63. The four agencies in question were the CIA's National Photographic Interpretation Center, the imagery and dissemination functions of the Defense Intelligence Agency, the National Reconnaissance Office and the Defense Airborne Reconnaissance Office. Pat Cooper, 'New U.S. Spy Agency Melds Mapping, Imaging Services', *Defense News,* 14-20 Oct. 1996, p.68.
64. David A. Fulghum, 'Planning Moves Deep Into Predictive Process', *Aviation Week & Space Technology,* 18 June 2001, pp.175–6.
65. Gary Waters, 'Operational Intelligence: Lessons >From The Gulf War', in Anthony Bergin and Robert Hall (eds.), *Intelligence and Australian National Security* (Canberra: Australian Defence Studies Centre, Australian Defence Force Academy 1994) p.54; Berkowitz and Goodman, 'Why Spy – and How – in the 1990s?' (note 58) p. 273.
66. Barbara Starr, 'US Rapid-targeting Data System Deployed to Gulf', *Jane's Defence Weekly,* 18 Feb. 1998, p.4.
67. Pat Cooper, 'Air Force Stresses Big-Picture Reconnaissance', *Defense News,* 12–18 Aug. 1996, p.14.
68. *Preparing for the 21st Century* (note 43). Some analysts do not categorise sensor-derived targeting information as intelligence but such reservations seem largely semantic and fail to recognise the integrated nature of modern C4ISR systems. See, e.g., Handel, (ed.), *Intelligence and Military Operations* (note 37) pp.11–12.
69. Pat Cooper, 'Bosnia C2 System To Bridge Allied Communications Gap', *Defense News,* 12–18 Aug. 1996, pp. 29 and 34.
70. 'Defense Intelligence Carves a New Niche', *Signal,* Oct. 2001, pp.21–2.
71. This concept is articulated in Freedman, *The Revolution in Strategic Affairs* (note 2) p.11.
72. Tim Weiner, 'A Call for Complete Overhaul of CIA', *International Herald Tribune,* 4 June 1998, p.3. Admiral David Jeremiah is a former vice chairman of the Joint Chiefs of Staff.
73. After the US commander of 'Desert Storm', General H. Norman Schwarzkopf. John Ferris and Michael, I. Handel, 'Clausewiz, Intelligence, Uncertainty and the Art of Command in Military Operations', *Intelligence and National Security* 10/1 (Jan. 1995) p.50.
74. Bruce Berkowitz, 'Information Technology and Intelligence Reform', *Orbis* 41/1 (Winter 1997) p.114.
75. Ball, *Desperately Seeking bin Laden* (note 5) p.63.

76. Mark Gaylord, 'Money Laundering in Asia', in Ann Lodl and Zhang Longguan (eds.), *Enterprise Crime: Asian and Global Perspectives* (Chicago, IL: Office of Int. Criminal Justice with Shanghai Bureau of Justice and The East China Inst. of Politics and Law, Univ. of Illinois 1992) pp.82–3.
77. Bandwidth problems are being addressed and there is growing optimism that they will not be a serious constraint on the development of more capable intelligence architectures. Bandwidth capacity is doubling every four months compared with 18 months for computer power. 'Defense Intelligence Carves a New Niche', *Signal*, Oct. 2001, p.21.
78. William J. Broad, 'New Technology Pares Spies' Edge', *International Herald Tribune*, 21 Sept. 2001, p.15.
79. Information warfare is defined here 'as activities undertaken by governments, groups or individuals to gain electronic access to information systems in other countries either for the purpose of obtaining the data in such systems, manipulating or fabricating the data, or perhaps even bringing the systems down, as well as activities undertaken to protect against such activities'. *Preparing for the 21st Century* (note 43).
80. *Defense News*, 14–20 Oct. 1996, p.18.
81. This is certainly the belief of the former head of the US National Security Agency, Lt. Gen. Ken Minihan. Pat Cooper, 'DoD Directive Links Info War Intelligence, Operations', *Defense News*, 14–20 Oct. 1996, p.84.
82. Bradley Graham, 'In Cyberwar, A Quandary Over Rules and Strategy', *International Herald Tribune*, 9 July 1998, <www.int.com>. See also David A. Fulghum, 'Cyberwar Plans Trigger Intelligence Controversy', *Aviation Week & Space Technology*, 19 Jan. 1998, pp.52–3; David A. Fulghum, 'Computer Combat Rules Frustrate the Pentagon', *Aviation Week & Space Technology*, 15 Sept. 1997, pp. 67–8.
83. The Global Information Network is defined as 'a world-wide network of information sources, archives, consumers and architectures'. Freedman, *The Revolution in Strategic Affairs* (note 2) p.49.
84. Robert Steele quoted in Leonard Davis, 'Officials Question Sat Ability To Track', *Defense News*, 17–23 Sept. 2001, p.6.

Counter-Terrorism, Information Technology and Intelligence Change

MICHAEL HERMAN

Assume that terrorism with the destructive intent demonstrated on September 11, 2001 (9/11) will be a continuing threat, and not a one-off, and a threat is to Western capitalism as a whole, not just the United States (US). Assume also that a continuous information revolution of computers and electronic communications – referred to here simply as information technology (IT) – is really in progress and will continue, with government intelligence as an integral part of it. Should these two assumptions combine to make us think radically about intelligence? It is getting more money and attention everywhere. In the present British political idiom about public services, how is government to ensure that it delivers.

Well before 9/11 there was extensive American writing about the need for intelligence change. Some of it was about the perceived weaknesses of particular American organisations. The National Security Agency (NSA) was said to be fossilised; the new National Imagery and Mapping Agency (NIMA) should never have been created in the first place; the Defense Intelligence Agency had never found its real *métier*; the Central Intelligence Agency (CIA) to some writers was too civilian, and to others had become too oriented after the 1991 Gulf War to military support, while one or two argued that it should never have been created in the first place. The Director of Central Intelligence (DCI) at the apex of the structure was held to be ineffectual, without direct control of money and jobs. To some extent all this reflected the American national propensity for self-criticism; if anything is important enough, there must be ways of doing better.

This literature also had a strain of managerial radicalism in it, linked with the IT revolution. Information and information-handling were being transformed, and intelligence must follow suit. There was a consensus about the need for change, though less agreement on the direction. Robert Steele argued for re-thinking intelligence as a whole, putting far more emphasis on open sources and cooperation with non-governmental sources of information; a change in boundaries was needed 'away from a small group of secret government bureaucracies and toward a larger conception of a "virtual intelligence community" that harnesses the distributed intelligence of each nation, creating "smart nations"...Bureaucracies are bad. Secret bureaucracies are worse.'[1]

Others believed that, even if intelligence's boundaries remained unchanged, something drastic had to be done to its internal structure. Bruce Berkowitz and Allan Goodman represented this school of thought in claiming in 2000 that the information revolution pointed to a new 'decentralised, market-based, fluid model' for intelligence, the antithesis of all the bureaucratic regularities.[2] 'If it is to remain effective, the intelligence community will have to change – so much, that when these changes are completed, it will likely bear little resemblance to the organization created fifty years ago.'[3]

The 9/11 attack produced some changes. Terrorism was already a top priority but became the super-priority, and budgets have increased correspondingly. The political climate in which Western intelligence operates has altered, quite dramatically in the US and more subtly elsewhere. New overseas intelligence liaisons have become acceptable and have been developed. New legislative balances are being struck domestically between extended intelligence coverage on the one hand (and the admissibility of its evidence in legal processes), and citizens' privacy on the other.

Most of these changes are not new in kind, and reinforce the developments of the last decade towards increased international cooperation and military intervention in an increasingly turbulent and dangerous world. But 9/11 has meant a change of national mood, which the subsequent US concentration on Iraq has intensified and not dissipated. According to President Bush's National Security Strategy presented on 20 September 2002, 'intelligence – and how we use it – is our first line of defense against terrorists and the threat posed by hostile states',[4] and despite policy differences America's allies are following this general lead. It would be surprising if the mood has not had some influence in Russia, China and elsewhere outside the nominal Western camp. Intelligence is riding high worldwide and will continue to do so.

This has been accompanied in the US by renewed calls for intelligence reform, yet since 9/11 these have remained largely unfocused. American Congressional post-mortems have not got very far and did not secure the administration's cooperation. The Executive and Legislature have been embroiled in action rather than reflection, and the pace of events has given most commentators too many other things to think about. British criticism of intelligence over 9/11 has been muted for similar reasons, and because it became known that the Joint Intelligence Committee (JIC) had actually warned ministers in July 2001 that plans for the Al-Qaeda attacks were in the final stages of preparation, though the timings, precise targets and methods were not known.[5]

This lack of focus may change. President Bush has endorsed the need for intelligence reform, including better warning capabilities.[6] Eventually there may be time for governments to stand back and consider lessons coolly, though at the time of writing one would not bet on it.

Be that as it may, the case for a rethink remains. Global terrorism poses many requirements, but the assumptions set out at the beginning of this article point to what may be the a central issue. If the IT revolution is a 'given', does it have a direct bearing on counter-terrorism? If so, does it point to applying technology in a gradual and evolving way, or to the more radical approach suggested in the pre-9/11 literature? And if the latter, in what direction? These are the questions for this article, using British and American examples to illustrate general issues for intelligence everywhere.

COUNTER-TERRORISM AND INFORMATION MANAGEMENT

Counter-terrorist intelligence is nothing new, but its importance now warrants regarding it as an intelligence discipline in its own right, with equal standing to the accepted 'political', 'military' and 'economic' categories of collection and product. Like these other categories it serves policy-making and decision-taking at all levels: strategic, operational and tactical. Its most important and direct value is in providing pre-emptive tactical warning of terrorist action, though even this may not result in immediately observable action such as arresting terrorists or capturing their *matériel*. Warnings may be effective defensively rather than offensively, as illustrated in Dame Stella Rimington's claim in 1994 that the security forces in Northern Ireland were by then frustrating four out of every five attempted terrorist attacks, without necessarily disrupting the terrorist units involved.[7] Warning may also be used defensively at the general operational level of updating the threat assessments that gear defensive security policies to the best estimates of risks and vulnerabilities. Intelligence success in the short and long terms may be simply in contriving that nothing happens.

Nevertheless counter-terrorism in most of its applications operates characteristically on twin tracks of timeliness: on one track the long-term research and source development characteristic of 'difficult' targets, and speedy reaction on the other track. It combines the patience of counterespionage's detective work and counterintelligence's penetration of the adversary with the agility of military intelligence's wartime tactical applications and the 'quick response' aspects of law enforcement. It needs a scholarly attention to detail and objectivity, yet the destructiveness of 9/11 emphasised the intensity with which it has to work; tactical warning must be given in time. In this respect counter-terrorist intelligence comes close to counter-terrorist action, and the two are sometimes almost indistinguishable; yet they need to be considered separately. 'Counter-terrorism' is used here for convenience, but relates throughout to intelligence and not action taken on it.

As such, counter-terrorism's tradecraft embodies the central importance of secret sources; the identifying and tracking of people (rather than the military accent on equipment, for example); and, now, a combination of specific expertise on difficult languages and terrorist culture with a more general global-mindedness. Terrorism's global disposition and reach requires a comparably global counter-terrorist reaction. The merging of 'domestic' and 'foreign' intelligence is even more complete now than in earlier, more geographically constrained campaigns such as those against the IRA.

Most of these features are reflected in a notable current account written by a member of the British Security Service's International Counter Terrorist Branch.[8] He argues that counter-terrorist intelligence is neither a chess game against a single enemy, nor is it like completing a jigsaw puzzle, unless it is accepted that the picture is fragmentary and fleeting with many pieces in the box that fit nowhere. For the 'needle-in-a-haystack' search for clues, he prefers a metaphor of tracing threads and weaving patterns. The raw material is itself variegated and extensive, including:

secret intelligence such as the intercepted communications of known terrorists; secret intelligence on those, perhaps overseas, known to have been involved in terrorist support activity in the past; reports from overseas security organisations (again of highly variable quality and sometimes politically coloured) on actual or possible terrorist planning; police reports, for instance of suspicious movements through ports; allegations from 'walk ins' who claim to have inside knowledge of terrorist plans; calls from members of the public reporting their suspicions; media statements by spokesmen for terrorist groups or their sympathisers. The quantity of material coming in is immense – and to some extent driven by market forces. If someone is willing to pay for counter-terrorist intelligence then you can be sure that someone else is willing to supply it – manufacturing it first if necessary.

On this material

the job of the intelligence officer is to identify those strands that are worth pursuing and then to pursue them until either they are resolved, or they start to look flakey and not worth pursuing, or there is nothing more that can usefully be done. It is a risk management process. The number of potential leads that can be followed is virtually infinite. On the other hand, covert investigation is extremely resource-intensive and impinges on the human rights of the subject. The threshold for such investigations is therefore high and the number of investigations necessarily limited. Consequently many potential leads have to be discounted. Decisions on which leads to pursue are vital, but they are also complex and rich in judgement.

Some American discussion – both before and after 9/11 – has had a different focus: on improving collection, with a special emphasis on human sources. Some writers have portrayed human sources (Humint) as the answer to terrorism. Even in Britain a usually sensible MP has managed to bring a political bias into urging this need for more Humint: '...instead of recruiting more establishment-type Oxford and Cambridge graduates, MI6 needs recruits who will mix easily in the coffee bars of Kandahar'.[9]

Such sentiments have an element in them of naivety and the search for panaceas. Good human sources are of course worth their weight in gold; success in the UK's battle against the IRA depended in large measure upon them. The American commentators may indeed have been correct in arguing that the CIA's Directorate of Operations had become demoralised in the 1990s by persistent public and congressional criticism and lack of managerial support. But even the best Humint – and the extensive liaison with foreign services it often entails – will not provide a magical solution on targets of the Al-Qaeda kind. Hence the importance of the analogy of thread-developing and weaving, searching and making connections in many different kinds of information: secret and non-secret, domestic and foreign, with many different provenances. Counterintelligence is particularly all-source and holistic.

This makes it a 'natural' for advanced IT. Technology is affecting all parts of the intelligence process, from collection (and its targets' defences against it, as through the commercial availability of encryption systems) through processing and analysis to delivery to customers. But its special relevance to counter-terrorism is probably its expanding scope for searching large swathes of data and making connections in them, in ways previously impossible: a revolution in the scope for bringing all evidence together automatically for the process of testing and developing the possible 'threads'. There is the obvious parallel with police methods; no murder investigation in Britain would now take place without an IT system to handle the evidence. But for counter-terrorism the need is for much wider searches in databases with many different levels of IT compatibility and sophistication.

Here a current military analogy is relevant. The literature since the 1991 Gulf War on the so-called Revolution in Military Affairs (RMA) has centred on IT's ability to develop a 'system of systems' to knit together the separate IT of Intelligence, Surveillance and Reconnaissance and other information sources, to provide immediate and common 'situational awareness' of the battlespace, a form of 'network-centric' warfare in which information is shared and readily available at all relevant levels of command.[10] The suggestion here is that counter-terrorism can have its comparable IT vision: a 'system of systems' to make all the different kinds of relevant data accessible by every counter-terrorist analyst at every IT workstation.[11]

Analysts would still specialise in particular targets or particular kinds of evidence, but would have a more comprehensive and immediate view of all relevant material, including 'collateral' from unusual sources, than has ever been possible by traditional methods, with a correspondingly increased and more timely ability to 'thread' and 'weave' connections in the evidence. Work on counter-terrorism would produce better insights, more sensitive steerage of investigation and quicker tactical warning. IT's potential and terrorism's threat combine to suggest this as a strategic vision. If so, how then do we get from here to there?

INSTITUTIONAL BARRIERS

The vision is of revolutionising information flows across inter-institutional boundaries. (Improved flows within organisations may be almost as important, but are not considered here.) The boundaries are of two different kinds. One is between the different organisations for collection and analysis in what is dubbed the 'intelligence community' – officially designated by Executive Order in the US, and corresponding with membership of the JIC in the UK. Thus the boundaries within the community between the CIA's 'foreign' intelligence and the Federal Bureau of Investigation's (FBI) 'domestic' intelligence appear on present showing to have been a key factor in the failure to provide warnings of 9/11. The other kind of boundary is between this intelligence community and other bodies outside it. Both kinds of boundary pose the same problem: 'the difficulty of achieving horizontal integration in a vertically funded world',[12] in which vertical authority and prerogatives create tensions between immediate institutional interests and the broader common good; common interests compete with turf dominance.

Intra-Intelligence Barriers

On the intelligence community itself, American writers have extensively criticised the 'stovepiping' effects of the separate agencies, in which single-source intelligence is passed up to the top without sufficient all-source integration, and without sufficient cooperation in the steerage of collection. They point to the production and marketing of single-source rather than all-source material, the prevalence of inter-agency rivalry and demarcation problems, and the difficulty of pursuing community rather than sectional interests. As an earlier example of stovepiping in the present writer's experience, American satellite imagery in the Cold War was a technical and professional miracle, but its handling in separate organisations with separate security regulations meant that it was difficult for anyone to integrate it properly with other technical collection.

There must be some suspicion that this stovepiping has become a convenient whipping boy in the American writing for almost every kind of shortcoming. Intelligence puts a special emphasis on reliability, and organisational divisions are needed to maintain varied kinds of special expertise and establish rules of accountability. Intelligence cannot just be an all-source free-for-all. The issue is not the existence of the stovepipes but their number, their length and the arrangements for junctions with others.

Nevertheless the problem remains of vertical institutional barriers. The intelligence agencies that developed in the course of the twentieth century are remarkably powerful, autonomous and resilient. In Britain the pattern of the separate agencies, distinct from military intelligence and police forces, dates back essentially to the post-World War I reorganisation of 1919 which established the Security Service and Secret Intelligence Service (SIS), and gave Signals Intelligence (Sigint) a position of some independence under SIS's chief; and this structure has been unaffected by the incessant reorganisation of the rest of the public sector over the past 30 years.

Something of the same relative stability has applied in the US; the creation of the NIMA has been the only major institutional innovation since the establishment of the Defense Intelligence Agency and National Reconnaissance Office in the early 1960s. Institutional separation is very deeply entrenched. After practical experience of the American intelligence community and the separate institutions within it, Gregory Treverton memorably commented on it that 'community describes precisely what it is not: it is somewhere between a fiction and an aspiration'.[13]

Separate and long-standing institutions of any kind develop proprietary instincts about 'their' information, but in the case of intelligence these have been multiplied many times over by the secrecy needed for source protection. Intelligence in the half-century after World War II developed an ever-increasing labyrinth of special classifications and compartments, designed explicitly to control information flows; justifiably so, in the light initially of the scale of Soviet espionage and subsequently of leakages to the media, but with damage nevertheless to intelligence's effectiveness.[14]

Partly for these security reasons intelligence over the same period regularised the conventions of inter-agency exchanges. Intelligence information was either included in the formally 'published' product which agencies sent to their 'customers', or remained as 'unpublished' material in agency files and was not available to others. Intelligence as a whole developed its philosophy of output as a service to 'customers' outside the community, rather than to 'collaborators' inside it; and IT was planned essentially on that single-agency basis, and not for community access. The community could connect separate items of published information, but it had no means of connecting individual items which did not meet publication thresholds on their own and hence lay unpublished in two, three or four different agencies, but might have been significant if put together.

There were good reasons for all these developments. But one result was the growth of some formality and rigidity in intelligence dissemination. I have written elsewhere of the ways in which the institutional boundaries between single-source and all-source analysis could impede what intellectually is really an all-embracing search for truth, ideally a *jeu sans frontières*.[15] Something of an earlier informality of that kind can be found in R. V. Jones' account of British scientific and technical intelligence between 1939 and 1945,[16] but there was rather less place for it in the long years of peace that followed.

Extra-Intelligence Barriers

Similar considerations apply to horizontal flows between the intelligence community and bodies outside it. Counter-terrorism needs ad hoc access to some data normally quite unrelated to it: perhaps company data, driving licence applications, passenger lists and manifests as examples. (The American government research programme of Total Information Awareness envisages a matching of much more extensive personal data to trace terrorists, including *inter alia*, passport and visa applications, criminal, education and housing records, travel and transportation information, as well as personal identity data like fingerprints and iris scans.)[17] Much more regular contact is certainly needed with the law enforcement agencies in which specialised 'intelligence' is becoming a new quasi-community in its own right. In Britain this is led and coordinated by the National Criminal Intelligence Service (NCIS); in the US the connection between the intelligence community and law enforcement is encapsulated in the dual roles of the FBI, though there are many other law enforcement agencies. In both countries the secret agencies of the 'old' intelligence communities have increasing links with this 'new' law enforcement intelligence on subjects like drugs trafficking, and counter-terrorism has made these connections more important. An example is the study of terrorist funding, said to be performed in Britain principally by the NCIS.[18] Even apart from these connections between intelligence specialists, law enforcement bodies as a whole are necessarily close to terrorism, and are both prime customers for intelligence on it and contributors of the information they gather themselves. Terrorism accentuates the need for horizontal information access between these two communities; IT provides the potential for doing so.

So the IT vision of an overarching 'system of systems' and a counter-terrorist *jeu sans frontières* really has two parts: within the intelligence community itself (let us call it the 'Mark 1' system), and between the community and other bodies, particularly in law enforcement (the 'Mark 2' equivalent). For reasons that will be apparent, this article concentrates on Mark 1, even though for counter-terrorism some aspects of Mark 2 are equally important.

Realising the Information Technology (IT) Vision

For the intelligence community itself (the Mark 1 system) a simplistic answer would be to reorganise; to solve the problem of IT interoperability by following the modern fashion for 'agile organisation' and moving all those working on counter-terrorism into a new organisation geared exclusively to that target. There was some suggestion of this in the recent hearings of the British Parliament's Defence Committee – not the Intelligence and Security Committee – and the idea has been floated by some American politicians.

It is not completely without merit. The main intelligence agencies are often seen as specialists in particular methods and material – Humint, Sigint, imagery and other smaller specialisations – yet the security services among them are in reality specialists in a subject: covert threats to internal security. It would be interesting to consider, counterfactually, whether Britain in 1969 would have been wise to create a more interdisciplinary, target-driven counter-terrorist organisation of this kind, perhaps under the Security Service, if it had known that Irish terrorism was to be a main national preoccupation for at least the next 30 years. So reorganisation now on these lines for counter-terrorism is not entirely out of the question; indeed it is to be hoped that small centres of expertise on Islamic terrorism have already been created somewhere. But wholesale reorganisation around terrorism seems impractical, for far more reasons that can be adumbrated here. Treverton, though quite radical on intelligence reform, put it neatly before 9/11: 'the capacities embedded in existing intelligence organizations are both powerful and hard to create, so caution is called for in demolishing them in favor of something new while we are yet so uncertain of the world we will confront'.[19] The private sector, with different traditions of reorganisation and organisational fluidity, might well reorganise, but can run greater risks of disaster than governments.

Even more hesitation must apply to facilitating the Mark 2 system through reorganising the intelligence community to include more weighty representation for law enforcement. Some of this is already provided, by the FBI's full membership of the American community and the NCIS's attendance at the British JIC when necessary. In Britain the various police forces' Special Branches have also always had feet in the two worlds of intelligence and policing. Giving the many law enforcement organisations a stronger representation in the machinery of the 'old' intelligence world would be possible, but quite a change. Despite its involvement in counter-terrorism, law enforcement is still directed principally against crime for financial gain, intrinsically rather different from intelligence's main targeting on the world of international politics, potential and actual violence and national security as a whole.[20] The objectives and cultures of the two communities are different, and some continued separation is probably sensible, rather than expanding the JIC, for example, into a new mega-community. Possibly a deconstruction of the present intelligence community may eventually be called for, as is perhaps suggested in Robert Steele's analysis, but it is difficult to see this in the short or medium term.

Counter-terrorism may indeed call for some overlap or revised demarcation between the FBI and CIA, but on the whole the intelligence and law enforcement communities should retain their separate identities. Indeed one effect of 9/11 may be to reverse slightly the trend of recent years towards more coverage by the 'old' intelligence communities of their 'new' criminal targets. This conservative view applies even more to redrawing institutional boundaries between intelligence and government information-gathering outside law enforcement.

So the IT vision should be applied to broadly the present intelligence structures and not to revamped arrangements. On purely technical grounds this should not pose special problems. The whole concept of an overarching 'system of systems' is geared precisely to coping with organisational diversity and the heterogeneous IT that it produces. For such a system an American writer on military command and control distinguishes the different stages of *interoperability*, *integration* and *interdependence*, and argues that these are achievable through a suitable central effort with three characteristics: first, 'a substantive blueprint for centralised guidance and decentralised execution', which 'allows local flexibility to accommodate local needs'; second, dedicated funds to support progress in 'core activities, such as exercise, experimentation, and interoperability or integration augmentations [to already existing systems]'; and, third, 'developing trust over time' by 'pushing for the common good' and 'providing funding for "common good" investments'. Interoperability should be regarded as 'a process rather than a decision'.[21]

These axioms seem equally applicable to IT for counter-terrorism. They all relate to matters of management, human attitudes and the right kind of central oversight, rather than technological limitations. They accord with the private sector doctrine that IT revolutions promote managerial revolutions, but depend on managerial acts of faith to initiate them properly. IT provides the possibility of new 'virtual' communities of analysts, but the opportunities will not be grasped without a commitment to new ways of working. Managers have to 'think out of the box' of well-tried preconceptions. So the managerial 'vision thing' for the IT vision is a matter of cultural change, putting new wine into the old bottles of a largely unchanged structure. But anyone can talk of cultural change. What does it actually mean for counter-terrorism?

This is where the Mark 1 and Mark 2 solutions diverge. The present writer's belief is that a campaign for cultural change is possible and desirable within the normal intelligence community; that the Mark 1 system of systems could be pursued with visionary enthusiasm. He is doubtful whether a cultural change of this kind spanning both intelligence and segments of law enforcement and other government data is possible or indeed desirable. Law enforcement intelligence is a developing specialisation, but in democracies it seems undesirable as well as impractical to conflate responsibilities geared to national security too closely with law enforcement's main task of 'crime-busting'. Better horizontal flows between the two specialisations are indeed needed for counter-terrorism; the point was made repeatedly in President Bush's national address in September 2002.[22] But it will need to be pursued on a more pragmatic basis than in the Mark 1 vision. Suggestions in this sense are made later in this essay. Otherwise it now concentrates on the vision for the intelligence community itself.

CULTURAL CHANGE AND THE INTELLIGENCE COMMUNITY

The essentials of intelligence culture need to be maintained: in particular the assumption that intelligence is dedicated to understanding and forecasting objectively, with some freedom from the responsibilities of policy advice, decision-taking and execution. Intelligence has to be close to policy with only a wafer-thin gap from it, but with a gap nevertheless between making key intelligence judgements and deciding what to do about them. This is not peculiar to intelligence, but applies equally to other government information specialisations – the British Office for National Statistics, for example. But it is particularly relevant to counter-terrorism where threat assessment and tactical warning are necessarily close to action, and some distinction between intelligence and action needs to be preserved. I have argued separately that this characteristic needs propagating as a 'world standard' for intelligence everywhere, but that is not the theme here.[23]

Nevertheless, if intelligence is to realise IT's potential, data needs to become seen more often as a common asset of 'virtual communities', and not a single-agency possession. This is in some ways a frightening vision, violating most of the canons of clear responsibilities, source protection and avoidance of duplication. It would need very careful handling in many ways, including the preservation of professional standards in the citing of evidence; otherwise there could be analytical chaos. Yet it must be recognised that, even with the importance of source protection, intelligence's traditional distinction between 'published' reports and 'unpublished' material limits horizontal flows more than is always necessary. Secrecy breeds an unusually intense sense of belonging, but to the agency, not the abstraction of the community. Other agencies may be partners but are sometimes seen also as competitors. Yet serving one's intelligence collaborators may sometimes be more important nationally than serving one's non-intelligence customers, and the needs of the two for accessing data may be quite different. The IT vision for counter-terrorism points to a heightened degree of 'community consciousness'.[24]

This is not a special problem for intelligence, but applies to all kinds of public service. According to an academic writer on public administration, getting agencies to work together is a matter of behaviour and process, rather than structure. It needs 'managerial craftsmanship'. Collaboration is not going to happen overnight, but is a long-term process that turns on 'creating a climate of trust and joint problem solving'. The writer describes this as building up an 'Interagency Collaborative Capacity'. If true of all government, secrecy and history make the difficulties apply to intelligence in spades.[25]

In encouraging a greater 'community' aspect of intelligence culture something can be learned from the three armed services' progress over the past 50 years with what the British call 'jointery'. Military power has been increasingly recognised as a unity, and not as separate categories of land, sea and air operations; recent British defence doctrine for expeditionary warfare is a current example. The military have adapted accordingly. Military specialisations and separateness have not been superseded, but have come to be seen increasingly as parts of some larger whole. Navies, armies and air forces still prize formal responsibilities and command intense single-service loyalties, very similar to those of intelligence agencies; but these have been accommodated in recent years with the development (in the British case) of joint force commanders, a mixed-service helicopter force, RAF aircraft deployed on naval carriers, and the creation of some other fully integrated joint-service organisations, including some in intelligence.

The shift of assumptions has been facilitated by a mixture of doctrine, training linked with appropriate personnel policies and central influence. Community measures to emphasise intelligence's unity might be considered under these same general headings.

Doctrine

Intelligence has little in the way of comprehensive doctrine. The streetwise wisdom of the civilian agencies is rarely formulated in doctrinal terms. Military intelligence has its doctrine, but it is purpose-designed for military settings and training, bringing control to the confusion of battle. In so far as there are received assumptions about intelligence as a whole, they tend to emphasise 'rational' frameworks: the military intelligence cycle, the importance of customers' requirements and priorities; the role of EEIs (essential elements of information); collection plans; 'intelligence architecture'. Democratic accountability and legislation have also contributed a characteristic emphasis on the roles and propriety of individual agencies. Thus the British Parliament's Intelligence and Security Committee recently felt it right to publicise its regret that GCHQ accounts are not acceptable to the Comptroller and Auditor General, since audit 'cannot correlate the physical assets...with the supporting accounting records'. Resource accounting has 'highlighted the poor asset tracking system' and 'forced a culture change'[26] – not the kind of cultural change advocated here to combat terrorism. Academic writing has contributed substantially to a more subtle understanding of the intelligence community, but has said relatively little about the problems of inter-agency relationships within it.

Professional doctrine cannot be invented overnight. But to reflect the 'community consciousness' advocated here two general points might be developed.

The first is that intelligence's roles of truth-seeking and truth-marketing do not lend themselves entirely to an apparently 'rational' and controllable view of its dynamics. All successful knowledge processes seem to thrive on a degree of creative disorderliness and opportunism, sacrificing some order and control for the greater good of creativity and insight. Intelligence is not divisible into neat boxes. Both collection and analysis need initiative, as well as responses to formal requirements. There has to be some kind of order, control and direct responsiveness to customer needs, and developing 'intelligence architecture' with these objectives has been a worthy discipline. But perhaps the architecture has to be baroque or rococo, rather than classical. The knack of success is striking the right balance between entrepreneurial local initiative and central control.

The second, related, point is that the accepted typologies of agency specialisations are correct as far as they go, but are simplifications. Some inter-agency boundaries are rooted in history rather than rational divisions of effort. Where boundaries do follow distinctive differences in skills, the different kinds of covert collection still support each other synergistically more extensively than is often acknowledged; code-breaking for example has been greatly influenced historically by the acquisition of data by Humint and other means, as in the breaking of the German Enigma cipher in World War II. Some kinds of modern technical collection – line-tapping, bugging, outputs from remote sensors, computer hacking, perhaps 'deep mining' of the Internet – defy any neat single-agency categorisation, though the US has devised the term Masint (Measurement and Signature Intelligence) to cover some of them. Collection is partly a set of techniques, but is also a capability for opportunistic information-gathering by any means that come to hand, as illustrated in the impressive Cold War history of the CIA's Directorate of Science and Technology.[27] Similarly, most worthwhile single-agency analysis actually has an all-source purview. Mutual support between its different elements is a key element of intelligence power. Depending on the effectiveness of inter-agency cooperation, this national power is something more (or less) than the sum of its parts.

Human Resources

Organisational culture is influenced in a host of practical ways, and there can be no simple template for promoting community consciousness. But some practical measures could spring from turning accepted assumptions about intelligence organisations on their head. Almost all nations view civilian intelligence employment as a matter of working in one specialist organisation separate from others, with its own distinctive recruitment, training, pay, conditions, career prospects and promotion procedures. The general assumption is that intelligence is a single-trade profession. In the UK the individual organisations have been quite good at training and attachments that expose their professionals to the 'real world' outside intelligence, and they have also had some leaders brought in from other parts of government. But historically they have had fewer exchanges within the intelligence community itself; no one except Sir Dick White has ever been head of two British agencies in succession, and as far as can be judged from published CVs no other head of agency has ever worked for any length of time in any of the others. In the US there is more mobility at the top level, but single-agency careers still appear to be the norm below it.

Yet the assumption that a professional life is based on a single agency is not incontestable. In another not totally dissimilar field Britain has a single Government Statistical Service deployed in a variety of government departments. It is not impossible to visualise intelligence similarly as a single (admittedly larger) National Intelligence Service, divided for convenience into its separate components, each with their individual and distinctive skills and characteristics, but with common conditions, experience and standards where practicable. The military intelligence specialists would necessarily be in a rather different position, but they too could be accommodated in the vision. New ways of developing and utilising a more community-based professionalism might then suggest themselves, for example:

- Provision for 'equal opportunities' in pay and prospects between those in small intelligence organisations and those in larger ones. For many years in Britain it was argued that the small Defence Intelligence Staff found it more difficult to recruit and keep people of high talent than the other, larger members of the intelligence community. If analysis now needs more attention than formerly, why not start by offering it parity with the wider intelligence community in pay, prospects and opportunities for inter-agency promotion?

- Mobility of specialist skills between organisations. Linguists are the most obviously redeployable specialists; a system of common recruitment and conditions might facilitate movement to meet changing operational needs. Similarly there may be advantages in making some provision for voluntary switching between specialisations, hypothetically, for example, between Sigint and imagery interpretation.

- Common training at various levels. The different elements of the US community each have their own powerful training organisations, and invite selected members of others to their course; but it is puzzling to the outsider that the US, as the intelligence superpower, does not have a single national intelligence staff college for the whole community. Britain might consider some ad hoc joint service training of this kind; so too could smaller countries. At lower levels, individual British agencies are said to have applied modern management training exercises to produce better internal communication and 'bonding'; perhaps this training could also be applied on a community basis to produce the same effects on inter-agency relations.

- Planned cross-postings as part of the career development of future senior officers; experience in another intelligence agency would be a desideratum for senior promotions in the parent organisation. This was a recommendation in 1996 of the American Brown-Aspin Commission on Intelligence, but seems to have vanished without trace.

These suggestions apply directly to the intelligence community; the Mark 1 IT vision and not the Mark 2. Yet viewing intelligence professionalism in this more integrated way could have a bearing on the latter. There is no reason why the intelligence specialists in law enforcement should not have some place in a wider intelligence career structure, and some advantage if they were. The professional techniques and standards are virtually identical with some of those in the intelligence community. Horizontal data access between this 'old' community and its newer law enforcement counterpart would be encouraged by more staff exchanges and progressions. The writer has argued separately for a wider all-source analyst career in Britain on 'difficult' foreign areas, a career which would perhaps include the research and analysis professionals in the Foreign and Commonwealth Office.[28] The inclusion of law enforcement intelligence specialists would add another dimension. To put such bread-and-butter proposals into a wider context: governments' need to work with intelligence's techniques and objectivity against difficult targets – whether terrorism, crime or the many others – is increasing. Twenty-first-century governments need to treat intelligence power with increasing seriousness. This means reviewing the ways in which they deal with the profession of those who elect to be part of it.

It may well be argued that informal arrangements already exist for most of the above; that standardisation between agencies is the last thing intelligence needs in an age of devolution in other government services; that the sheer size of intelligence communities precludes this approach in the US and UK (though not in smaller countries, especially where intelligence structures are still evolving); that with modern mobility the idea of careers and career prospects is outmoded – people apply for particular jobs and then move on. All this may be true. Nevertheless, if IT has the technological potential to revolutionise counter-terrorism and intelligence in general, some radical thinking about intelligence's human dimensions is called for to realise it.

Central Influence

At a technical IT level, introducing the 'system of systems' approach considered here needs a central overview with a capacity to develop blueprints, provide funding, and kick-start and oversee the concept generally. At a human level the complementary move towards greater community consciousness requires a similar central influence. Some actual central authority is needed for both, but providing any authority of this kind is a problem for intelligence almost everywhere.

In the US the future of this 'centre' still remains largely a matter of guesswork. Thus 9/11 has given an impetus towards central direction; the present DCI appears to exercise considerable personal authority; and enhanced power for the post figured among the recently stated Presidential objectives.[29] But it is too early to say whether central authority will be permanently strengthened. The new Department of Homeland Security may be improving intelligence's cooperation with law enforcement, though if changes have been made they have not yet received much publicity. At a technical level within the intelligence community itself its Intelink (its own intranet) may already contain some elements of a 'system of systems', and the defence-oriented Joint Worldwide Intelligence System is said to demonstrate a considerable degree of community collaboration. But American intelligence and law enforcement as a whole may just be too large and diverse to preclude any real change in the centre.

In Britain the authority within intelligence has moved in recent years towards the post of Intelligence Coordinator, which has been filled in varied ways and is now combined with that of the JIC Chairman. Worries were expressed some time ago by the Parliamentary Committee about a perceived 'void in the centre',[30] though British arrangements there have been so fluid in recent years that judgements should probably be deferred. It is, however, a good sign that the Cabinet Office team tasked with developing community IT has recently been strengthened.

Moreover, 9/11 has recently produced one UK development which may be significant both for intelligence and for much wider areas of counter-terrorism. A new Cabinet Office post has been created at top, Permanent Secretary level with responsibility for intelligence and security matters including defence against terrorism, and the occupant (Sir David Omand) will be able to influence not only IT in the 'old' intelligence community but also to encourage bridges between it and law enforcement. He is operating in the wider context of the present British government's longer-term commitment to 'joined up government' – the use of IT to simplify its dealings with citizens by eliminating multiple contacts with different departments – so presumably he will have some influence over inserting counter-terrorism's requirements into this IT strategy, with suitable safeguards.

Nevertheless the practical difficulties and the problems of reconciling counter-terrorist IT with individual privacy and legal constraints in modern democracies are enormous.[31] Creating a common pool of data on terrorism, with all manner of safeguards, can be pursued in the intelligence community with visionary enthusiasm, and one hopes it will be. By contrast its extension to areas of law enforcement and other government information, though equally relevant, still probably has to be pursued more pragmatically. Outside the intelligence community the vision of the common IT pool is still probably a vision too far.

CONCLUSIONS

Effective counter-terrorist intelligence seems to lend itself particularly to advanced IT. Intelligence is often seen as a matter of human brainpower. But bringing technology properly to bear is now of at least equal importance. Counter-terrorism appears to put a special emphasis on accessing and relating different kinds of data residing in different organisations. Developing IT 'systems of systems' to provide interoperability, integration and interdependence between these separate databases may be the key to greater overall effectiveness.

Modern writing on the information revolution suggests that the real problems in exploiting it to the full are managerial and human rather than technical. Managers are urged to 'think out of the box' in these matters. In this spirit this essay suggests shifts in the concept of 'intelligence power', incorporating:

- Doctrine that emphasises the unity of this power, and lays less emphasis on formal divisions in its processes and the separate disciplines within it.

- Practical personnel policies designed to develop a more holistic view of the intelligence profession and thereby promote the greater 'community consciousness' needed to develop community IT to the full.

- The right degree of central influence and leadership backed by an appropriate degree of authority.

This approach is advocated as the managerial/human component of developing an IT 'system of systems' for the intelligence community itself. It does not offer a solution to the (greater) problems of providing this community with IT interaction with law enforcement and other government data relevant to counter-terrorism, but its proposals could have some useful spin-off effects in that direction.

NOTES

I am particularly indebted for advice from the late Colonel K.R. Cunningham, US Army War College. I am also grateful for helpful comments from John Morrison and Robert Steele. Responsibility for the views expressed is of course mine.

1. Text of address by Robert David Steele at St Antony's College, Oxford, 12 June 2002. For his views in detail, see the speaker's *On Intelligence: Spies and Secrecy in an Open World* (Oakton, VA: OSS International Press 2001).
2. Bruce D. Berkowitz and Allen E. Goodman, *Best Truth: Intelligence in the Information Age* (New Haven, CT/London: Yale UP 2000) p.92.
3. Ibid. p.98.
4. As reported in *The New York Times*, 20 Sept. 2002.
5. Intelligence and Security Committee, *Annual Report 2001–2002*, Cm 5542 (London: Stationery Office 2002), para. 65.

6. *The New York Times* (note 4).
7. S. Rimington, Richard Dimbleby Lecture, *Security and Democracy* (London: BBC Educational Developments 1994) p.9.
8. Published in *Security Monitor* (London: RUSI 2002).
9. Paul Keetch, MP (Liberal Democrat) at the Royal United Services Institute, 11 Sept. 2002.
10. For a discussion of RMA and references to its literature, see Michael Herman, *Intelligence Services in the Information Age: Theory and Practice* (London and Portland, OR: Frank Cass 2001) Chap. 3.
11. Part of the vision could also be to link intelligence assessment automatically to menus and options for decision-taking; a counter-terrorist equivalent of the military 'sensor to shooter' harnessing of battlespace IT. But this is not pursued here.
12. Victor A. DeMarines, 'Exploiting the Internet Revolution' in Ashton B. Carter and John P. White (eds.), *Managing Defense for the Future* (Cambridge, MA/London: MIT Press 2001) p.77.
13. Gregory F. Treverton, *Reshaping National Intelligence in an Age of Information* (Cambridge: CUP 2001) p.xiii.
14. The present American Defense Secretary is said to have complained recently to the DCI that his briefing on national missile defence had been chaotic since, because of compartmentalisation, no analyst could present the total picture. (I am grateful to Robert Steele for this example.)
15. Herman, *Intelligence Services in the Information Age* (note 10) Chap. 12.
16. R.V. Jones, *Most Secret War: British Secret Intelligence 1939–1945* (London: Hamish Hamilton 1978). See, e.g., his account of work on German rocket developments on pp.332–48.
17. Vertic, *Trust and Verify* (no.103, July–Aug. 2002) p.8 (Journal of Verification Research, Training and Information Centre).
18. Other current British examples of intelligence and law enforcement connections on terrorism are the National Counter Terrorism and Security Office (NaCTSO) manned jointly by police and Security Service officers, and the Police International Counter Terrorist Unit, also with Security Service representation (Cabinet Office Report, *The UK and the Campaign against International Terrorism: Progress Report* (Sept. 2002). <http://cabinet.office.gov.uk/reports/terrorism>.
19. Treverton, *Reshaping National Intelligence in an Age of Information* (note 13) p.249.
20. Admittedly the discipline of detecting terrorists is not unlike law enforcement's detection of serial killers; but these are still a small minority of criminals.
21. DeMarines, 'Exploiting the Internet Revolution' (note 12) pp.76–7.
22. *The New York Times* (note 4).
23. Herman, *Intelligence Services in the Information Age* (note 10) Chap. 1.
24. For earlier discussion of 'community consciousness', and background, see Michael Herman's *Intelligence Power in Peace and War* (Cambridge: CUP 1996) Chap. 17.
25. The summary is of conclusions in E. Bardach, *Getting Agencies to Work Together: the Practice and Theory of Managerial Craftsmanship* (Washington DC: Brookings Institute 1998) quoted by Wayne Parsons, 'Modernising Policy-Making for the Twenty-First Century: the Professional Model', *Public Policy and Administration* 16/10 (Autumn 2001).
26. Intelligence and Security Committee, *Annual Report 2001–2002* (note 5), paragraph 41.
27. Jeffrey T. Richelson, *The Wizards of Langley: Inside the CIA's Directorate of Science and Technology* (Oxford: Westview 2001).
28. Herman, *Intelligence Services in the Information Age* (note 10) pp.86–90.
29. *The New York Times* (note 4).
30. Intelligence and Security Committee, *Annual Report 2001–2002* (note 5), paragraphs 23,41.
31. For a discussion of the political problems of data security and data privacy in the British objective of 'joined up government' on routine matters, see Christine Bellamy, 'Implementing Information-Age Government: Principles, Progress and Paradox', *Public Policy and Administration* 15/1 (Spring 2000).

9/11: The Failure of Strategic Intelligence

MELVIN A. GOODMAN

One week after the attack on the Pentagon and the World Trade Center, National Security Adviser Condoleeza Rice told the press corps, 'This isn't Pearl Harbor.' No, it was worse. Sixty years ago, the United States (US) did not have a director of central intelligence or 13 intelligence agencies or a combined intelligence budget of more than $30bn to provide early warning of enemy attack. And just as intelligence was divided and diffuse on the eve of Pearl Harbor, there was no genuine intelligence community on the eve of September 11, 2001.

There is another significant and telling difference between Pearl Harbor and September 11. Less than two weeks after the surprise attack on Pearl Harbor, President Franklin D. Roosevelt appointed a high-level military and civilian commission to determine the causes of the intelligence failure. Following the September 11 attacks, however, President George W. Bush, CIA Director George Tenet and the chairmen of the Senate and House intelligence committees were adamantly opposed to any investigation or postmortem. The president's failure to appoint a statutory inspector general at the Central Intelligence Agency (CIA) from January 2001 to April 2002 deprived the agency of the one individual who could have started an investigation regardless of the director's opposition. Overall, the unwillingness to begin a congressional inquiry for nearly eight months increased the suspicion that indicators of an attack had gone unheeded.

The eventual Senate and House intelligence committee investigation of the September 11 failure, which began in June 2002, was mishandled at the outset. The original staff director for the investigation, former CIA inspector general Britt Snider, had the stature and experience for the job, but he was soon pushed out by former Senate intelligence committee chairman Richard Shelby (Republican-Georgia), a staunch critic of CIA director Tenet but never an advocate for reform of the intelligence community. The staff itself seemed too small and inexperienced to do the job seriously. The August 2002 decision of the chairmen of the Senate and House intelligence committees, Senator Bob Graham (Democrat-Florida) and Representative Porter Goss (Republican-Florida), to order an aggressive Federal Bureau of Investigation (FBI) investigation of the joint committee, ostensibly to uncover leaks of classified information, marked a blatant violation of the separation of powers between the executive and legislative branches. Much time was lost as senators and representatives debated whether committee members should submit to unprecedented polygraph examinations, a move designed to placate the Bush administration.

President Bush never wanted an intelligence investigation of September 11, neither congressional nor independent, and established roadblocks to an independent investigation of the intelligence community. He did not permit his secretaries of state and defense to testify to the joint congressional investigation in public session and wanted the investigation to be quick and dirty. According to Senator Shelby, the administration has 'delayed cooperating fully, knowing it (the committee) has a deadline to meet'.[1]

To make matters worse, the congressional oversight process has broken down over the past ten years, and there is no sign that the appropriate committees are willing to scrutinize the intelligence community. Senator Charles Grassley (Republican-Iowa) says 'Everyone's in awe of them [intelligence agencies]. Everyone just melts in their presence, and so they have always gotten a long leash.' Republican David Obey (Representative-Wisconsin) agrees, adding that congressional oversight has been 'miserable'. Republican Saxby Chambliss (Representative-Georgia) conceded that the congressional intelligence committees have a 'share in the blame for not providing better oversight'.

Nevertheless, the preliminary report of the joint intelligence committee did an excellent job of ferreting out evidence documenting the failures at CIA and the FBI.[2] The report describes a director of central intelligence who declared a war on terrorism in 1998, but allocated no additional funding or personnel to the task force on terrorism; an intelligence community that never catalogued information on the use of airplanes as weapons; a CIA that never acknowledged the possibility of weaponizing commercial aircraft for terrorism until two months after the attacks on the World Trade Center and the Pentagon.

We now know from the preliminary report that the timely use and distribution of intelligence data could have prevented the terrible acts of terrorism in 2001. And the refusal of the White House and the CIA to declassify the information provided to the president before the attacks, which has already been reported in the international press, suggests that important information did make its way to the highest levels of government. Two days after the report was published, the Bush administration reversed itself and endorsed the creation of a separate, independent commission to study the intelligence failure.[3]

FAILURES OF INTELLIGENCE

The failure to anticipate the September 11 attacks – and the reluctance to thoroughly investigate this failure – is merely the latest in a long series of CIA blunders, consistently followed by the inability of the intelligence committees to conduct oversight. Over the past half-century, US presidents have accepted the poor performance of the CIA, presumably because the agency offers a clandestine and relatively inexpensive instrument for American foreign policy. President Dwight Eisenhower employed the CIA in a series of covert actions in Guatemala, Iran and Cuba that contributed to instability in these countries and complicated US bilateral relations in the Caribbean and Southwest Asia. Subsequent covert operations in Indonesia, Congo, Angola and Chile followed a similar pattern. In the field of intelligence analysis, there was no warning for the 1973 October War, the 1982 Israeli invasion of Lebanon or the 1983 terrorist bombings that killed 250 US marines and destroyed the US embassy in Beirut. Intelligence missed the Iranian revolution and the fall of the Shah in 1979, Iraq's invasion of Iran in 1980 and the Iraqi invasion of Kuwait in 1990.

In the 1980s, CIA director William Casey politicized the intelligence analysis of the CIA and orchestrated the Iran-contra scheme that seriously embarrassed the Reagan administration. Deputy director Robert Gates failed to receive confirmation as CIA director in 1987 because the Senate Select Committee on Intelligence did not believe his denials of knowledge of the Iran-Contra affair. When he was confirmed in 1991 after a second nomination, he garnered more negative votes than any director in the history of the CIA because of his role in the politicization of intelligence on the Soviet Union. Casey and Gates were directly responsible for the CIA's poor analytical record in dealing with Soviet issues throughout the 1980s, from the failure to foresee the Soviet collapse to the revelation that CIA clandestine officer Aldrich Ames had been a Soviet spy for nearly a decade, altogether the greatest intelligence failure in the history of the agency until the terrorist attacks in 2001. In an unguarded moment in March 1995, Gates admitted that he had watched Casey on 'issue after issue sit in meetings and present intelligence framed in terms of the policy he wanted pursued'.[4] There has never been a better definition of politicization by a former director of central intelligence.

The performance of the intelligence community did not improve in the 1990s. When the CIA missed Indian underground nuclear testing in 1998, Director George Tenet stated, 'We didn't have a clue'.[5] This failure to monitor Indian testing and Tenet's inexplicable testimony that the CIA could not guarantee verification of the treaty led to the Senate's unwillingness to ratify the Comprehensive Test Ban Treaty. The CIA also failed to anticipate the third-stage capability of the North Korean Taepodong missile, which was tested in August 1998, leading to congressional calls in the US for a national missile defense and Japanese suspension of talks to establish diplomatic relations with North Korea.[6] Since 1998, CIA analysis of Third World missile programs has taken on a worst-case flavor, exaggerating the national security threat to the US and politicizing the intelligence data in the process.

The CIA has been particularly weak on the terrorism issue. In 1986, Casey and Gates created the conceptually-flawed Counter-Terrorism Center (CTC). They believed that the Soviet Union was responsible for every act of international terrorism (it was not), that intelligence analysts and secret agents should work together in one office (they should not) and that the CIA and other intelligence agencies would share sensitive information (they did not). The CIA and FBI provided no warning of terrorist attacks on the World Trade Center in 1993, US military barracks in Saudi Arabia in 1996, US embassies in East Africa in 1998 or the USS *Cole* in 2000.

The CTC never understood the connection between Ramzi Ahmed Yousef, the coordinator of the 1993 World Trade Center attack, and the Al-Qaeda organization until it was too late. And the CTC expected an attack abroad, not at home. Not even the foiled plot to bomb Los Angeles International Airport in December 1999 led the CIA and the FBI to heighten concerns over the ability of Al-Qaeda to strike inside the US.[7] President Bill Clinton's national security adviser, Samuel Berger, told the joint intelligence inquiry in September 2002 that the FBI repeatedly assured the White House that Al-Qaeda lacked the ability to launch a domestic strike.

The September 11 attacks exposed the inability of analysts and agents to perform strategic analysis, challenge flawed assumptions and share sensitive secrets. No agency in the intelligence community could imagine a terrorist operation conducted inside the US, using commercial airplanes as weapons, although Al-Qaeda had planned such operations in the mid-1990s in Europe and Asia. The CIA was tracking Al-Qaeda operatives but never placed them on the immigration service Watch List; the FBI failed to track Arab men attending flight schools who were behaving in a suspicious fashion.

The CIA has always been slow to pass along sensitive information to other intelligence agencies because of the risk of releasing information that could be embarrassing or the tendency to place the needs of counter-intelligence (protecting sources and methods) over the needs of counter-terrorism. In typical fashion, the CIA actually received sensitive information from the Malaysian intelligence service on two hijackers, who then lived openly in San Diego, but the CIA was slow to pass names to the FBI and the FBI dropped the ball in the US. One of the hijackers was listed in the San Diego phone directory and the other used a credit card in his own name; both were active at the San Diego Islamic Center. Either one of these hijackers could have led the FBI to at least 11 of the 19 hijackers and the plan to hijack and weaponize commercial airliners. The CIA never informed the State Department that one of these men, Khalid al-Midhar, held a multiple-entry visa to get into the US and should be placed on the Watch List to prevent future re-entry. Nevertheless, without the benefit of classified information and foreign liaison, the Congressional Research Service of the Library of Congress and University of Pennsylvania Professor of Political Science Stephen Gale did anticipate hijacking of commercial aircraft and warned both the CIA's National Intelligence Council and the Department of Transportation.[8]

Since September 11, the Bush administration's global policy of unilateralism has involved the CIA in controversial covert operations, including political assassinations, despite the ban on such actions by presidential executive order since 1975. US unilateralism and fear of the CIA are major components of the anti-Americanism that is sweeping across Europe, the Middle East and Southwest Asia. CIA Director Tenet's unprecedented diplomatic role in the Middle East peace process revives the suspicion that a CIA director has put the nation's strategic intelligence at the service of a political agenda. His intense involvement with both Palestinian and Israeli security forces places him at the center of the policy process in the Middle East and compromises the collection of intelligence against both sides.

Tenet is serving the policy interests of the Bush administration in other ways as well, resorting to worst-case analysis to describe the threats that confront America in order to justify the deployment of a national missile defense and the US withdrawal from the Anti-Ballistic Missile Treaty, a cornerstone of US arms control policy since 1972. Without new data, CIA analysts have begun asserting that Iran, Iraq and North Korea are moving closer to a nuclear capability that would threaten the US. The administration's pressure on the CIA to produce intelligence data to justify a war against Iraq led to greater politicization of intelligence, and the emphasis on preemptive attack led to dubious demands on the CIA to produce intelligence justification for warfare. Tenet previously told the White House in 1998 that the CIA had sufficient data to justify attacking a pharmaceutical plant in Khartoum, Sudan, although his own operational specialists were skeptical of the intelligence.

STRUCTURAL FLAWS

One reason for the consistent failures of the intelligence community is the organizational discontinuity at both the CIA and FBI. The CIA has an operational mission to collect clandestine intelligence and conduct covert action; it also analyzes and publishes national intelligence estimates. The agency cannot perform both missions well and the operational demands of the agency have often politicized the intelligence analysis. This has happened in such regions as Central and South America, where the CIA covered up human rights abuses, and South and Southwest Asia, where the agency failed to analyze reports of strategic weapons programs.

The FBI also suffers from a bipolar mission. Its traditional law enforcement mission involves reacting to crimes that have already occurred. Its counter-terrorism mission, by contrast, requires a proactive role – ferreting out threats to national security before they occur. Under former FBI director Louis Freeh, the FBI remained hostile to the inexact world of analysis and intelligence that is the basis of any investigation of international terrorism. Walter Lippmann reminded us 70 years ago that it is essential to 'separate as absolutely as it is possible to do so the staff which executes from the staff which investigates'.[9]

Turf issues abound. The protection of 'sources and methods' has been an obstacle to information sharing, with the CIA and the FBI having a long history of poor communication. Intelligence agencies and the Pentagon often lock horns. The Director of Central Intelligence (DCI) is responsible for foreign intelligence, but lacks control and authority over 90 per cent of the intelligence community, including the National Security Agency (NSA), the National Imagery and Mapping Agency (NIMA) and the National Reconnaissance Office (NRO), which are staffed and funded by the Department of Defense (DoD).

The priorities of the DCI and those of the Pentagon are quite different. Previous DCIs, particularly Gates and John Deutch, harmed the CIA by de-emphasizing strategic intelligence for policymakers and catering instead to the tactical demands of the Pentagon. The CIA produces fewer intelligence assessments that deal with strategic matters and emphasizes instead intelligence support for the warfighter. Gates ended CIA analysis on key order-of-battle issues in order to avoid tendentious analytical struggles with the Pentagon; Deutch's creation in 1996 of NIMA at the DoD enabled the Pentagon to be the sole interpreter of satellite photography. In its short history, NIMA has been responsible for a series of major intelligence disasters, including the failure to monitor Indian nuclear testing in 1998, the bombing of the Chinese embassy in Belgrade in 1999 and the exaggeration of missile programs in North Korea, Iran and Iraq.

The Pentagon uses imagery analysis to justify the defense budget, to gauge the likelihood of military conflict around the world and to verify arms control agreements. In creating NIMA, Deutch abolished the CIA's Office of Imagery Analysis and the joint DoD-CIA National Photographic Interpretation Center, which often challenged the analytical views of the Pentagon and monitored arms control agreements that would have been impossible without CIA's capability to do so.

Worst of all, the Bush administration has referred to a 'marriage' between the Pentagon and the CIA, which suggests that intelligence continues to be subordinated to Pentagon priorities. The CIA's worst-case analysis on global issues is being used to justify the highest peacetime increases in defense spending since the record-level increases of the Reagan administration as well as the construction of a national missile defense system. In justifying the use of force against Iraq, it appears that the policy community is ignoring Tenet's role of supplying intelligence as director of central intelligence and is turning to Secretary of Defense Donald Rumsfeld, who actually controls both imagery collection and analysis.

One of the CIA's major missions, covert action, remains a dangerously unregulated activity. There are no political and ethical guidelines delineating when to engage in covert action, and previous covert actions have harmed US strategic interests, placing on the CIA payroll such criminals as Panama's General Manuel Noriega, Guatemala's Colonel Julio Alpirez, Peru's intelligence chief Vladimiro Montesinos and Chile's General Manuel Contreras. Although President Bush, like every other president since Gerald Ford, has signed an executive order banning political assassination, exceptions have been made in the covert pursuit of Iraqi President Saddam Hussein and former Afghanistan Prime Minister Gulbuddin Hekmatyar, who received CIA assistance in the 1980s.

In 1998, the US and the CIA used the cover of the United Nations (UN) and the UN Special Commission (UNSCOM) to conduct a secret operation to spy on Iraqi military communications as part of a covert action to topple Saddam Hussein. Neither the UN nor UNSCOM had authorized the US surveillance, which Saddam Hussein cited as justification for expelling the UN monitors. As a result, the US and the UN lost their most successful program to monitor and verify Iraq's nuclear, chemical and biological programs, compromising the credibility of multilateral inspection of weapons of mass destruction. In that same year, the CIA produced spurious intelligence data to justify the US bombing of a pharmaceutical plant in the Sudan, one of the few countries willing to help the Clinton administration arrest Osama bin Laden.[10] President George Bush's speech to the UN on 12 September 2002 contained no new information on Iraqi military capabilities, particularly weapons of mass destruction. In view of the high priority on intelligence collection against Iraq, the speech was devoid of information on any recent developments in Iraq.

Finally, a comparison of the CIA and the State Department reveals skewed US priorities. Today, the CIA has approximately 16,000 employees, more than four times the number at the State Department, and the intelligence community budget is nearly ten times that of the State Department. As a result of cutbacks, the State Department has closed important posts in South America, the Balkans, Southwest Asia and Africa, and has increased the practice of posting political amateurs with deep pockets to key ambassadorships. It is no wonder that the role of the State Department has significantly diminished in such key functional areas as arms control and disarmament and such key regional areas as the Middle East and South Asia. Meanwhile, the CIA has received large increases in its budgetary authority, although one of the CIA's first directors, Allen Dulles, emphasized that 'the bulk of intelligence can be obtained through overt channels' and that if the agency got to be a 'great big octopus it would not function well'.[11]

The intelligence community, moreover, could learn a great deal from the State Department, where foreign service officers cannot advance through the system or receive prestigious positions without mastering foreign languages. On the other hand, the chronic shortage of language experts in the intelligence community is the Achilles heel of all the collection and analytic agencies. The FBI lacked the means to translate documents found in the wake of the murder of Rabbi Meir Kahane that could have provided significant intelligence to about the role of Al-Qaeda. (A vigorous pursuit of the Kahane case might have prevented both attacks on the World Trade Center, since the assassin was at the center of a terrorist conspiracy with links to the Middle East and the US.) NSA lacked the means to translate important messages prior to September 11 that mentioned 'Tomorrow is zero hour'. The CIA has the weakest language capabilities of all the intelligence agencies, with only one Farsi speaker in the embassy in Tehran, for example, when the embassy was seized in 1979. The situation has improved negligibly in the past two decades.

WHAT IS TO BE DONE?

What the CIA and the intelligence community should be, what it should do and what it should prepare to do are less clear than at any time since the beginning of the Cold War. Throughout the Cold War, the need to count and characterize Soviet weapons systems and the search for indications of surprise attack focused the efforts of the CIA. These goals disappeared with the collapse of the Berlin Wall in 1989 and the dissolution of the Soviet

Union in 1991. Major steps must be taken to design an intelligence infrastructure to deal with terrorism, the major security threat in the twenty-first century. The ongoing contentious debate over the role of the new Department of Homeland Security masks the far greater need to reform the intelligence community. Such reforms include demilitarizing the intelligence community, resolution of key turf issues and reform of covert operations.

It is essential that the intelligence community provide an alternative source of information and intelligence to the decision-making community. Currently, the uniformed military dominates the collection and analysis of sensitive intelligence, which means that the CIA is no longer a check on the military bureaucracy as it was during the Vietnam War and arms control decision-making in the 1960s and 1970s. In these years, civilian analysts were a more objective and balanced source of intelligence than their military counterparts in assessing threats to the US and the military capability of state and non-state actors. Since the 1991 Gulf War, the CIA has not played a major role in military intelligence. According to a former senior CIA analyst, Richard Russell, 'the absence of an independent civilian analytic check on military intelligence threatens American civilian control of the military instrument for political purpose'.[12]

Retired General Brent Scowcroft, the head of the President's Foreign Intelligence Advisory Board, has conducted a comprehensive review of the intelligence community for President Bush and favors transferring budgetary and collection authority from the Pentagon to a new office that reports directly to the DCI.[13] These agencies include NSA, which conducts worldwide electronic eavesdropping; NRO, which designs spy satellites; and NIMA, which analyzes satellite pictures and data, and produces maps. Secretary of Defense Donald Rumsfeld opposes this transfer and has created a new position of undersecretary of defense for intelligence to preempt such reform. Congressional approval of this new position would preserve the status quo and close the narrow window of opportunity for more extensive reform proposals under consideration by the joint intelligence committees of the House and Senate.

It is crucial that the CIA strengthens links across the intelligence community in order to share intelligence. Unfortunately, the agency places too much emphasis on the compartmentalization of intelligence and the 'need-to-know', which are obstacles to intelligence sharing. The failures at Pearl Harbor in 1941 and the terrorist attacks in 2001 could have been prevented with genuine sharing of sensitive intelligence information. But this information tends to move vertically within each of the 13 intelligence agencies instead of horizontally across them. The FBI and the CIA have never been effective in sharing information with each other or with such key agencies as the Immigration and Naturalization Service, the Federal Aviation Agency, the Border Guards and the Coast Guard, which are on the front line in the war against terrorism. There is no guarantee that the CIA and FBI will share raw reporting on terrorism with the new Department of Homeland Security.

Even if the 13 agencies and departments of the intelligence community were willing to share information, their anachronistic computer systems would not allow it. The FBI computer system is particularly unable to move and recall data, because former director Louis Freeh believed that computer technology was overrated and too expensive. The State Department computer system is from another age, which means that American embassies overseas regularly issue visas to likely terrorists because consular officials cannot obtain up-to-date information. And State Department computers are not linked to the CIA, the FBI or the Immigration and Naturalization Service.

To minimize the politicization of intelligence work, covert operations and intelligence gathering should be separated. The Directorate of Operations is responsible for clandestine activities. It relies on secrecy, hierarchy and the strict enforcement of information on a need-to-know basis. It is involved in the policy-making process. The Directorate of Intelligence is devoted to analysis. It helps set the context for people who formulate policy but it should not be involved in the making of policy. The FBI should be split into two agencies, with a Domestic Counter-Terrorism Service reporting directly to the DCI.

The Bush administration and Congress have responded in classic bureaucratic fashion to the September 11 failure, throwing lots of money at the problem to find a solution. The defense budget for 2004 exceeds $400bn, an increase of nearly 30 per cent since 2000. The intelligence budget will increase by 20 per cent in 2003, climbing toward $40bn. The defense budget protects the current force structure and ongoing weapons modernization programs, and assigns top priority to deploying a national missile defense. Most of the intelligence budget pays for collection resources – including a profusion of electronic data and images from planes, ships, ground stations and satellites, along with clandestine human intelligence collection. These increases have little to do with countering terrorism and are reminiscent of President Dwight Eisenhower's warning against the military-industrial complex in 1961.

THE NEED FOR GLASNOST

CIA Director Tenet has reversed the modest steps toward greater openness that were instituted by several of his predecessors. At his confirmation hearings in 1997, Tenet promised to continue the policy of openness, but he also emphasized that it was time for the agency to stop looking over its shoulder at its critics and to increase its clandestine role in support of national security. Accordingly, he has withheld thousands of sensitive documents detailing covert operations in Chile that took place more than 25 years ago, despite demands for openness by former president Bill Clinton and secretary of state Madeleine Albright. Tenet argued that releasing these documents would compromise covert sources and methods; more likely, he feared that declassification would embarrass the US both by revealing the efforts of the Nixon administration to overturn a constitutionally-elected government and by exposing the details of the Letelier/Moffitt murders during the Ford administration.

Both the CIA and FBI were derelict in not providing important information to the Justice Department and the congressional committees about the espionage activities of Aldrich Ames and Robert Hannsen on behalf of Soviet and Russian intelligence. Former CIA director Gates (1991–93) did not share with the White House the fact that a CIA operative had compromised every agency operation aimed at the former Soviet Union. Former CIA director James Woolsey (1993–95) never punished those officials who failed to monitor Ames. And former director Deutch (1995–97) upheld a decision to revoke the security clearance of Richard Nuccio, the State Department whistle blower who tried to expose CIA lying when he revealed a suspected murderer on the CIA's payroll in Guatemala.

Sadly, the US Senate, led by Senator Shelby, then director of the Senate intelligence committee, aggravated the situation in September 2000, when it passed a bill that would have criminalized the disclosure of all 'properly classified' information, thus creating an official secrets act. It is already a crime to disclose classified information about nuclear weapons codes, intelligence communications and the names of covert agents. The CIA initially convinced the Senate to criminalize all leaks of classified information, and President Clinton's Justice Department was persuaded to reverse its position and support the measure.

'Properly classified' information is too broad a category; even the Pentagon Papers were 'properly classified'. Far too much information is classified, and the recent disclosures on the role of the CIA in Chile demonstrate that a great deal of information is classified to cover up government embarrassments and CIA misdeeds. Opposition to the bill was bipartisan, but when the House of Representatives did not block it in a House-Senate conference, the threat of another 'torment of secrecy' akin to the worst days of the Cold War was anticipated. Fortunately, President Clinton vetoed the bill in November 2000, dealing a major setback to CIA Director Tenet, one of the main proponents of the bill. Clinton chose to protect his legacy and the public's right to know rather than endorse the zeal of his CIA director.

Former Senator Daniel Moynihan's 1995–96 commission on secrecy concluded that the American public both needs and has a right to a full accounting of the history of US covert operations. A presidential executive order to extend openness to intelligence matters is required, along with congressionally mandated limits on the intelligence community's prerogative, to conceal information. Senator Shelby, then minority director of the Senate intelligence committee, stopped just short of accusing the CIA and the intelligence community of slowing the flow of information to the congressional investigation of September 11.[14] A balancing test between public interest and national security must be part of the classification/declassification process, and this would include judicial review of CIA denials to release of information under the Freedom of Information Act.

The CIA should not be able to hide behind its secret budget and remain in violation of Article I/Section 9 of the Constitution, which demands that a 'regular Statement and Account of the Receipts and Expenditures of all public money shall be published from time to time'. The overall intelligence community budget (now greater than $35bn) was declassified only in 1997 and 1998, but the CIA budget (nearly $3.5bn) has never been declassified. The CIA now maintains that, because of the openness in those two years, the release of old budget figures would 'help identify to other governments – including governments very hostile to the United States – trends in intelligence spending' that may permit correlations 'between specific spending figures and specific intelligence programs'.[15]

The intelligence community, particularly the CIA, faces a situation comparable to that of 55 years ago, when President Harry S. Truman created the CIA and the National Security Council. As in 1947–48, the international environment has been recast, the threats have been altered, and as a result the institutions created to fight the Cold War must be redesigned. If steps are not taken to improve the intelligence community, we can expect more terrorist operations against the US. Certainly the self-aggrandizing behavior of the FBI and CIA in not investigating the intelligence and operational failures of the collapse of the Soviet Union, the espionage careers of Aldrich Ames and Robert Hannsen, and the terror attacks of September 11 does not auger well for the future of intelligence in the US.

In Joseph Conrad's novel, *The Secret Agent* (1907), there is a minor character, an anarchist called the professor, whom no one dares to touch because he has wired himself to a powerful bomb. The novel ends with a view of the mad professor walking like a 'pest in the street full of men'. This grotesque vision, familiar to many in Israel, Colombia and Lebanon, is now a clear and present danger to Americans. This vision brings home to us that, in the long run, it will be law enforcement agencies and the local police that and will win the war on terrorism, and they will require intelligence collection and analysis from an intelligence community that must be rebuilt.

NOTES

A version of this article appears in the forthcoming *Power Trip* (Seven Stories Press, 2003). The author's views are his own and do not necessarily reflect the opinions of the Department of Defense or the National Defense University.

1. James Risen, 'White House Drags its Feet on Testifying at 9/11 Panel', *New York Times*, 13 Sept. 2002, p.10.
2. Joint Inquiry Staff Statement, Part I, Joint Inquiry Staff, 18 Sept. 2002, <www.nytimes. com>.
3. *New York Times*, 23 Sept. 2002, p.1.
4. *Boston Globe*, 29 Sept. 2002, p.11.
5. *Wall Street Journal*, 13 May 1998, p.22.
6. Ronald E. Powaski, *Return to Armageddon: The United States and the Nuclear Arms Race, 1981–1999* (NY: OUP 2000) p.226.
7. *New York Times*, 23 Sept. 2002, p.11.
8. *Washington Post*, 19 May 2002, p.9.
9. Walter Lippmann, *Public Opinion* (New Brunswick, NJ: Transaction Publishers 1997) p.386.
10. *New York Times*, 21 Sept. 1998, p.1.
11. Peter Grose, *Gentleman Spy: The Life of Allen Dulles* (Boston, MA: Houghton Mifflin 1994) p.292.
12. Richard Russell, 'CIA's Strategic Intelligence in Iraq', *Political Science Quarterly* 117/2 (2002) p.207.
13. *Washington Post*, 9 Sept. 2002, p.17.
14. Allison Mitchell, 'In Senate, a Call for Answers and a Warning on the Future', *New York Times*, 10 Sept. 2002, p.1.
15. *Washington Post*, 7 Oct. 2002, p.16.

All Glory is Fleeting:
Sigint and the Fight Against
International Terrorism

MATTHEW M. AID

The impact of terrorism is currently far more limited by the failure or
unwillingness of terrorists to exploit new technologies and complex
vulnerabilities than by the inherent difficulty in conducting much more lethal
attacks. The problem is not a lack of credible means to an end, but rather the
lack of a real-world Doctor No or Professor Moriarty.
Anthony Cordesman

The surest guarantee of disappointment is an unrealistic expectation.
Thomas Patrick Carroll

Despite the passage of time since the deadly terrorist attacks of September 11,
2001, it remains extremely difficult to objectively discuss the important role
that Signals Intelligence (Sigint) has played, and must necessarily continue to
play, in the war against terrorism. Naturally, the single largest impediment to
an educated discussion of the subject is the secrecy that surrounds virtually
all aspects of contemporary Sigint operations. The US government and its
partners have released virtually no primary documentation about the role
played by intelligence in the events leading up to the bombings in New York
City and Washington, DC, and the congressional public hearings on the
performance of the US intelligence community prior to September 11 left
much unsaid because of security considerations.

This essay seeks to set out what is known or can be reasonably
established about the role that Sigint played in the events leading up to the
terrorist attacks on September 11, 2001. It focuses on the performance of
America's Sigint organization, the National Security Agency (NSA), and
also discusses the potential future role of Sigint in the war on terrorism.

SIGINT AND THE CHANGING WAR ON TERRORISM IN THE 1990S

In order to understand the role that Sigint played in the war against
international terrorism in the 1990s, and more specifically NSA's

intelligence collection operations against Osama bin Laden and the Al-Qaeda organization, it is essential to understand the global context within which Sigint had to operate in the early 1990s.

The Cold War, which had shaped world politics for more than 40 years, came to an abrupt end with the dismantling of the Berlin Wall in 1989–90, and the subsequent collapse of the Soviet Union in 1991. With the end of the Cold War, virtually all Western intelligence services, including virtually every agency making up the US intelligence community, were pared down to 'peacetime levels'. Between 1991 and 1998, congressionally-ordered budget cuts forced the US intelligence community to reduce its size by 22.5 per cent, meaning that more than 20,500 men and women lost their jobs; and the US intelligence budget was slashed from about $34bn to $27bn. NSA, the single largest and most expensive component of the US intelligence community, lost one third of its staff between 1991 and 1996, and its budget was slashed by 35 per cent from $5.2bn to less than $3.5bn.[1] We now know that these cuts, especially the loss of so many of the agency's most talented managers, had a devastating impact on NSA's ability to perform its mission. According to a declassified congressional study: 'One of the side effects of NSA's downsizing, outsourcing and transformation has been the loss of critical program management expertise, systems engineering, and requirements definition skills.'[2]

NSA was not the only Sigint service feeling the pinch. The British Sigint organization, the Government Communications Headquarters (GCHQ), was also forced to pare down its operations and reorganize itself in the early 1990s in order to deal with the new geostrategic threats and changes in global telecommunications technology.[3] In 1992, GCHQ Director Sir John Adye informed his staff that he had ordered a three-year study into a 'redirection of effort' for the agency, which led to the closure of several GCHQ stations; GCHQ's civilian staff of 7,000 was cut by about ten per cent.[4] Another study completed in 1995 revealed that GCHQ was still overmanned, inefficient and cost more than it was producing in the way of hard intelligence.[5] This study resulted in further substantial cuts in the size and budget of GCHQ. Between 1995 and 2000, GCHQ's staff was cut from 5,500 to only 4,600 civilian and military personnel.[6]

The intelligence struggle against international terrorism also changed dramatically with the end of the Cold War. In the fall of 1991, Yasser Arafat and the leadership of the Palestinian Liberation Organization (PLO) agreed to participate for the first time in political dialog with Israel. This dialog, which was brokered by the Norwegian government, led to the signing of the so-called Oslo Accord on the front lawn of the White House on 13 September 1993. With the creation in 1995 of an autonomous Palestinian governing entity, the Palestinian Authority (PA), on the West Bank and the

Gaza Strip, acts of international terrorism by Palestinian terrorists fell dramatically in the early 1990s. With the support of virtually all frontline Arab states, including Saudi Arabia, the PLO ceased its sponsorship of terrorist activities and recognized the State of Israel. The Oslo Accord also effectively emasculated the more radical Palestinian organizations that opposed reconciliation with Israel, such as those led by George Habash and Abu Nidal, who fell into disfavor with the countries which had previously supported them. As a result, their terrorist activities came to an almost complete standstill.

Given the dramatic decline in Middle Eastern terrorism, the scale of intelligence resources dedicated to monitoring worldwide terrorist activities by the US and other Western intelligence agencies, especially in the area of Sigint, fell precipitously in the first half of the 1990s as more pressing intelligence targets ate up a higher percentage of the available collection resources.[7] NSA and other Western Sigint services continued to monitor terrorist activities, albeit with significantly fewer resources than before.[8]

Western intelligence services had to adapt and readjust the nature and extent of their collection activities to deal with the changing and more diffuse global terrorist threat. For example, NSA's counter-terrorist Sigint mission in the early to mid-1990s was complicated by the wide geographic dispersion and disparate nature of the new terrorist targets that it was being asked to cover. There was the continued threat posed by state-sponsored terrorism, especially from Iran. For instance, Sigint intercepts of Iranian government message traffic between Tehran and the Iranian embassies in Paris, France and Berne, Switzerland, confirmed that Iranian secret agents operating from the Iranian embassy in Berne had murdered former Iranian prime minister Shahpour Bakhtiar on 8 August 1991 in Paris.[9] According to press reports, NSA Sigint intercepts, together with Human Intelligence (Humint) provided by the Central Intelligence Agency (CIA) station in Khartoum, led to the 14 August 1994 arrest in the Sudan of the Venezuelan-born terrorist Ilyich Ramirez Sanchez, better known as 'Carlos' or 'The Jackal', and his subsequent extradition to France to stand trial for murder. In 1997, 'Carlos' was sentenced to life imprisonment by a French court for the 1975 killing of two French security officers and a Lebanese national.[10]

Then NSA had to devote Sigint collection resources to monitoring the activities of the new generation of smaller but more violent terrorist organizations, including the Iranian-backed Shi'ite organization Hizballah (Party of God) based in Lebanon, the Egyptian group Islamic Jihad, the Palestinian terrorist organization Hamas, the Shining Path in Peru, Abu Saayef in the Philippines, and the tiny 50-man 'November 17' organization in Greece. Probably the most important terrorist target for the US intelligence community, including NSA, during the early and mid-1990s was Hizballah because of its previous attacks on American targets in Lebanon during the 1980s and its close ties to the Iranian government.[11] NSA Sigint intercepts dating as far back as 1983 revealed that the Iranian ambassador in Damascus, Muhammad Mohtashami-Pur, managed and financed a significant portion of the terrorist activities of Hizballah.[12]

On 17 June 1987, an American journalist with ABC News named Charles Glass, the son of the Lebanese Defense Minister, Ali Osserian, and their Lebanese driver, were kidnapped by members of Hizballah on the road between Sidon and Beirut in southern Lebanon. After pressure was brought to bear on the kidnappers by the Syrian government, the two Lebanese men were released, but Glass was not let go until two months later. According to press reports, GCHQ's listening post at Ayios Nikolaos on Cyprus intercepted the communications traffic between the Iranian ambassador in Damascus and the Iranian Foreign Ministry in Tehran as they debated what to do with Glass, strongly suggesting that the Iranian government was behind the kidnapping.[13] NSA and GCHQ were reportedly able to successfully listen to the tactical radio communications of Hizballah forces in Lebanon because they sometimes used insecure walkie-talkies to coordinate their operations against Israel from bases in southern Lebanon.[14] Intercepts of diplomatic communications traffic in July 1991 revealed that some Arab states were pressuring Hizballah to release the remaining American and British hostages then being held by the organization in eastern Lebanon.[15] Sigint intercepts reportedly implicated Hizballah in the March 1992 bombing of the Israeli embassy in Buenos Aires, Argentina, which killed 29 people. The intercepts reportedly showed that Iranian officials had acquired the plastic explosives used by Hizballah in the attack.[16]

The new generation of Palestinian terrorist organizations, such as Hamas, posed an entirely different set of problems for Sigint in the 1990s, especially for the Israeli intelligence services. Arguably, no country has more experience with Sigint monitoring of terrorist organizations than Israel. Over the past decade, Israel's national Sigint organization, Unit 8200, has developed highly sophisticated techniques for monitoring Palestinian terrorist activities in the Gaza Strip and on the West Bank, using both conventional and unconventional Sigint collection systems fused together with Humint. At the same time that the Oslo Accord was being signed in Washington in September 1993, Unit 8200, then commanded by Brigadier General Hanan Gefen, began secretly constructing a network of intercept sites adjacent to the West Bank and the Gaza Strip to spy on the soon-to-be-created Palestinian Authority.[17]

Israeli intercepts of telephone transmissions led Israeli agents to Hamas' principal bomb maker, Yehia Ayyash, popularly known as 'The Engineer'. Ayyash was the mastermind behind seven terror bombings inside Israel during 1994 and 1995 that killed 55 Israelis. Using a combination of intelligence gathered by both Sigint and Humint, the Israelis eventually caught up with Ayyash, tracking him down to a hideout in the Gaza Strip. The 29-year-old Ayyash was killed in Gaza in January 1996 by an exploding cellphone planted on him by Israeli intelligence.[18] In 1996, at the height of the first Intifada in the Palestinian territories, Unit 8200 spent millions of dollars to build a network of special intercept antennas located within Israeli hilltop settlements throughout the West Bank to intercept cellular telephone calls coming from the Palestinian-controlled territories. Naturally, the cellphone numbers of key PA and terrorist suspects were monitored around-the-clock. Computers at Unit 8200's headquarters north of Tel Aviv scan the calls looking for key words of intelligence significance, as well as track the locations of the cellphones of PA officials.[19] In 1999, PA security officials discovered that the Israelis had planted miniature listening devices inside the cellular telephones used by PA officials, which enabled Israeli eavesdroppers to listen to everything the phone's owner said, even when the phone was switched off.[20]

During the wave of fighting between Israel and the PA in 2002, Israel used its electronic eavesdropping prowess to try and prevent terrorist attacks, as well as proactively attack key officials of the PA who they held responsible for the violence. Press reports indicate that Israeli Sigint has for years intercepted all of the telephone calls, faxes and emails coming in and out of Yasser Arafat's headquarters complex in Ramallah. According to Israeli intelligence officials cited in these reports, the intercepts reportedly prove that Arafat has financed the terrorist arm of his Fatah organization, the Al-Aqsa Martyrs' Brigade, knowing that this unit would conduct terrorist attacks inside Israel.[21]

Israeli newspapers have alleged that Israel has intercepted telephone calls from the PA Preventive Security Service chief in Gaza, Muhammad Dahlan, or his deputy, Rashid Abu-Shibak, in which they reportedly ordered terrorist attacks on Israeli targets. The Israeli newspapers have alleged that the recordings were made by the CIA, although this would seem unlikely given the political sensibilities involved.[22] PA security officials quickly determined that the success of Israeli attacks on their leadership was due in large part to Unit 8200's ability to monitor their cellphone conversations. This led PA officials to ban the use of cellphones among their senior members on the West Bank in the spring of 2002 during the height of the fighting between Palestinian and Israeli troops in and around Jenin.[23]

Countries other than the US also extensively used Sigint to combat terrorism in the 1990s. Historically, Britain's foreign intelligence service (MI6) and security service (MI5) have always devoted a greater percentage of their intelligence collection resources to countering the terrorist threat than Britain's Sigint organization, GCHQ, because of the Irish Republican Army's (IRA's) minimal international presence. But beginning in the early 1990s, GCHQ began devoting a small but increasing amount of intercept and processing resources to monitoring international terrorist activities around the world.[24] A section within GCHQ's K Division produced a weekly Top Secret Codeword document called the 'Travel Digest', which detailed the movements as reflected in Sigint of individuals including international terrorists on watch lists prepared by MI5, MI6 and other law enforcement bodies in Britain.[25]

In January 1996, GCHQ intercepted orders from the Iraqi representative to the United Nations (UN) in Geneva, Barzan al Tikriti (Saddam Hussein's half-brother and former head of the Iraqi secret service from 1980 to 1985) transferring $10 million from Switzerland to the London bank account of an Iraqi businessman. British authorities believed this money was destined to be used to counter the activities of Iraqi dissident groups based in London, including the assassination of key dissidents.[26] In the late 1990s, under pressure from the other members of the British intelligence community, GCHQ began cooperating more closely with the British domestic security service, MI5, and other law enforcement bodies in monitoring the activities of terrorist organizations operating in Britain or threatening British interests abroad.[27]

NSA AND THE NEW INTERNATIONAL TERRORISTS

Despite the marked decline in Palestinian and Middle Eastern state-sponsored terrorism in the 1990s, there were clear signs that a new and more dangerous actor in the terrorism arena was beginning to take shape. On 26 February 1993, a powerful bomb hidden inside a rented truck blew up in the basement parking garage of the World Trade Center's North Tower in New York City, killing six people and injuring more than 1,000 others. Unlike the terrorist attacks of the previous three decades, the World Trade Center bombing was carried out by a small group of Muslim extremists living in the US led by Ramzi Ahmed Yousef, a 36-year-old Pakistani national who had studied electronics and chemical engineering in England. What made this group unique is that they planned and executed the bombing without the benefit of any discernible support from a state sponsor or overseas parent organization other than ties to radical organizations based in the Pakistani city of Peshawar.[28]

Following the 1993 World Trade Center bombing, NSA and the rest of the US intelligence community were ordered to increase the level of intelligence coverage of terrorism, with emphasis on the host of Muslim extremist organizations then known to be operating with impunity in Peshawar.[29] How much in the way of additional Sigint collection and processing resources NSA dedicated to this new target cannot be definitively determined, but a former senior NSA official indicated that the Sigint collection and processing resources dedicated to the terrorist problem by the agency at the time were relatively modest when compared with the substantially larger collection resources being devoted to higher-priority transnational intelligence targets, such as trying to stem the flow of illegal narcotics from Latin America and countering the proliferation of weapons of mass destruction around the world.[30]

By all accounts, NSA and its partners reacted slowly to the changing terrorist threat. Part of the reason that NSA experienced difficulty focusing on terrorist activities at the time was that the agency was experiencing considerable internal turmoil. Thousands of NSA's employees were in the process of either retiring early or being let go as part of the previously mentioned 'reduction in force' of the agency. Among the casualties were many of NSA's most experienced senior managers, analysts and technical personnel, including key analysts who had specialized in international terrorism.[31] As part of an effort to reduce duplication of effort and improve the efficiency of the agency's global Sigint effort, in February 1992 NSA drastically reorganized its Operations Directorate (DDO), which managed the agency's worldwide Sigint collection, processing, analysis and reporting activities.[32]

THE EMERGENCE OF AL-QAEDA AS A THREAT

Despite the slightly greater effort being devoted to monitoring terrorist activities in the mid-1990s, it was to take several years before Osama bin Laden and Al-Qaeda were to resonate loudly within the US intelligence community. According to former US intelligence officials, Osama bin Laden did not become a viable target entity as far as the US intelligence community was concerned until sometime in 1994, when intelligence reports began to circulate indicating that bin Laden's organization, Al-Qaeda (which in Arabic means 'The Base'), was providing financial support to Muslim extremist organizations in the Middle East and elsewhere around the world.[33]

Unfortunately, getting timely and accurate intelligence information about bin Laden's activities proved to be an extremely difficult proposition for the US intelligence community, with a recent US congressional report admitting that Al-Qaeda 'proved an exceptionally difficult target for US intelligence'.[34]

In general, spying on terrorist organizations historically has always has been an extremely difficult proposition. A 1997 study by the US Defense Department's Defense Science Board stated that, 'Because of the very high security consciousness of transnational groups, there is generally insufficient, verifiable information available about transnational adversary operations, membership, and other important details. Moreover, these groups often come from countries in which the United States has no human intelligence capabilities.'[35]

Sigint collection against Al-Qaeda was a particularly difficult task given the unorthodox nature of the organization.

First, Al-Qaeda is, from an organizational standpoint, a very different actor from the Palestinian and Lebanese-based terrorist organizations that US intelligence and its partners had previously spied on. Unlike the rigidly organized and bureaucratic Palestinian terrorist organizations of the twentieth century, all of which were state-sponsored to one degree or another, Al-Qaeda was a truly transnational phenomena in that it was not dependent on support from state sponsors. With a reported net worth of about $250 million, Osama bin Laden did not have to depend on the largesse of state sponsors for his survival or ability to conduct terrorist operations.[36] Vincent Cannistraro, the former head of the CIA's Counterterrorism Center, went so far as to describe Al-Qaeda in an interview as representing 'the privatization of international terrorism'.[37]

Second, Al-Qaeda has depended on unconventional sources of financing over the past decade to fund its worldwide operations. There is no question that bin Laden has dug deep into his own personal fortune over the past ten years to finance Al-Qaeda. But available information suggests that bin Laden has largely spent his personal inheritance over the past ten years, and today his personal net worth is nowhere near the $250m that has been reported previously in the press.[38] Prior to September 11, 2001, evidence suggests that Al-Qaeda depended on a combination of extortion and voluntary donations from wealthy Arab businessmen for most of its financing. The unconventional nature of Al-Qaeda's financial operations made it an extremely difficult organization to monitor since it is not dependent on conventional bank accounts and wire transfers as previous state-sponsored terrorist organizations were.[39]

Third, Al-Qaeda has remained since its inception a relatively small, loosely-knit confederation of Islamic fundamentalist terrorist organizations from all over North Africa, the Middle East, the former Soviet Union and Asia, with bin Laden acting as the organization's nominal titular head or 'Sheikh'. More properly stated, Al-Qaeda is...a network of networks of networks, in which terrorists from various organizations and cells pool their resources and share their expertise. This loose and amorphous confederation of disparate organizations did not have the clear lines of communication or a centralized command structure, such as that provided by an army general or a corporate chief executive officer. The network is, instead, a 'combination of convenience', with groups joining or departing, depending on their interests and the needs of their particular operations ... with bin Laden acting as a facilitator, financier and source of training and logistical support for these organizations.[40] The unstructured nature of Al-Qaeda made Sigint collection against it extremely difficult since, as two intelligence scholars have correctly observed: 'The problem with clandestine organizations is that, unlike governments or conventional military [forces], they very rarely have an organized operational communications network.'[41]

Fourth, from a Humint perspective, trying to penetrate the Al-Qaeda organization was, and remains, a difficult proposition given its unusual internal makeup. Al-Qaeda is a religious, non-political organization that views the US and its friends and allies as intractable and implacable foes. As such, its members tend to be fervent followers of the politico-religious dogma espoused by bin Laden despite their relative lack of higher education and intellectual sophistication. Traditional espionage recruiting lures for potential agents, such as financial inducements and sexual favors, generally do not work with Muslim fundamentalists, who comprise the vast majority of Al-Qaeda. As demonstrated by the behavior of Al-Qaeda prisoners being held at the US naval base at Guantanamo Bay, Cuba, interrogators have learned the hard lesson that the fanatical disposition of Al-Qaeda members has meant that it is near impossible to 'turn' these individuals into American spies, much less get useful and reliable intelligence information from them. A natural predisposition to distrust outsiders has also made it extremely difficult to penetrate Al-Qaeda with agents from the outside.[42]

And fifth, compartmentalization of information within the organization meant that even if agents were successfully planted inside Al-Qaeda, the likelihood that they would be able to produce high-level intelligence information was very low unless the source was close to bin Laden or held a very high-ranking post within the organization.[43] A recently released congressional report confirmed, based on a review of available classified intelligence information, that only a select few individuals within the upper echelons of Al-Qaeda knew the details of the organization's terrorist operations.[44] For example, it would appear based on videotaped admissions by bin Laden himself that the Al-Qaeda operatives who participated in the September 11, 2001 terrorist attacks in the US did not know what their target was until just before they boarded their aircraft. In a November 2001 videotape captured by US forces in Afghanistan and released to the public on 13 December 2001, bin Laden told his associates: 'The brothers who conducted the operation, all they knew was that they have a martyrdom operation and we asked each of them to go to America, but they didn't know anything about the operation, not even one letter. But they were trained and we did not reveal the operation to them until they are there and just before they boarded the planes.'[45]

SIGINT AND AL-QAEDA

The available evidence suggests that the CIA's clandestine service was unable to penetrate Al-Qaeda. The inherent difficulty of spying on an organization such as Al-Qaeda was compounded by the fact that the CIA failed to mount an aggressive effort to infiltrate bin Laden's organization in Afghanistan prior to the September 11, 2001 bombings. The almost complete absence of American Humint sources within Al-Qaeda, recently declassified studies have determined, left the US intelligence community largely blind as to bin Laden and his lieutenants' intentions prior to 9/11. The absence of Humint sources also left the US intelligence community largely dependent on information of varying reliability received from foreign intelligence services and Sigint before 9/11.[46] Because of the historic tendency on the part of American intelligence analysts to be skeptical of the reliability of intelligence reporting from foreign intelligence services, by the mid-1990s Sigint had become by far the most important source of intelligence about bin Laden and Al-Qaeda within the US intelligence community.[47]

Much of NSA's Sigint emphasis on bin Laden during the early 1990s was directed at trying to trace the sources of Al-Qaeda's finances, since bin Laden was widely suspected by the US intelligence community at the time of being nothing more than a financier of international terrorist activities.[48] The thinking inside the US intelligence community at the time was that NSA was well-suited to perform this task because of the agency's success in the 1980s tracking terrorist finances. In 1981, NSA began intercepting financial data transmissions concerning money transfers that were being carried by three large international wire-transfer clearinghouses: the Clearing House Interbank Payments Systems (CHIPS), which was a worldwide computer network run from New York City that was used by 139 member banks in 35 countries to transfer money in US dollars from one bank to another; the CHAPs network based in London, which handled wire transfers paid in British pounds sterling; and the SIC financial network in Basel, Switzerland, which handled wire-transfers that were based on the Swiss franc.[49]

By monitoring these international banking clearinghouses, NSA was able to develop much useful intelligence during the 1980s concerning terrorist activities, as well as information about the financing of illegal drug trafficking, money laundering, illegal technology transfer to Soviet bloc countries, nuclear proliferation and international debt issues in the Third World.[50]

For example, according to Dr Norman Bailey, the Special Assistant for National Security Planning in the National Security Council from 1981 to 1983, after the La Belle Disco bombing in West Berlin on 5 April 1986, NSA analysts reviewed thousands of intercepted money wire transfers carried by the three banking clearinghouses and discovered that the Libyan government was financing Palestinian and other international terrorist organizations. The intercepted wire transfers revealed that in 1985, the Libyan government had wired $60 million to bank accounts controlled by million international terrorist and guerrilla organizations, including $20million apiece to the Red Brigades in West Germany, the IRA and the M-16 guerrilla organization in Columbia.[51]

As early as 1994, NSA turned its financial tracking capabilities onto the Al-Qaeda target. Intercepts began to indicate that bin Laden was involved in financing a broad range of terrorist activities around the world. For example, Sigint intercepts in the mid-1990s revealed that some wealthy Saudi Arabian businessmen were directly involved in financing terrorist operations, such as Al-Qaeda and Muslim insurgents in the southern Philippines. Among the intelligence collected were electronic wire transfers moving large sums of money from bank accounts in Europe to the Philippines.[52] In December 1995, the British were able to track electronic wire transfers from the bank accounts of bin Laden companies in Khartoum to a London-based cell of a fundamentalist Muslim terrorist organization called the Algerian Armed Islamic Group (GIA).[53] According to an October 2001 news account, NSA Sigint intercepts revealed that beginning in 1996, the Saudi Arabian government secretly began sending large sums of money to Al-Qaeda, reportedly to ensure that bin Laden kept his terrorist activities out of Saudi Arabia.[54] All of these intelligence reports were based on intercepts of electronic wire transfers from bank accounts in the Middle East and South Asia known to be controlled by bin Laden or his operatives.[55]

It would appear that NSA and its partners focused their efforts on monitoring bin Laden's telephone traffic being carried by the Umm Haraz satellite ground station outside the Sudanese capital of Khartoum, which handled all international telephone traffic coming in and out of the Sudan being relayed by Intelsat or Arabsat communications satellites in orbit over the Indian Ocean. Beginning in 1995, NSA analysts identified a series of telephone numbers belonging to telephones that were used by Osama bin Laden or his key lieutenants. By monitoring these telephone numbers around-the-clock, especially calls coming in and out of bin Laden's office at his ranch outside Khartoum, NSA analysts began to slowly derive some very useful intelligence information about bin Laden and the activities of his fledgling Al-Qaeda organization.[56]

For example, NSA intercepted a telephone call on the afternoon of 13 November 1995 from an Al-Qaeda operative to bin Laden, who was staying at his ranch at Soba, 20 miles southeast of Khartoum. The caller indicated to bin Laden that an attack on an American target (which was not identified) was about to take place. A half-hour later, a bomb hidden inside a van exploded in Riyadh, Saudi Arabia, killing five American contractors working for the Saudi National Guard. The clear implication of the intercept was that bin Laden and Al-Qaeda were behind the bombing.[57]

Seven months later, NSA intercepted a series of telephone calls that showed that bin Laden's organization was involved in the 25 June 1996 bombing of the Khobar Towers in Dhahran, Saudi Arabia, which killed 19 American military personnel. The day after the Khobar Towers bombing occurred, 26 June 1996, NSA intercepted a series of congratulatory phone calls to bin Laden's ranch in the Sudan from, among others, the leader of the Egyptian Islamic Jihad organization, Ayman al-Zawahiri, and the head of the Palestinian Islamic Jihad group, Ashra al-Hadi. That same day, bin Laden called Mohammed al-Masari, a Saudi dissident living in London. The NSA transcript of the call reportedly caught bin Laden telling al-Masari that the 1995 Riyadh bombing was 'the first action, Dhahran was the second and that more was coming'.[58] It should be noted, however, the an indictment filed in June 2001 at the US District Court in Alexandria, Virginia, by the US Department of Justice alleged that Hizballah and the Iranian government, not Al-Qaeda, had planned and carried out the Khobar Towers attack.[59]

Despite these successes, it would appear that NSA was experiencing considerable difficulty monitoring bin Laden. A 1 July 1996 CIA report lamented that, 'We have no unilateral sources close to bin Laden, nor any reliable way of intercepting his communications... We must rely on foreign intelligence services to confirm his movements and activities.'[60]

As noted above, spying on terrorist organizations is inherently difficult, and the same holds true for Sigint. Testifying before Congress in 2002, NSA Director, General Michael Hayden admitted that 'cracking into these targets is hard – very hard – and Sigint operations require considerable patience – sometimes over years – before they mature'.[61] Interviews with former US intelligence officials suggest that the difficulties NSA was experiencing in the mid-1990s trying to monitor bin Laden's communications were due to a combination of technical factors. NSA's Sigint collectors had a difficult time trying to identify the telephone lines that bin Laden and his chief lieutenants were using to communicate with each other on operational matters other than the phone at bin Laden's ranch outside Khartoum. Intensive efforts were made to search the telecommunications spectrum looking for other communications links being used by Al-Qaeda members, but with little success. Despite not using encryption to protect its communications, Al Qaeda utilized a crude but effective communications security procedure of rarely using the same communications means twice. A former intelligence analyst recalled being exhilarated after identifying a particular telephone number being used by an Al-Qaeda operative in Southwest Asia, only to be disappointed when it was not used again. The analyst recalled going home one night and being confronted by his teenage daughter, who was distraught because her boyfriend had not called her. All he could tell her was that he knew exactly what she was going through, but could not tell her why.[62]

THE FALLACY OF HIGH-TECH TERRORISM

In 1996, bin Laden was forced out of the Sudan by the Sudanese government. He moved his base of operations to Afghanistan, where he was protected by the fundamentalist Taliban regime. Former US intelligence officials confirm that bin Laden's move to Afghanistan turned out to be a godsend from an intelligence point of view, since it made Sigint coverage of his activities significantly easier than it had been when he was living in the Sudan.[63]

Afghanistan, which was bin Laden's principal base of operations between 1996 and 2001, was a particularly difficult environment for American Humint collectors to operate in. Afghanistan was a closed society controlled by a fundamentalist regime that did not brook dissent of any kind, with public execution being a typical punishment for even the slightest infraction of the Taliban regime's numerous strictures. The US government had no embassy in Kabul, and therefore no on-the-ground intelligence presence inside Afghanistan throughout the 1990s. This forced the CIA to depend on the generosity of neighboring Pakistan and its intelligence service, the Inter-Service Intelligence (ISI), for much of the Humint intelligence available to the US intelligence community. ISI's reliability was fair at best given the agency's deep ties to the Taliban regime in Kabul. It should therefore come as no surprise that a 1996 American congressional study recognized that insofar as intelligence coverage of so-called 'rogue states' was concerned, and Afghanistan qualified as such, Humint 'played a secondary role to Sigint' as the primary source of intelligence information for American intelligence analysts.[64]

A detailed review of available information clearly demonstrates that despite its very public operational accomplishments over the past decade,

Al-Qaeda was nowhere near as professional, disciplined or as sophisticated as the Palestinian terrorist organizations of the 1960s, 1970s and 1980s, or even the secretive Hizballah in Lebanon and Hamas in Gaza and the West Bank. Unlike their Palestinian counterparts, many of whom received advanced training in intelligence and security procedures in East Germany and the Soviet Union during the Cold War, most of Al-Qaeda's senior officials and operatives have had little if any prior professional training or experience. As such, Western intelligence analysts found that many of the operational procedures and tactics employed by Al-Qaeda bordered on the amateurish, such as the abysmally poor communications security discipline exhibited by the organization's members throughout the 1990s.[65]

The public record shows that over the past decade bin Laden and his operatives broke virtually every basic tenant of good spying tradecraft, the most important commandment of which was and remains never to speak about one's operations using communications means that can be intercepted. As will be demonstrated below, this cardinal rule, which is beaten into every junior intelligence officer around the world in the first week of their beginner's training course, was repeatedly violated by bin Laden and his operatives throughout much of the 1990s. Not surprisingly, NSA and its partners quickly discovered this chink in bin Laden's armor and exploited it to best advantage over a period of many years prior to September 11, 2001. British author Philip H. J. Davies has written that during an 'off-the-record' February 1996 briefing given to British academics by a senior British intelligence officer, a question was asked as to whether Sigint had declined in importance in the years since the end of the Cold War. The intelligence officer stated that exactly the opposite was true, adding that, 'If anything it is even more important. More terrorists and drug barons are using cellular phones and satellites to talk to each other than ever before.'[66]

It took years of mind-numbing research to identify phone numbers used by bin Laden's operatives, but once identified American Sigint analysts found that Al-Qaeda operatives in Europe and elsewhere tended to talk ceaselessly on their phones, sometimes referring to pending operations and even identifying fellow operatives. One of the fallacies that writers and commentators in the West have latched on to since the attacks of September 11, 2001 is the concept that bin Laden and Al-Qaeda were significant users of high technology, including encryption and high-tech telecommunications technology. Some pundits have even suggested that Al-Qaeda used extremely advanced technology such as steganography (hiding textual information in pictures) in order to convey orders to operatives around the world. It turns out that nothing could be further from the truth. Instead, Al-Qaeda operatives used simple word codes or disguised their meaning using 'flowery language' when referring to their operations on the telephone.[67] When captured in Karachi in September 2002, Ramzi Binalshibh, allegedly one of the planners of the 9/11 terrorist attacks, had in his possession a laptop computer containing reams of valuable information about Al-Qaeda activities, none of which he had apparently bothered to encrypt.[68]

One does not have to dig very deep to discern that the telecommunications options available to bin Laden and his operatives in Afghanistan prior to the US-led invasion in late 2001 were few and far between. One could make the argument that if one was to choose a place best suited from which to run a global terrorist network, Afghanistan would probably rate near the bottom of available choices. The impoverished state of the country, and the backwardness of the Taliban regime which ruled it, meant that the country had virtually no telecommunications infrastructure. As of late 2001, conventional landline telephone service in Afghanistan was practically nonexistent except in a small number of government offices in Kabul. Most of the Soviet-made telecommunications equipment installed during the 1980s had been allowed to fall into disrepair during the civil strife in Afghanistan during the 1990s. According to data compiled by the UN, Afghanistan had only 29,000 telephones in the entire country, which equates to 0.14 phones per inhabitant of the country (22 million inhabitants in 1999). Almost all of these phones were located in the cities of Kabul and Kandahar. This placed Afghanistan almost last in the UN rankings, with the country possessing fewer telephones per capita then even impoverished Bangladesh. It should therefore come as no surprise that there were virtually no fax machines in Afghanistan, no fiber-optic cable telecommunications lines, nor was there any cellular telephone service whatsoever prior to the US-led invasion.[69]

Moreover, in July 2001 the Taliban regime declared the Internet 'unholy' and banned its use throughout Afghanistan because it carried 'obscenity, vulgarity and anti-Islamic content'. Even Afghan government departments were banned from using the Internet. It should be noted that there was practically no Internet usage in Afghanistan prior to the ban because of an almost total lack of computers in the country. This meant, of course, that email connections in and out of Afghanistan were non-existent prior to September 2001.[70]

Without these tools, Al-Qaeda members living in Afghanistan were forced to use satellite telephones to communicate with the outside world. They were among the few people in impoverished Afghanistan who could afford these relatively expensive telecommunications systems. Naturally, this led NSA to monitor virtually all satellite phone calls coming in and out of Afghanistan beginning in the mid-1990s.[71]

In November 1996, one of bin Laden's operatives living in the US, Ziyad Khalil, purchased a Inmarsat Compact M satellite telephone and more than 3,000 hours of prepaid satellite time from a company in Deer Park, New York, for $7,500.[72] The sat-phone worked by bouncing phone calls off an Inmarsat communications satellite parked in orbit over the Indian Ocean. The sat-phone was assigned an international telephone number.[73] Khalil purchased the telephone and satellite time using the credit card of Dr Saad al-Fagih, a 45-year-old Saudi-born surgeon who headed the Movement for Islamic Reform in Arabia, which is headquartered in London. This satellite phone was shipped to another bin Laden sympathizer living in Herndon, Virginia, named Tariq Hamdi, who sent the set to Dr al-Fagih in England. Al-Fagih arranged for the satellite phone to be transported to bin Laden in Afghanistan.[74]

For two years, this satellite phone was the primary means of communications for bin Laden and his military operations chief, Muhammad Atef, who used it to keep in touch with their operatives and sympathizers around the world.[75] According to court records filed in New York City, between 1996 and 1998 bin Laden logged more than 2,200 hours of satellite time talking on this phone, which is the equivalent of more than 91 hours a month over a two-year time period. Phone records show that bin Laden made a total of 260 calls from Afghanistan on the satellite phone to 27 different telephone numbers in Britain.[76] The number called most often by bin Laden (143 telephone calls over a two-year period) was to a house in the London suburb of Dollis Hill belonging to Khaled al-Fawwaz, who according to US law enforcement officials acted as bin Laden's point man and public relations outlet in Britain. Fawwaz and another London-based individual who was called frequently by bin Laden, Ibrahim Eidarous, are currently in a British prison awaiting extradition to the US to stand trial for their alleged role in the 1998 Nairobi-Dar es Salaam embassy bombings. After Britain, telephone records show that the countries bin Laden called most often were Yemen (more than 200 calls), Sudan (131 calls), Iran (106 calls), Azerbaijan (67 calls), Pakistan (59 calls) and Saudi Arabia (57 calls). Only six calls were made to the US, and none to Iraq, which Bush administration officials have long suggested was involved in supporting Al-Qaeda terrorist activities. Telephone records show that bin Laden only stopped using the satellite phone in October 1998, two months after the August 1998 embassy bombings in East Africa.[77]

Former NSA officers recall that many of the bin Laden telephone intercepts were, at best, banal and of relatively low intelligence value. For instance, many of the calls to and from bin Laden's satellite phone dealt with repeated attempts by the publicity-driven exiled Saudi financier to generate favorable press coverage of Al-Qaeda from influential Arabic-language newspapers and television broadcast networks in England and Yemen.[78]

But other intercepts helped foil bin Laden terrorist plots around the world. In 1997, information in part developed from NSA communications intercepts allowed the CIA to disrupt two terrorist attacks on American embassies overseas, as well as foil three terrorist plots that were in the initial stages of planning.[79] In 1998 Sigint was credited with helping foil seven potential attacks by Al-Qaeda terrorists on American diplomatic or military establishments overseas, including a planned terrorist attack on American forces stationed at Prince Sultan Air Base in Saudi Arabia.[80] Also in 1998, intelligence obtained from Sigint as well as human sources allowed the CIA to prevent the hijacking of an American airliner.[81] In August 1998, the US intercepted telephone conversations between bin Laden in Afghanistan and his senior operatives around the world as they plotted a series of terrorist attacks against American targets.[82]

In late 1996, a joint NSA-CIA Special Collection Service team operating from the US embassy in Nairobi began intercepting telephone calls and fax transmissions coming in and out of five telephone numbers in Nairobi, Kenya, which analysts had deduced belonged to members of the Al-Qaeda organization who had established an operating cell in East Africa. Two of the telephone numbers in Nairobi being monitored belonged to a bin Laden-controlled relief organization called the Mercy International Relief Agency, and one was a cellular telephone line. Court records show that NSA was still intercepting telephone calls and faxes passing through these telephone numbers as late as August 1998.[83] Four of the calls on the sat-phone went to the Nairobi telephone number of one of the bombers, Wadih al Hage. All of these calls were intercepted by US intelligence. At al Hage's 2001 criminal trial held in federal court in New York City, prosecutors read into the record the transcripts of two intercepted 1997 telephone calls from bin Laden's military deputy in Kandahar, Afghanistan, Muhammad Atef, to al Hage, as well as excerpts of a February 1997 call from al Hage to another co-conspirator, Muhammad Sadeek Odeh.[84]

In August 1998, NSA intercepted messages among bin Laden operatives which confirmed that Al-Qaeda was directly involved in the bombings of the American embassies in Nairobi, Kenya and Dar es Salaam, Tanzania, on 7 August 1998, which killed 224 people (12 of whom were Americans) and injured thousands more. One intercepted conversation among bin Laden operatives in Africa, which took place just before the bombings, caught one of the operatives saying that 'something bad was going to happen' and that the operatives were 'going to get out of the area'. After the attack, NSA intercepted another conversation among bin Laden officials, wherein one angry operative stated that the attack had killed too many Kenyans and Tanzanians, and not enough Americans. Another intercept revealed that bin Laden and his senior commanders were to have a meeting at a training camp outside the town of Khost in southeastern Afghanistan on 20 August 1998.[85]

US retaliation for the attacks was not long in coming. On 20 August 1998, the Al-Qaeda Kili al-Badr training camp at Khost and five other facilities in eastern Afghanistan were leveled by 66 Tomahawk cruise missiles fired by US Navy warships operating in the Arabian Sea. A few hours earlier, NSA had intercepted a satellite phone call made by bin Laden from the Kili al-Badr camp, which helped determine the target for the retaliatory strike (Clinton administration officials later denied that bin Laden was the target of the attack). Bin Laden survived the attack unscathed. Another 13 cruise missiles fired by US Navy warships cruising in the Red Sea destroyed the El Shifa pharmaceutical plant outside the Sudanese capital of Khartoum, which a soil sample obtained by a CIA operative reportedly indicated was manufacturing precursor chemicals for VX nerve gas. A postmortem examination of intelligence information showed, however, that the plant was making nothing more harmful than a generic form of the drug ibuprofen for headaches.[86]

After news reports in 1998 revealed that NSA and its partners were listening to his phone conversations, in February 1999 bin Laden reportedly ceased using his satellite telephone to communicate with his subordinates and sympathizers outside of Afghanistan.[87] According to Indian intelligence reports, after the fall of 1998 bin Laden conveyed his orders to his operatives around the world by sending operatives across the border to Peshawar, Pakistan, where they used public telephones at hotels and other commercial establishments in the city to transmit bin Laden's orders to his operatives around the world.[88] Bin Laden finally was forced to realize that the mounting toll of failed or blown operations was caused by his own poor operational security practices and those of his senior lieutenants.[89]

THE DAYS OF WINE AND ROSES

In his October 2002 testimony before Congress, NSA Director, Lieutenant General Michael Hayden cryptically stated: 'You are also well aware that the nation's Sigint effort has successfully thwarted numerous terrorist attacks in the past. While our successes are generally invisible to the American people, *everyone* knows when an adversary succeeds. NSA *has had* many successes, but these are even *more* difficult to discuss in open session.'[90] What General Hayden was referring to was the fact that while bin Laden may have ceased using his satellite telephone shortly after the 1998 East Africa bombings, evidence shows that his lieutenants and operatives around the world did not follow his example, and continued talking openly about their activities on satellite and cellular phones and other telecommunications means. As a result of these operations, between 1998 and September 2001, 'some notable successes' were achieved against Al-

Qaeda, including the thwarting of planned attacks on American targets in the US, Europe and the Middle East.[91]

Part of the reason for the improvement in results coming out of NSA was a reorganization of NSA's management structure. In 1997, responsibility for managing and coordinating NSA's global Sigint efforts against international terrorism was moved to a newly created operations analysis organization called the Global Issues and Weapons Systems Group, or W Group, then headed by Michael S. Green. W Group was responsible for Sigint collection on a host of transnational issues, including international terrorism, as well as counterintelligence issues, international drug trafficking, international organized crime and illegal alien smuggling communications traffic.[92] A unit within W Group, designated W9B, was the NSA Terrorism Customer Service Center, which served as the primary interface between NSA's collectors and analysts and the agency's intelligence consumers.[93] Concurrent with these organizational changes, NSA dedicated more Sigint intercept and processing resources to monitoring Al-Qaeda activities following the August 1998 East African bombings.[94]

One of the Sigint sources that proved to be of high intelligence value for NSA was intercepts of calls to a telephone number in Yemen that belonged to an Al-Qaeda operative named Ahmed al-Hada.[95] US intelligence had identified this number after interrogating one of the captured planners of the August 1998 East Africa bombings, Muhammad Rashed Daoud al-Owhali. Sigint coverage of al-Hada's telephone calls began in the fall of 1998. Intercepts of calls coming in and out of al-Hada's home in Sana'a revealed that he acted as an information clearing house, relaying messages between bin Laden and his lieutenants in Afghanistan and Al-Qaeda operatives around the world. Al-Hada's home was also used to plan terrorist operations, including the October 2000 attack on the destroyer USS *Cole*, as well as serve as an Al-Qaeda logistics center.[96]

Also in 1999, a team of CIA operatives working for the Special Collection Service (SCS), the joint CIA-NSA clandestine Sigint collection unit, slipped into southeastern Afghanistan to emplace a remote-controlled Sigint collection system near a series of Al-Qaeda camps close to the town of Khost.[97]

According to publicly-available information, these and other Sigint sources generated reams of actionable intelligence during the years 1999 and 2000. In early 1999 the British intercepted telephone calls from a senior bin Laden operative named Said Mokhles to cohorts in Britain, indicating that bin Laden's terrorist organization was examining the possibility of attacking the British embassy in Brussels, Belgium.[98] In June 1999, the US State Department temporarily closed six American embassies in Africa after intelligence reports, including Communications Intelligence (Comint) intercepts, revealed the bin Laden operatives were in the final stages of preparing an attack on an American diplomatic target in Africa. The intercepts of conversations by bin Laden operatives revealed that bomb-making materials had been transported to Africa for the attack.[99] By early July 1999, intercepted Al-Qaeda communications traffic revealed that bin Laden operatives were preparing another operation, this time in Western Europe. Other intercepts reportedly showed that Saudi billionaire Sheikh Khalid bin Mahfouz, owner of the National Commercial Bank, and the Dubai Islamic Bank were hiding and moving bin Laden's money.[100] In mid-July 1999, communications intercepts indicated that bin Laden was planning to hit a major American 'target of opportunity' in Albania. As a result, planned trips to Albania by Secretary of State Madeleine Albright and Secretary of Defense William Cohen were hastily canceled.[101]

Despite the successes of the previous two years, it was only a matter of time before Al-Qaeda finally succeeded. On 12 October 2000, Al-Qaeda suicide bombers attacked the US Navy destroyer USS *Cole* as she lay at anchor in the port of Aden, Yemen. Seventeen sailors were killed in the blast and another 39 wounded. On the same day that the attack on the USS *Cole* occurred, NSA issued an intelligence report based on Comint intercepts warning that terrorists were planning an attack in the region. However, the NSA warning message was not received by consumers until well after the attack had taken place.[102]

Two weeks after the attack on the USS *Cole*, on 25 October 2000, new NSA intercepts of Al-Qaeda message traffic indicated that further attacks on American forces in the Persian Gulf were in the offing, leading the Pentagon to place US forces in Bahrain and Qatar on the highest state of alert. No attack took place, but these alerts based on Sigint intercepts became the norm for US forces stationed overseas during the next year.[103]

It should be noted that the US was not the only country monitoring the terrorist activities of Al-Qaeda. According to the 2002 annual report of the British Parliament's Intelligence and Security Committee, it was not until 2000 that bin Laden finally became 'a major preoccupation' of GCHQ. By the spring of 2001, GCHQ was making headway exploiting bin Laden's communications traffic.[104] In March 2001, Italian law enforcement officials arrested a Tunisian national named Essid Sami Ben Kemais and five other Al-Qaeda members operating in Italy based in large part on intercepts of their cellular telephone calls by the Italian antiterrorist agency, the Divisione Investigazione Generali e Operazioni Speciali (DIGOS). Further investigation by the Italian authorities determined that these men, some of whom had fought against Russian forces in the breakaway province of Chechnya, comprised an important cell in bin Laden's European network.[105]

SIGINT AND THE SEPTEMBER 11, 2001 TERRORIST ATTACKS

We now know that in the year prior to the September 11, 2001 bombings, NSA did intercept an increasing volume of Al-Qaeda messages which indicated that bin Laden was planning a major operation against American targets. Most US intelligence analysts concluded that the threat was primarily to US military or diplomatic installations overseas, particularly in the Middle East and Persian Gulf. In late 2000, NSA intercepted a message, wherein an Al-Qaeda operative reportedly boasted over the phone that bin Laden was planning to carry out a 'Hiroshima' against the US.[106] Beginning in May and continuing through early July 2001, NSA intercepted at least 33 messages indicating that Al-Qaeda intended to conduct in the near-term future one or more terrorist operations against US targets.[107] In some of the intercepted message traffic, bin Laden operatives reportedly referred to an upcoming operation using a series of code words and double talk to disguise what they were talking about, but no specifics of the operation were revealed in the messages. But the intercepts did reveal increased activity levels, including the movement of key Al-Qaeda operatives.[108]

During the summer of 2001, the volume of NSA intercepts of Al-Qaeda communications traffic continued to surge, with the nature of threats implied in these intercepts suggesting that an operation against one or more American targets was imminent, although no specifics as to date, time and place of the threatened attacks was reportedly ever given. But some of these intercepts were so threatening that they forced the US government to take drastic measures to protect American personnel stationed overseas. In June 2001, Sigint intercepts led to the arrest of two bin Laden operatives in the Middle East who were planning to attack US military installations in Saudi Arabia. At about the same time, another Al-Qaeda agent, who was planning an attack on US diplomatic facilities in Paris, was captured with the help of Sigint.[109] On 22 June 2001, US military forces in the Persian Gulf were placed on alert after NSA intercepted a conversation between two Al-Qaeda operatives in the region which indicated that 'a major attack was imminent', although no specifics as to the date, time or place of the attack were given in the intercept. But as a result, all US forces in the Middle East were placed on the highest state of alert, a military exercise in Jordan was cut short, and all US Navy ships docked in Bahrain, homeport of the US Fifth Fleet, were ordered to put to sea immediately.[110]

In July 2001, advance warning provided by Sigint intercepts allowed American and allied intelligence services to disrupt planned Al-Qaeda terrorist attacks in Paris, Rome and Istanbul.[111] In August 2001, either NSA or GCHQ reportedly intercepted a telephone call from one of bin Laden's chief lieutenants, Abu Zubaida, to an Al-Qaeda associate believed to be in Pakistan. According to press reports, the conversation centered on an

operation that was to take place in September, as well as the possible
ramifications stemming from the operation. About the same time, bin Laden
telephoned another associate inside Afghanistan and discussed the
upcoming operation. Bin Laden reportedly praised the other party to the
conversation for his role in planning the operation. For some reason, the
intercepts were reportedly never forwarded to intelligence consumers,
although this contention is strongly denied by NSA officials.[112] Just prior to
the 9/11 bombings, several European intelligence services reportedly
intercepted a telephone call that Osama bin Laden made to his wife who was
living in Syria, asking her to return to Afghanistan immediately.[113]

Finally, on 10 September 2001, the day before the US attacks took place,
either NSA or GCHQ intercepted two messages involving a telephone number
in Afghanistan known to be used by senior Al-Qaeda officials. Buried within
the intercept transcripts were hints which, although extremely vague,
indicated that an Al-Qaeda terrorist attack was going to occur in the immediate
future. In the middle of the first conversation one of the speakers reportedly
said that, 'The big match is about to begin'. In the second intercept, another
unknown speaker was overheard saying that, 'Tomorrow was "zero hour"'.
NSA translated the messages on 12 September 2001, the day after the terrorist
attacks in New York City and Washington DC, took place.[114] According to a
congressional report, 'These intercepts did not provide any indication of
where, when or what activities might occur. Taken in their entirety, it is
unclear whether they were referring to the September 11 attacks.'[115]

EVALUATION OF NSA'S COUNTERTERRORIST INTELLIGENCE
ACTIVITIES

Given what we know now, what judgments can one make about NSA's
performance in the war against terrorism prior to the attacks of September
11, 2001? As will be shown below, Sigint's performance against
international terrorism in the 1990s can only be described as mixed.

NSA and the September 11 Attacks

Since the terrorist bombings of September 11, 2001, government officials,
legislators and pundits around the world have tried to determine if the
bombings could have been prevented by better intelligence work. The
preliminary conclusion to be drawn is that the US intelligence community
did not miss any so-called 'red flags' indicating that terrorist attacks on New
York and Washington were imminent. In a 12 July 2002 statement to the
press, Congressman Saxby Chambliss of the House Permanent Select
Committee on Intelligence, stated: 'This was such a closely held,
compartmentalized act of devastation that was carried out by the terrorist

community that we don't know of any way that it could have been prevented.'[116] Congressman Chambliss' evaluation is confirmed by the June 2002 annual report of the British Parliament's Intelligence and Security Committee, which after taking testimony from British intelligence officials and reviewing the classified documentary record, concluded: 'The [intelligence] Agencies have told us that they had no intelligence forewarning... specifically about the 11 September attacks on the USA. A subsequent re-examination of material across the intelligence community did not find any that, with the wisdom of hindsight, could have given warning of the attacks.'[117]

Does NSA itself and/or its Sigint partners bear any responsibility for the alleged intelligence failure leading up to the terrorist attacks of Septembers 11, 2001? Some commentators in the US and Europe have chosen to blame NSA in part or in whole for the intelligence failures leading up to the bombings 9/11. Is the criticism of NSA, and Sigint in general, deserved? The available primary source material suggests that NSA did not commit any egregious errors in the days and months leading up to the attacks. A recently released congressional report concluded: 'Prior to 11 September 2001, NSA had no specific information indicating the date, time, place, or participants in an attack on the United States.'[118] Moreover, it would appear that NSA performed better than the rest of the US intelligence community prior to 9/11, although this judgment is not universally shared within the US intelligence community.[119]

A July 2002 report prepared by a subcommittee of the House Permanent Select Committee on Intelligence was critical of NSA's performance prior to 9/11 attacks, stating that NSA failed 'to provide tactical and strategic warning' of the attacks.[120] NSA's response to this criticism was that it collected no intelligence upon which it could have provided a warning of the attacks. Despite all of the 'indications' of an impending Al-Qaeda attack that were appearing in Sigint prior to the September 11, 2001 attacks, NSA officials candidly admitted that 'NSA had no Sigint suggesting that al-Qa'ida was specifically targeting New York and Washington, DC, or even that it was planning an attack on US soil. Indeed, NSA had no knowledge before September 11th that any of the attackers were in the United States'.[121]

A US intelligence official quoted in a newspaper interview neatly summarized the conundrum surrounding NSA's performance prior to the September 11, 2001 attacks, stating: 'The good news is we didn't miss it. The bad news is it wasn't there to be missed.'[122]

Over-Dependence on Sigint

Some pundits have argued that prior to September 11, 2001, the US intelligence community was too dependent on Sigint and placed too little emphasis on Humint. Ephraim Halevy, the former head of the Israeli foreign intelligence service, the Mossad, has harshly criticized the US intelligence community's heavy dependence on Sigint, arguing that, 'Sigint has turned into the ultimate judge of reality, and the power of the other disciplines are used to confirm, cross-reference, and supplement [Sigint]. Sigint has become the high priest of intelligence and... blinded those deciphering the signs.'[123]

This is a legitimate criticism of the overall performance of the US counter-terrorist intelligence effort, and raises important questions about why the CIA and the Pentagon's Defense Humint Service (DHS) did not attack Al-Qaeda and other terrorist targets with greater gusto prior to September 2001. The Israeli military's experience fighting Hizballah in southern Lebanon during the 1990s only serves to reinforce the notion that Sigint is no substitute for good Humint in counter-terrorist operations, especially when the terrorist groups in question limit their use of telecommunications in order to preserve operational security.[124]

For almost a decade, government and congressional officials, senior American intelligence officers and a host of public commentators have pressed for greater emphasis on Humint. For example, in 1998 former CIA director James Woolsey told a subcommittee of the US Senate Committee on the Judiciary that Humint was essential for combating terrorism. He and others who testified before the committee acknowledged that Humint collection on terrorism was expensive, hard to achieve and oftentimes involved the recruitment of 'unsavory individuals'.[125]

One overall conclusion to be derived from the available documentation is that Sigint was the US intelligence community's principal source of 'actionable' information about terrorist activities prior to September 11, 2001. Available evidence indicates that the performance of the CIA's clandestine service's against international terrorist activities began to markedly deteriorate in the mid-1990s, just as bin Laden and Al-Qaeda were becoming increasingly important intelligence targets.

An internal CIA assessment conducted in 1994 found that Humint was 'the most important source of intelligence' on international terrorism.[126] But by the end of the 1990s, internal US intelligence community assessments showed that Sigint had surpassed, if not supplanted, Humint as the primary source of intelligence reporting on international terrorism. In 2001, a former senior Pentagon official told Congress that since the early 1990s, Sigint 'has provided decision-makers with the lion's share of operational counter-terrorism intelligence'.[127]

Another document indicates that by the end of the 1990s Sigint had become the most consistent producer of hard intelligence against the so-called transnational targets, that is, international terrorism, narcotics trafficking, arms control compliance, weapons proliferation and international economics.[128] A congressionally-funded report issued in June 2000 stated that, 'The National Security Agency (NSA) is America's most important asset for technical collection of terrorism information.'[129]

Sigint as a Passive Collector

On the negative side, Sigint was used solely as a passive collection source, and not as an active means by which terrorists could be rooted out and destroyed by other intelligence and security agencies. An American counterintelligence official complained that 'NSA's position was that it was solely an intelligence collector, and that it was the responsibility of the CIA and the FBI to use the Sigint it was producing to get the [terrorists]'.[130]

NSA's reluctance to become more actively involved in the counter-terrorism fight stemmed from the agency's traditional culture as an intelligence collector. In the past, NSA officials have taken the position that it was more important to collect intelligence on the targets being monitored than to disrupt or destroy them, which would result in the loss of the source.[131] For example, in 1997 Pentagon officials complained that NSA still was reluctant to give the military the intelligence information that it needed to do its job because of concerns about compromising the security of the agency's sources. This led one Pentagon official to charge that: 'long-entrenched civilian NSA employees are still fighting the Cold War and are more worried about maintaining security than improving tactical warfighting capabilities'.[132] These restrictions have placed extreme burdens on the counter-terrorist action agencies and effectively prevented them from using the intelligence gathered by NSA to go after terrorist organizations.

There were officers within NSA who, prior to September 11, strongly advocated making Sigint more freely available to those tasked with combating Al-Qaeda, but existing policy and security considerations prevented this policy from being acted upon. Moreover, a former NSA official argued that since NSA is only an intelligence collection agency, it is the responsibility of the agency's military and civilian consumers to use the information to attack terrorist groups and their members. Only since 9/11 attacks have 'the gloves come off', and Sigint is now actively being used to destroy Al-Qaeda cells around the world.[133]

Strategic Direction

Former and current US intelligence officials complain, probably with some justification, that the guidance that they received over the past decade from the Director of Central Intelligence (DCI) Sigint Committee in terms of priorities regarding Sigint collection on international terrorism were oftentimes and vague and ambiguous. It was left to NSA to try to interpret the consumers' will into concrete tasking directives to NSA's Sigint collectors. Moreover, many of the tasking requests received from US law enforcement agencies on terrorism, such as from the Federal Bureau of Investigation (FBI) and US Secret Service, conflicted with mission tasking received from US intelligence community members.[134] This lack of clearly defined set of counter-terrorism tasking requirements from the DCI Sigint Committee resulted in NSA being swamped by some 1,500 formal tasking requirements from dozens of intelligence consumer agencies, many of which were non-specific in nature (one consumer agency tasked NSA with 'all intelligence on Middle East terrorist groups') which the agency could not cover with the limited resources at its disposal.[135]

Part of the reason for this anomaly is that the tasking guidance received from NSA's consumers through the DCI Sigint Committee in Washington, DC, was oftentimes contradictory or confusing, leaving it up to NSA officials to determine how best to cover specific terrorist targets and what resources to dedicate to the problems at hand.[136] The tasking conundrum was due to the fact that by 1997 the number of federal agencies involved in one way or another in counter-terrorism had jumped from only a handful to more than 40, each of which had their own parochial interests.[137]

Resource Allocation to the Counter-Terrorism Mission

A pointed criticism of NSA's counter-terrorist Sigint effort raised in a July 2002 report by the House Permanent Select Committee on Intelligence (HPSCI) is that in the years prior to September 11, 2001, NSA did not dedicate enough Sigint collection and processing resources to the counter-terrorist mission.[138] Past and present NSA officials have admitted that there is some truth to this charge insofar as they believe that NSA could have devoted more resources to monitoring worldwide terrorist threats. But the officials stated that this could only have been accomplished by diverting precious Sigint intercept and processing resources from other equally important targets which were competing with international terrorism for the attention of NSA's interceptors and analysts.[139]

A related criticism leveled by some members of Congress is that NSA paid insufficient attention to Al-Qaeda. Congressman Saxby Chambliss (Republican-Georgia) of the HPSCI has stated that though NSA monitored 'large volumes of phone calls from the part of the world where Al-Qaeda was located... the problem was, they didn't focus on Al-Qaeda' to the degree that intercepts were not being identified and processed quickly enough.[140] In testimony before Congress in October 2002, NSA Director, General Michael Hayden rejected this criticism, stating that NSA did, in fact, focus its efforts and resources on Al-Qaeda after DCI George Tenet 'declared war' on Osama bin Laden in 1998.[141]

The truth probably lies somewhere in between these two positions. According to the recently released final report of the joint congressional inquiry into the handling of intelligence prior to the September 11 attacks:

> NSA and other agencies learned valuable information from intercepting terrorist communications and prevented several planned attacks. Indeed. Numerous officials throughout the policy and Intelligence Community told the Joint Inquiry that Sigint was a valuable source of information on al-Qa'ida, Exploitation of terrorist communications, however, was uneven at best and suffered from insufficient investment. Al-Qa'ida was only one of several high priority targets and a difficult one.[142]

It is true that two significant problems that NSA faced when it came to Sigint collection on international terrorists were money and resources. Three independent government commissions that examined the terrorist threat in the late 1990s all concluded that the US intelligence community needed to devote more resources to intelligence coverage of terrorism, which naturally required that the priority assigned to intelligence coverage of international terrorism needed to be elevated.[143] But somehow, these public calls for a higher priority to be placed on intelligence on international terrorism got muddled in the transmission to NSA. Moreover, the House and Senate intelligence committees did not allocate to NSA increased funding for more resources to dedicate to international terrorism. According to US intelligence officials, NSA did not have sufficient resources to conduct a comprehensive, large-scale global counter-terrorism target development program, that is, dedicating a certain number of collection and processing resources to find and develop new terrorist communications targets beyond those that were already known and being exploited.[144]

This issue is potentially the most troubling since it raises the specter that NSA and other Sigint services may not be able to sustain the current level of effort against terrorism targets for anything more than the duration of the current crisis. Since 9/11, NSA, GCHQ and other Sigint services have succeeded in increasing the level of resources dedicated to coverage of international terrorism only by stripping personnel, equipment and other collection and processing resources away from other critical targets, such as the Balkans.[145] The danger is that this level of effort cannot be sustained indefinitely because of financial considerations and the likelihood of another crisis breaking out somewhere else in the world, requiring another reapportionment of finite Sigint resources away from the international terrorism mission. The fear in some quarters is that once the current crisis abates, the services will quietly return to their pre-September 11 target coverage.[146]

Sigint Processing Problems

It is now widely recognized that Sigint agencies around the world are being stretched to the limit by what can only be described as 'information overload'. According to the International Telecommunications Union (ITU), in the last five years, the volume of international communications traffic has doubled from 61.7 billion minutes in 1995 to 120.9 billion minutes in the year 2000.[147] By 2002, it was estimated that international telephone traffic would have grown to 157.1 billion minutes, which equates to a growth rate of 15 per cent per annum.[148] Moreover, Sigint collection technology has improved to the point where it is indeed possible to gain access to much of this worldwide communications traffic. As of 1995, the various Sigint collection systems owned by NSA were capable of intercepting the equivalent of the entire collection of the US Library of Congress (1 quadrillion Bits of information) every three hours.[149]

But as the volume of worldwide communications traffic has increased, and the efficiency of the Sigint collections systems have concurrently improved, the result has been that it has become increasingly difficult for even the largest and best funded of the world's Sigint organizations to process, analyze and disseminate the vast amount of incoming data.[150] This is not a new phenomenon. During Operation 'Desert Storm' in 1990–91, the volume of Iraqi intercepts being collected by NSA's Sigint satellites alone reportedly surpassed the ability of NSA's computers, analysts and linguists to process.[151] According to news reports, during the 1999 military operations in Kosovo, NSA experienced great difficulty processing and getting to its consumers the huge volumes of perishable Sigint data that it was collecting on the operations of the Yugoslav Army.[152]

By the late 1990s, NSA analysts were drowning in the ever-increasing volume of intercepts pouring into the agency's headquarters at Fort Meade. By the mid-1990s, NSA was only processing approximately one per cent of the intercepts being received at Fort Meade, down from approximately 20 per cent in the late 1980s.[153] The net result was that NSA's Director, Lieutenant General Michael Hayden, was forced to admit in 1999 that, 'NSA currently collects far more data than it processes, and its processes more data than it reports.'[154]

What this means is that in reality, the primary problem facing Sigint today and in the near future is not collection, but rather the processing, analysis and reporting of this information. A 1996 US congressional report delineated the problem this way: 'The ability to filter through the huge volumes of data and to extract the information from the layers of formatting, multiplexing, compression, and transmission protocols applied to each message is the biggest challenge of the future.'[155] In addition, it is becoming harder to find the few nuggets of intelligence gold amid the growing amount of material being intercepted every day.[156] A 1999 study commissioned by the US Senate Permanent Select Committee on Intelligence described the problem as being comparable to trying to find 'needles in the haystack, but the haystack is getting larger and larger'.[157]

The implication is that Sigint's ability to perform its counter-terrorist mission may be in jeopardy. A June 2000 congressional report stated that NSA was unable to 'translate the rising volume of terrorist traffic into intelligence, putting the US at increased risk for attacks'.

Personnel Shortages

Another serious failing identified by the HPSCI in its July 2002 report was NSA's critical shortage of intelligence analysts specializing in terrorism and of linguists who understood critical Middle Eastern and South Asian languages in the years leading up to the terrorist bombings of September 11, 2001.[158] The final report of the congressional Joint Inquiry into the September 11 intelligence failures found that: 'personnel employed in the [NSA] counterterrorism organization were largely static over several years, despite repeated efforts by local managers to increase the number of linguists and analysts. General Hayden testified that in hindsight he would have liked to have doubled his resources against al-Qa'ida.'[159]

Postmortem examinations following every foreign crisis have consistently found that the US intelligence community's linguistic resources were grossly deficient. In a letter to the *Washington Post*, former Illinois Senator Paul Simon stated that: 'In every national crisis from the Cold War through Vietnam, Desert Storm, Bosnia and Kosovo, our nation has lamented its foreign language shortfalls. But then the crisis goes away, and we return to business as usual. One of the messages of September 11 is that business as usual is no longer an acceptable option.'[160]

This conclusion may surprise some since NSA has the single largest pool of qualified linguists in the entire US government, dwarfing the linguistic resources of the CIA and the FBI combined. As of the end of 2001, NSA employed almost 4,000 civilian translators and controlled some 7,000 active duty military cryptologic linguists, for a total of approximately 11,000 men and women who were qualified translators in 115 different languages. In addition, there are nearly 3,500 military Reserve and National Guard linguists, many of whom have spent extended tours on active duty in recent years performing so-called 'live environment' cryptologic missions around the world.[161]

Despite these seemingly impressive statistics, it turns out that all has not been well within the agency's linguist population for more than a decade.

First, NSA let go of many of its best analysts and linguists, especially those who spoke Russian or Eastern European languages, during the first half of the 1990s as part of the congressionally-mandated general reduction-in-force at NSA following the end of the Cold War.[162]

Second, during the heady economic boom years of the 1990s, NSA and the military found it difficult to recruit individuals who spoke foreign languages, largely because the pay levels being offered were far below what was being paid in the business community.

Third, NSA and the military found it near impossible to retain the analysts and linguists they had because of the lure of better pay, more interesting work and a less frantic work schedule in the private sector. For its part, the US Congress consistently failed to authorize higher reenlistment bonuses and other benefits needed in order to help retain these linguists. Many of the departing military cryptologic linguists cited misapplication of their skills while in the service, such as being used as recruiters, administrative clerks and drivers instead of what they were trained for. This led a US Army linguist to write: 'Is it any wonder then why linguist retention remains a weak point for the Army?'[163]

As a result, every year during the 1990s more than 75 per cent of the military's linguists finishing their term of enlistment chose to leave the service rather than reenlist for another tour of duty. In 1998, only 23.3 per cent of the Army's first term linguists chose to reenlist. Since it took the military 18 months and up to $123,000 to train each linguist, these wholesale departures constituted a massive loss of talent and investment that could easily be prevented through greater investment in these vital personnel resources.[164]

The result was that by late 2001 NSA's linguistic talent pool was in a state of turmoil. NSA and the military were suffering from severe imbalances in their linguist population, having too many linguists in some languages, such as French, Spanish, Russian and Serbo-Croatian, and suffering from severe shortages in a host of other critical languages. For instance, as of the fall of 2001 the US Army was missing more than 25 per cent of its Korean and Chinese cryptologic linguists.[165]

Knowledge of these deficiencies was not limited solely to NSA insiders. In April 2000, the congressional oversight organization, the General Accounting Office (GAO), issued a report noting the critical shortage of linguists at NSA. Despite the GAO's findings, in the two years after the report was issued the number of NSA linguists in key language billets had dropped even further.[166] This finding was confirmed by a 2001 report by the National Commission on Terrorism, which found that NSA and other US intelligence agencies were suffering from 'a drastic shortage of linguists', which was making it difficult to translate raw information into useful intelligence in the war against terrorism.[167] At the time of the September 11, 2001 bombings, NSA was substantially lacking in experienced Arabic,

Pashto and Dari linguists.[168] The agency reportedly only had four linguists fluent in the languages spoken in Afghanistan (Pashto, Dari, Uzbek and Turkmen), including only one who spoke Pashto, the primary language spoken in Pakistan and Afghanistan.[169]

Analytic Shortcomings

NSA officials also found that NSA's W Group, the operations analysis group at Fort Meade which handles, among other subjects, international terrorism, has consistently suffered from pervasive shortages of intelligence analysts and area specialists to adequately handle the reams of intercepts being produced on terrorist targets.[170] A recently declassified congressional report revealed that throughout 2001, NSA's counter-terrorism office had a standing request for dozens of additional analysts, but because of tight purse strings the report revealed that, 'there was little expectation that such a large request would be satisfied'.[171] These shortages of analysts and linguists clearly hindered the collection and processing of Sigint relating to international terrorism over the past decade. Thousands of intercepts piled up unread by analysts at NSA headquarters because there were not enough qualified linguists to translate them. This meant of course that NSA's analysts never got to see the vast majority of the products that NSA's intercept platforms were forwarding to Fort Meade.[172]

Moreover, the shortage of experienced analysts in W Group at Fort Meade meant that much of what the translators did reduce to English never was read, analyzed or reported to intelligence consumers. According to a report prepared by the HPSCI, 'At the NSA and CIA, thousands of pieces of data are never analyzed, or are analyzed "after the fact", because there are too few analysts; even fewer with the necessary language skills.'[173]

Problems with Dissemination

Historically, because of the need to protect sensitive intelligence sources, NSA's Sigint intercepts were given extremely limited distribution within the highest levels of government and the military, and even then, only on a need-to-know basis.[174] FBI and other law enforcement officials have complained repeatedly that when they did receive Sigint reports from NSA, the restrictions placed on their use by NSA were so onerous that they could not be used. For example, NSA has historically forbidden the FBI and other US law enforcement agencies from using Sigint if such use would compromise NSA's sources and methods. As one might imagine, these restrictions have frustrated FBI and US Department of Justice officials since the end of World War II.[175] Within the US intelligence community Sigint intercepts relating to international terrorist organizations were deemed to be some of the most sensitive materials then being produced by NSA. For instance, during the 1980s counter-terrorist Sigint being produced by NSA was deemed so sensitive that the US intelligence community assigned this specific category of Comint intercept the codename 'Spectre', which severely limited access to this compartment of intelligence information to a very select few high-level intelligence customers in Washington DC.[176]

Prior to the September 11, 2001 terrorist attacks, access to Sigint on terrorism within the US intelligence community was circumscribed by the high classification levels assigned to these materials, which restricted the number of personnel who could have access to this intelligence as well as how it could be used. A congressional staff study found that 'Poor information systems and the high level of classification prevented FBI field officers from using NSA and CIA data'. In other words, many of the intelligence consumers who needed the information the most were not able to see it because they had no access to computer systems carrying the NSA materials, or were not cleared for access to Sigint.[177]

Problems With Inter-Agency Cooperation and Coordination

During congressional hearings held in October 2002, witnesses from the CIA and FBI openly complained about NSA's 'unwillingness' to share information with its customers.[178] As before, there would appear to be some truth to these accusations. FBI officials have alleged that NSA occasionally refused to accept mission-tasking requests from the FBI if the request did not specify that the information was needed for 'foreign intelligence' purposes only, earning NSA a reputation for being generally unresponsive to requests for information from American law enforcement agencies.[179] A congressional report found that because of legal restrictions on the dissemination of intelligence information to law enforcement agencies, NSA 'began to indicate on all its reporting that the content could not be shared with law enforcement personnel without the prior approval of the FISA [Foreign Intelligence Surveillance Act] Court'.[180] For example, every NSA Sigint report relating to international terrorism in the 1990s contained the following caveat on its cover: 'This information is provided for intelligence purposes in an effort to develop potential investigative leads. It cannot be used in affidavits, court proceedings, subpoenas, or for other legal or judicial purposes.'[181]

NSA's response to these accusations was that it routinely provided significant amounts of intelligence information to US law enforcement agencies. In the early 1990s, NSA expanded the size and scope of its inter-agency cooperation with other US intelligence and law enforcement organizations in the field of terrorism. Beginning in 1992, NSA intelligence analysts began spending multi-year tours of duty at the FBI helping the bureau fight terrorism.[182] As of the fall of 2002, the FBI alone received some

200 Sigint reports a day from NSA.[183] After the 1993 World Trade Center bombings, a sizeable number of NSA intelligence analysts were posted for the first time with the CIA's Counterterrorist Center (CTC) at CIA headquarters in Langley, Virginia, where they helped direct intelligence collection against terrorist targets and analyzed Sigint materials forwarded to CTC from NSA concerning international terrorist groups.[184] But NSA Director General Michael V. Hayden also was forced to admit that, 'We have been able to be more agile in sharing information with some customers (like the Department of Defense) than we have with others (like the Department of Justice)', adding that congressional and court-imposed legal restrictions did in fact impede his ability to freely convey intelligence information to law enforcement agencies such as the FBI.[185]

NSA had its own set of problems in working with the FBI. Congressional reports indicate that a poorly defined division of labor between NSA and other US intelligence services and law enforcement agencies hindered the counter-terrorism effort prior to the September 11, 2001 attacks. NSA officials were particularly critical of the FBI, which failed to coordinate its efforts with NSA in order to identify and find Islamic militants associated with Al-Qaeda and other terrorist organizations operating in the US. As a result of the lack of cooperation between NSA and the FBI, according to a congressional report, NSA did not use a particularly sensitive Sigint collection resource that would have been particularly useful in locating Al-Qaeda operatives working in the US.[186] Commenting on the overall state of relations between NSA and the FBI, one senior American intelligence official stated that, 'Our cooperation with our foreign allies is a helluva lot better than with the FBI.'[187]

Regardless of the veracity of the conflicting accusations, it is clear that these inter-agency conflicts hampered the free-flow of intelligence information between NSA and the US law enforcement community, and impaired the US counter-terrorist effort in general. As a 1996 congressional report aptly put it, 'These internecine squabbles between agencies seriously undermine the country's ability to combat global crime in an effective manner and must be ended.'[188]

HUNTERS RATHER THAN GATHERERS

What has changed since the September 11, 2001 attacks is that NSA's counter-terrorist Sigint program has been transformed from a purely passive intelligence collection effort to an interactive source that is being used to hunt down and destroy terrorist cells around the world. NSA's Director, General Michael Hayden, described his agency's new doctrine as 'hunters rather than gatherers'.[189]

One does not have to look far to find evidence that Sigint is now being actively used to locate Al-Qaeda terrorists. Shortly after the US began supporting the Northern Alliance forces in Afghanistan in October 2001, NSA and its partners apparently began intercepting all satellite telephone calls coming in and out of Pakistan, where US intelligence officials believed most of the fugitive Al-Qaeda and Taliban officials had fled. It did not take long before this collection program began to yield results. On the night of 27 March 2002, Pakistani security forces captured one of bin Laden's chief lieutenants, Abu Zubaida, along with 19 other Al-Qaeda operatives in the eastern Pakistani city of Faisalabad. The house where Abu Zubaida was hiding was located when American intelligence operators in Pakistan intercepted a series of satellite phone calls from Afghanistan to the Al-Qaeda leader's hideout in Faisalabad.[190]

In July 2002, an intercepted satellite telephone conversation led Pakistani security forces to a shanty town outside Karachi, where they arrested a 33-year-old Kenyan named Sheikh Ahmed Salim, who was wanted by US authorities for his role in the 1998 embassy bombings in Kenya and Tanzania.[191] In September 2002, an intercepted satellite phone call led Pakistani paramilitary police to the hideout in a suburb of the Pakistani port city of Karachi of Yemeni-national Ramzi Binalshibh, who was one of the Al-Qaeda planners of the 9/11 terrorist bombings in the US.[192] In what has been described publicly as an important intelligence coup, in February 2003 intercepted emails and satellite telephone communications led US and Pakistani security officials to the hideout in the Pakistani city of Rawalpindi of reputed 9/11 mastermind Khalid Shaikh Muhammad. At 4.00 on the morning of 1 March 2003, heavily armed Pakistani security forces burst into Muhammad's hideout and arrested him and another key Al-Qaeda operative, Muhammad Ahmed al-Hawsawi, while they slept.[193]

Sigint is also being intensively employed to search out the sources of terrorist financing around the world. As noted earlier, many of the groups that comprise Al-Qaeda and other Middle Eastern terrorist organizations are dependent on sources of financing both within and from outside the Middle East. For example, Hizballah, Hamas and the Egyptian terrorist organization Gamaat al-Islamiyya conduct important fund-raising activities in the US, Canada and Western Europe among sympathetic immigrants, as well as purchase weapons and other materials overseas. Naturally, these activities are vulnerable to monitoring by Sigint collection.[194]

In July 2000, intelligence information, including Sigint collected by the Canadian Sigint service, the Communications Security Establishment (CSE), led the FBI to arrest a Hizballah support cell in Charlotte, North Carolina, led by a Lebanese-born American named Mohamad Youssef Hammoud. Court papers show that Hammoud and his brother Chawki raised money for Hizballah by operating an illegal cigarette smuggling ring. One of the intercepts introduced into the court record included the transcript of Mohamad Hammoud talking on the telephone with Sheik Abbas Harake, Hizballah's military commander. Other intercepts showed that Hizballah asked Mohamad Hammoud to purchase stun guns, mine detection devices, night vision devices, computers and advanced telecommunications equipment with the illegally-obtained proceeds.[195]

LESSONS LEARNED

The future of Sigint in the fight against terrorism can, in large part, be sketched by delineating the key lessons learned by American intelligence officials from their review of US intelligence performance prior to the September 11, 2001 terrorist attacks.

One of the lessons learned is that there is an urgent need for more clandestine or unconventional Sigint collection resources, because these collection resources can get better intelligence by getting closer to targets than most other sources. With the advent of new wireless communications technologies, such as cellular telephones and wireless paging systems, 'close-in' Sigint collection has become increasingly important in the past decade, while more conventional Sigint collection systems have diminished in value. Gregory F. Treverton, the former vice chairman of the US National Intelligence Council, wrote in the fall of 2001 that:

> Sigint will need to get closer to the signals in which it is interested. During the high Cold War, the Soviet Union sent many of its phone calls through microwave relay stations. Since private telephones were relatively few, intercepting those conversations with satellites yielded important insights into economic production and sometimes into military movements or lines of command. Now, though, with hundreds of communications bundled into fibre optic lines, there is less for satellites to intercept. If Sigint is to intercept those signals, it will have to tap into particular communications lines in specific places. It will have to collect keystrokes straight from a personal computer, before software encrypts the message.[196]

One of the premier practitioners of this arcane intelligence artform is the joint CIA-NSA clandestine Sigint collection unit, the Special Collection Service (SCS).[197] Headquartered in Beltsville, Maryland, the SCS has become an increasingly important intelligence collection resource in the past decade, intercepting foreign political, military and internal security telecommunications traffic from within American diplomatic establishments abroad, or by unconventional clandestine means in unfriendly 'denied area environments' where the US has no diplomatic representation.[198]

For example, in January 1999 the *Boston Globe* and the *Washington Post* revealed that the SCS had created a covert Sigint system to help UN weapons inspectors locate and destroy Iraqi weapons of mass destruction. This clandestine Sigint collection program began in February 1996, and consisted of commercially-available VHF radio intercept receivers provided by the CIA being secretly placed inside UNSCOM headquarters at Al-Thawra in the suburbs of Baghdad. In addition, sophisticated radio scanners hidden inside backpacks and the UNSCOM mobile ambulance were also used by the UN inspection teams when they operated in the field.[199]

Another lesson of the September 11, 2001 attacks is that it would seem to be imperative that intelligence services break down the barriers that have historically existed between Humint agencies and Sigint services. It is widely recognized that the deeply ingrained partisan attitudes among the differing intelligence and security agencies will be difficult to break down. For example, a former head of the FBI's domestic counter-terrorist unit was recently quoted in the press as saying: 'I'll take a live source any day over an electronic intercept.'[200] Regardless of whether intelligence consumers have personal preferences for Humint, Sigint or any other intelligence source, it is absolutely essential that intelligence analysts and consumers accept that all sources of intelligence fused together into an 'all source' intelligence product will be the only way to effectively combat terrorism.[201]

Partisans of Humint and Sigint must recognize and accept that there exists a synergistic cross-dependency between these two longtime competitors, and that in the post-September 11 world, one cannot survive without the other. The logic of greater cooperation between Humint and Sigint operators would seem to be obvious. Former CIA director John Deutch recently wrote in the journal *Foreign Policy* that: 'Cooperation between human and technical intelligence, especially communications intelligence, makes both stronger. Human sources ... can provide access to valuable signals intelligence ... Communications intercepts can validate information provided by a human source.'[202] Agreement on this point transcends international borders. British Foreign Secretary Robin Cook told Parliament in June 2000 that: 'The collection of signals intelligence and of human intelligence often bears its greatest fruit and best results when the two are put together.'[203] The former vice chairman of the US National Intelligence Council, Gregory Treverton, perhaps makes the strongest argument for greater inter-disciplinary cooperation, writing:

> [I]n the future spying will focus less on collecting information than facilitating its collection by technical means. The clandestine service

will gather secrets less through what its own spies hear than through the sensors those spies can put in place ... The United States probably breaks more codes by stealing code books than by breaking the codes with the National Security Agency's supercomputers and brainy mathematicians.[204]

There is a precedent for this sort of inter-disciplinary cooperation between Humint and Sigint collectors. During the 1980s, the US Army operated a clandestine intelligence unit called the US Army Intelligence Support Activity (ISA), which successfully combined Sigint and Humint intelligence collection resources into a single integrated organization capable of acting instantly on the information gathered by these collection assets.[205] In January 1982, Sigint technicians from ISA took part in the search for Brigadier General James Dozier, the highest-ranking American officer in Italy, who had been kidnapped from his home in Verona, Italy, by Italian Red Brigade terrorists on 17 December 1981. ISA operatives used helicopters equipped with sophisticated direction-finding gear to locate the Red Brigade terrorists holding Dozier, who was rescued unharmed.[206]

Then there is the critical need to improve Sigint's ability to handle the ever-increasing volume of communications traffic being intercepted. Publicly available sources suggest that partial technological solutions to these problems are available, albeit at considerable cost. Technology is presently available which allows computers to screen large volumes of communications for items of potential intelligence interest. Artificial intelligence algorithms, such as those used in today's Internet search engines, can be configured so as to identify intercepts which contain useful information based on keyword searches. This group of technologies is generically referred to as 'text and data mining'.[207]

Text and data mining, or as some call it 'electronic dumpster diving', is a relatively new concept using new computer processing systems and techniques for extracting information of intelligence-value from vast amounts of collected data in a timely manner.[208] The computers then collate, fuse and correlate the data in such a way as to make it easy to use and manage for intelligence analysts. If the software systems are properly set up, the computer databases can identify patterns not patently obvious from individual items of intelligence information, such as cluster analysis, link analysis and time series analysis.[209]

The applicability of data mining systems and techniques to Sigint are obvious. For example, data mining software currently available on the market can review in a matter of minutes millions of intercepted radio messages, telephone calls, faxes and email messages to find individual items of intelligence information, or identify patterns contained in the intercepts based on what search terms are programmed into the computer. With the proper voice recognition technology, these systems can also match voices contained in thousands of telephone intercepts, even if the speaker changes phones constantly while trying to avoid detection.[210]

Another lesson to be derived from NSA's performance prior to September 11, 2001 is that Sigint processing, reporting and analysis must become faster and more efficient if it is to be useful as a targeting tool against international terrorist organizations. According to the 2002 annual report of the HPSCI, 'The events of September 11th highlight the critical nature of Sigint analysis to understand the terrorist target, and moreover the need to be able to quickly exploit intercepted communications.'[211]

Finally, a major impediment to Sigint's future ability to effectively combat international terrorism is the evident lack of international cooperation among national Sigint agencies. In the recent past, NSA has certainly been guilty of being less than generous in its information-sharing arrangements with its friends and allies. But the US is not the only nation guilty of this infraction. For example, in Western Europe, where there is extensive cross-border cooperation among clandestine intelligence agencies and security services in the field of counter-terrorism, evidence indicates that multinational Sigint joint ventures are practically non-existent. A study by a European scholar found that in Europe 'WEU [Western European Union] intelligence cooperation has focused primarily on imagery intelligence (Imint), however, with a notable lack of emphasis on signals intelligence (Sigint), human intelligence (Humint), and tactical intelligence cooperation.'[212] This finding was confirmed by a recent European Union report, which stated: 'It has to be said that at the present time there is no real technical [intelligence] cooperation as each country takes the view that the electromagnetic situation in a given zone is a matter for its sovereignty. This means that any European potential will be confined to national equipment and approaches existing side by side.'[213]

The rationale for greater international Sigint cooperation against terrorism is a fairly simple one. The first is that the cost of maintaining a substantive national Sigint capability for most nations is very high, and is getting more expensive every day due to significant changes in worldwide telecommunications technology. Only a handful of the world's richest nations can afford to maintain a global Sigint intercept and processing capability, which provides a clear incentive for smaller nations to enter into cooperative joint ventures or information-sharing relationships with the larger and richer nations in order to gain access to the intelligence information that they collect.[214]

What makes these Sigint joint ventures attractive for the large nations is that it helps reduce their costs and enhances and extends the reach of their own national Sigint organizations. A report prepared by the Congressional Research Service in Washington DC, stated: 'In the post-Cold War environment, observers believe that Sigint cooperation with a number of friendly countries maximizes opportunities to obtain information regarding disparate regional threats from terrorist groups, narcotics traffickers, and dealers in nuclear and other substances used in the manufacture of weapons of mass destruction.'[215]

The second attractive quality for greater transnational Sigint cooperation is the regional expertise, technical skills and geographic access that many of the small national Sigint services possess in those parts of the world where the larger Sigint services heretofore have not trodden.[216] A 1996 US congressional report argued that greater international intelligence cooperation was essential, stating that other countries 'provide expertise, skills, and access which US intelligence does not have'.[217] For example, Russia's two Sigint services, the GRU and FAPSI, possess intercept facilities in the region that are better situated than those 'owned' by NSA, as well as a small but capable reservoir of Pashto and Dari linguists and Sigint analysts familiar with the region.[218]

After years of fighting Pakistani-backed Muslim guerrillas in the disputed state of Kashmir and Jammu, India has developed a significant level of expertise in monitoring the communications traffic of these groups. After September 11, 2001 the Indian government turned over to the US copies of satellite phone intercepts between Muslim guerrillas in Kashmir and their agents in Afghanistan, as well as other intelligence concerning links between the guerrillas and the Taliban and Al-Qaeda forces in Afghanistan.

This would suggest that NSA and its English-speaking partners must necessarily enter into more expansive cooperative Sigint relationships with new partners outside of the confines of the current UK/USA membership list. A CIA officer told an interviewer that: 'We've got to be serious about this: our intelligence world can't be this nice private club of English speakers any more.'[220]

The danger of broadened international Sigint cooperation, as with all intelligence liaison relationships, is that something could potentially go wrong with the relationship that would permanently sour the parties on current future intelligence sharing and cooperation. For example, some American officials have pointed out that much of the intelligence information that the US provided to Saddam Hussein's Iraq during its war with Iran in the 1980s, including Sigint intercepts, harmed the ability of the US intelligence community to monitor the Iraqi regime before, during and after Operation 'Desert Storm' in 1990–91.[221]

A 2002 report issued by a congressional subcommittee was critical of what it believed to be the CIA's 'over-reliance on foreign intelligence services' for counter-terrorism intelligence information.[222] Today, in the post September 11 world, the reigning school of thought within the US intelligence community is to become less reliant on liaison with foreign intelligence services, which will be a natural hindrance to further Sigint sharing and cooperation between the US and other nations.[223]

Sigint, whatever difficulties it faces, will remain an important tool for intelligence agencies in the ongoing war on terrorism. This review of the recent historical record suggests that new resources, new thinking and new ways of intra- and inter-government sharing of Sigint will be necessary. Technological obsolescence will not kill Sigint; inability to face necessary changes is the more dangerous threat.

NOTES

1. Matthew M. Aid, 'The Time of Troubles: The US National Security Agency in the Twenty-First Century', *Intelligence and National Security* 15/3 (Autumn 2000) p.6. See also *Statement for the Record by Lt. General Michael V. Hayden, USAF, Director NSA/CSS Before the Joint Inquiry of the Senate Select Committee on Intelligence and the House Permanent Select Committee on Intelligence*, 17 Oct. 2002, p.6.
2. Senate Report No. 107-351 and House Report No. 107-792, Report of the US Senate Select Committee and US House Permanent Select Committee on Intelligence, *Joint Inquiry Into Intelligence Community Activities Before and After the Terrorist Attacks of September 11, 2001*, 107th Congress, 2nd Session, Dec. 2002 (declassified and released in July 2003) p.76.
3. *Intelligence and Security Committee Annual Report 1998-99*, Nov. 1999, para. 18, <www.official-documents.co.uk/document/cm45/4532/4532-02.htm>.
4. Richard Norton-Taylor, 'GCHQ Facing Jobs Cuts', *Guardian*, 4 Feb. 1992, p.5.
5. Michael Herman, *Intelligence Power in Peace and War* (Cambridge: CUP 1996) p.37 fn6, p.38 fn8; Richard Norton-Taylor, 'Goal Posts Keep Moving in the Spying Game', *Manchester Guardian Weekly*, 1 Jan. 1995, p.8; James Adams and David Leppard, 'Spy Rivals Crow as GCHQ Faces Cuts', *Sunday Times*, 26 March 1995; 'Bad News for GCHQ', *Intelligence Newsletter*, 13 April 1995; 'New Boss at GCHQ', *Intelligence Newsletter*, 12 Oct. 1995.
6. House of Commons, Select Committee on Public Accounts, *Appendix 2: Supplementary Memorandum Submitted by HM Treasury (PAC 99-00/216)*, April 2000, <www.parliament.the-stationery-office.co.uk/pa/cm199900/cmselect/cmpubacc/556/556ap12.htm>.
7. Confidential interview.
8. Confidential interview.
9. Louis Lief, 'Murder, They Wrote: Iran's Web of Terror', *US News & World Report*, 16 Dec. 1991, p.67; Vincent Jauvert, 'Comment L'Amerique Nous Espionne', *Nouvel Observateur* 1779, 10 Dec. 1998, p.10.
10. Tom Bowman and Scott Shane, 'Battling High-Tech Warriors', *Baltimore Sun*, 15 Dec. 1995, p.22A.
11. Testimony of Cofer Black, former chief of Counterterrorist Center, Central Intelligence Agency, before the Joint Inquiry Staff, House Permanent Select Committee on Intelligence and Senate Permanent Select Committee on Intelligence, 26 Sept. 2002, p.9.

12. David Martin and John Wolcott, *Best Laid Plans: The Inside Story of America's War Against Terrorism* (NY: Harper & Row 1988) pp.105, 133; Jack Anderson, 'U.S. Was Warned of Bombing at Beirut Embassy', *Washington Post*, 10 May 1983, p.B15; R. W. Apple Jr., 'U.S. Knew of Iran's Role in Two Beirut Bombings', *New York Times*, 8 Dec. 1986, p.A16; Stephen Engelberg, 'U.S. Calls Iranian Cleric Leading Backer of Terror', *New York Times*, 27 Aug. 1989, p.16.

13. 'NBC Says U.S. Intelligence Shows Iran Ordered Glass's kidnapping', *Boston Globe*, 2 June 1987, p.17.

14. Scott Shane and Tom Bowman, 'America's Fortress of Spies', *Baltimore Sun*, 3 Dec. 1995, p.13A.

15. 'Now a "Grand Swap"?', *Newsweek*, 19 Aug. 1991, p.25.

16. Steven Emerson, 'Diplomacy That Can Stop Terrorism', *Wall Street Journal*, 22 July 1994, p.A10.

17. Amir Oren, 'Meanwhile, Back at the Muqata', *Ha'aretz*, 27 Sept. 2002.

18. Lisa Beyer, 'Death Comes Calling', *Time*, 15 Jan. 1996; Stacy Perman, 'Breaking a Terror Net', *Business 2.0 Magazine*, Dec. 2001, <www.business2.com/articles/mag/ 0,1640,35149,FF.html>. A detailed description of the Israeli manhunt for Ayyash can be found in Samuel M. Katz, *The Hunt for the Engineer* (Guilford, CT: The Lyons Press 2002).

19. Jamil Hamad and Ahron Klein, 'The Enemy Within', *Time International*, 27 Aug. 2001.

20 Kamal Qubaysi, 'Israel Accused of Spying Via Mobile Phones', *Al-Sharq Al-Aswat*, 22 Feb. 1999, FBIS-EAS-1999-0222.

21. Bill Saporito, 'The Scene of the Siege', *Time*, 8 April 2002, p.28.

22. Hagay Huberman, 'CIA Recording of Dahlan Ordering Terrorist Operations Said Passed On to Israel', *Hatzofe*, 13 April 2001, FBIS-NES-2001-0413.

23. David Eshel, 'Israel Hones Intelligence Operations to Counter Intifada', *Jane's Intelligence Review*, Oct. 2002, p.26.

24. CM 5542, Intelligence and Security Committee, *Annual Report 2001-2002*, June 2002, p.19; Michael Evans, 'Spy Centre "Monitored Maxwell Money Deals"', *The Times*, 16 June 1992.

25. Patrick Fitzgerald, 'All About Eavesdropping', *New Statesman & Society*, 29 July 1994, p.30.

26. 'Iraq's Money Transfer', *Intelligence Newsletter*, No. 284, 21 March 1996.

27. CM 4532, Intelligence and Security Committee, *Annual Report 1998-1999*, 1 Nov. 1999, <www.archive.official-documents.co.uk/document/cm45/4532/4532-02.htm>.

28. Yousef was later arrested in Feb. 1995 in a hotel in Islamabad, Pakistan. The month before, he had been forced to abandon his laptop computer in an apartment in Manila after he accidentally started a fire while mixing high explosives. When the NSA decrypted his hard drive, they discovered that Yousef intended to plant bombs on 11 American airliners and detonate the devices over the Pacific. In Jan. 1998, Yousef was sentenced to life in prison.

29. Shane and Bowman, 'America's Fortress of Spies' (note 14).

30. Confidential interview.

31. Aid, 'The Time of Troubles' (note 1), p.9.

32. The Directorate's largest component, A Group, which previously had covered the Soviet Union and the Communist states of Eastern Europe, was reorganized and reoriented towards intelligence gathering on Europe as a whole. B Group, which intercepted the communications of Asian communist nations, absorbed G Group, which had handled the rest of the world, including terrorism. From the merger came a new organizational entity called B Group, which essentially was tasked with intelligence coverage of the world except for Europe and Central Asia, including international terrorism. A new G Group was created, which was designated as the Collection Operations Group and assigned the mission of managing NSA's worldwide Sigint collection operations. Finally, a new group, the Cryptanalysis Group (Z Group), was created to centralize NSA's codebreaking activities under one roof. Memorandum for the NSA/CSS Representative Defense, *NSA Transition Book for the Department of Defense – Information Memorandum*, 9 Dec. 1992, Top Secret Edition, p. 22; *Naval Security Group Command Annual History 1993*, np, COMNAVSECGRU FOIA; Bill Gertz, 'Electronic Spying Reoriented at NSA', *Washington Times*, 27 Jan. 1992, p.A4; *National Security Agency Newsletter*, Aug. 1996, p.2.

33. Confidential interview.
34. Joint Inquiry Staff, House Permanent Select Committee on Intelligence and Senate Permanent Select Committee on Intelligence, Eleanor Hill, Staff Director, Joint Inquiry Staff, *Joint Inquiry Staff Statement, Part I*, 18 Sept. 2002, p.13.
35. Office of the Under Secretary of Defense for Acquisition & Technology, *The Defense Science Board 1997 Summer Study Task Force on DoD Responses to Transnational Threats*, Oct. 1997, Vol. I: Final Report, p.C-2.
36. Bill Gertz, 'Bin Laden's Several Links to Terrorist Units Known', *Washington Times*, 23 Aug. 1998, p.A1.
37. Ibid.
38. Bruce B. Auster, Kevin Whitelaw and Lucian Kim, 'An Inside Look at Terror Inc.', *U.S. News & World Report*, 19 Oct. 1998, pp.34–5.
39. Confidential interviews.
40. Frank J. Cilluffo, Ronald A. Marks and George C. Salmoiraghi, 'The Use and Limits of U.S. Intelligence', *The Washington Quarterly* (Winter 2002) p.66.
41. Shlomo Gazit and Michael Handel, 'Insurgency, Terrorism and Intelligence', in Roy Godson (ed.) *Intelligence Requirements for the 1980s: Counter Intelligence* (Washington DC: National Strategy Information Center 1980) p.136.
42. Confidential interviews.
43. Glenn Zorpette, 'Making Intelligence Smarter', *IEEE Spectrum*, Jan. 2002; Seymour M. Hersh, 'Missed Messages', *The New Yorker*, 29 May 2002; Thomas Patrick Carroll, 'The CIA and the War on Terror', *Middle East Intelligence Bulletin* 4/9 (Sept. 2002) p.2.
44. *Joint Inquiry Staff Statement, Part I* (note 34) p.13.
45. See the transcript of the Nov. 2001 Osama bin Laden videotape, filed in Kandahar, Afghanistan, on or about 9 Nov. 2001, in 'Caught on Tape', *ABCNews.com*, 13 Dec. 2001, <http://abcnews.go.com/sections/world/DailyNews/OBLtaperelease011213.html>.
46. David Johnston, 'Lack of Pre-9/11 Sources to be Cited as Intelligence Failure', *New York Times*, 17 July 2003, p.A1.
47. Confidential interviews. See also James Risen and David Johnston, 'Little Change in a System That Failed', *New York Times*, 8 Sept. 2002.
48. *Joint Inquiry Staff Statement, Part I* (note 34) p.13; Report of the US Senate Select Committee and US House Permanent Select Committee on Intelligence, *Joint Inquiry Into Intelligence Community Activities Before and After the Terrorist Attacks of September 11* (note 2) p.376.
49. *Frontline: Follow The Money*, transcript, Public Broadcasting System, 12 July 1989; Mark Urban, *UK Eyes Alpha* (London: Faber 1996) p.236.
50. Alan Friedman, 'The Flight of the Condor', *Financial Times*, 21 Nov. 1989.
51. *Frontline: Follow the Money* (note 49).
52. Jeff Gerth and Judith Miller, 'Funds for Terrorists Traced to Persian Gulf Businessmen', *New York Times*, 14 Aug. 1996, p.A1.
53. Robert Windrem, 'Bin Laden's Name Raised Again', *MSNBC*, 18 Oct. 2000, <www/msnbc.com/news/477832.asp>.
54. Seymour M. Hersh, 'King's Ransom: How Vulnerable are the Saudi Royals?', *The New Yorker*, 22 Oct. 2001, p.35.
55. Zorpette, 'Making Intelligence Smarter' (note 43).
56. Confidential interview.
57. Gertz, 'Bin Laden's Several Links to Terrorist Units Known' (note 36). See also Bill Gertz, *Breakdown: How America's Intelligence Failures Led to September 11* (Washington DC: Regnery 2002) p.7. The article specifically cites a NSA intercept for the intelligence. The book, published four years later, curiously does not mention Sigint as the source for the information.
58. Gertz, 'Bin Laden's Several Links to Terrorist Units Known' (note 36). See also Gertz, *Breakdown* (note 57) p.9. The 1998 Gertz article specifically cites NSA Sigint intercept for the intelligence about these phone calls. The 2002 book does not cite Sigint as the source for the information.

59. See FBI, press release and attached indictment, 21 June 2001, <www.fbi.gov/pressrel/pressrel01/khobar.htm>.
60. Gertz (note 57) p.10.
61. Report of the US Senate Select Committee and US House Permanent Select Committee on Intelligence, *Joint Inquiry Into Intelligence Community Activities Before and After the Terrorist Attacks of September 11, 2001*(note 2) p.380.
62. Confidential interview.
63. Confidential interviews.
64. US House of Representatives, Permanent Select Committee on Intelligence, *IC21: Intelligence Community in the 21st Century*, 104th Congress, 1996, p.187.
65. Auster *et al.*, 'An Inside Look at Terror Inc.' (note 38).
66. Philip H. J. Davies, 'Information Warfare and the Future of the Spy', *Information Communication and Society* 2/2 (Summer 1999).
67. Zorpette, 'Making Intelligence Smarter' (note 43); John Tagliabue, 'Cryptic Tapes From 2000 Hinted at Air Attacks in U.S.', *New York Times*, 30 May 2002, p.A1.
68. 'U.S. Landmarks Described', *ABCNEWS.com*, 17 Sept. 2002, <http://abcnews.go.com/sections/world/DailyNews/pakistan020917_arrest.html>
69. International Telecommunications Union, 'ITU Telecommunication Indicators', April 2000, <www.itu.int/ti/industryoverview/at_glance/KeyTelecom99.htm>. See also Paul Kaihla, 'Weapons of the Secret War', *Business 2.0 Magazine*, Nov. 2001.
70. 'Taliban Outlaws Net in Afghanistan', Reuters, 17 July 2001; R. Frank Lebowitz, 'Taliban Ban Internet in Afghanistan', Digital Freedom Network, 16 July 2001, <http://dfn.org/focus/afghanistan/internetban.htm>.
71. Confidential interview.
72. *United States of America v. Usama bin Laden et al.*, US District Court for the Southern District of New York, New York City, trial transcript, in 98 Cr. 1028, 1 May 2001, p.5290.
73. Ibid., p.5287.
74. Ibid. pp.5288–92.
75. Nick Fielding and Dipesh Gadhery, 'The Next Target: Britain?', *The Sunday Times*, 24 March 2002, p.1.
76. Ibid.
77. See Government Exhibits 48 and 321, attached to Trial Transcript for April 4, 2001, in
98 Cr. 1028, *United States of America v. Usama bin Laden et al.*, US District Court for the Southern District of New York, New York City.
78. Confidential interviews.
79. Walter Pincus and Vernon Loeb, 'CIA Blocked Two Attacks Last Year', *Washington Post*, 11 Aug. 1998, p.A16.
80. 'Terrorism Directed at America', *ERRI Daily Intelligence Report*, 24 Feb. 1999, <www.emergency.com/1999/bnldn-pg.htm>.
81. Walter Pincus, 'CIA Touts Successes in Fighting Terrorism', *Washington Post*, 1 Nov. 2002, p.A29.
82. 'Islam Rising', *The Atlantic Monthly*, 17 Feb. 1999.
83. Trial Transcript, 4 April 2001, p.3867, in 98 Cr. 1028, *United States of America v. Usama bin Laden et al.*, US District Court for the Southern District of New York, New York City; Trial Transcript, 17 April 2001, pp.4201–02, in ibid. See also Benjamin Weiser, 'U.S. to Offer Detailed Train of bin Laden in Bomb Trial', *New York Times*, 13 Jan. 2001, p.A1.
84. See Trial Transcript, 4 April 2001, p.3804, in 98 Cr. 1028, *United States of America v. Usama bin Laden et al.*, US District Court for the Southern District of New York, New York City; Trial Transcript, 1 May 2001, pp.5305–15, 5339, in ibid.; Trial Transcript, 2 May 2001, pp.5541–2, in ibid; Trial Transcript, 3 May 2001, pp.5604–05, in ibid.
85. Mark Matthews, 'Attacks' Timing Was Driven by Threats to US', *Baltimore Sun*, 21 Aug. 1998, p.1A; James Risen, 'Militant Leader Was a U.S. Target Since the Spring', *New York Times,* 6 Sept. 1998; Tim Weiner and James Risen, 'Decision to Strike Factory in Sudan Based Partly on Surmise', *New York Times*, 21 Sept. 1998; Gregory L. Vistica and Daniel Klaidman, 'Tracking Terror', *Newsweek*, 19 Oct. 1998; Bruce B. Auster *et al.*, 'An Inside Look at Terror Inc.' (note 38).

86. Vernon Loeb, 'A Dirty Business', *Washington Post*, 25 July 1999, pp.F1, F4; Paul McGeough, 'A Teacher of Terror', *Sydney Morning Herald*, 22 Sept. 2001, p.1.
87. Marian Wilkinson, 'Spy Stations Key to Australian Role', *Sydney Morning Herald*, 26 Sept. 2001, p.3.
88. 'Indian Daily: Musharraf Unlikely to Cooperate With US Forces' Hunt for UBL', *The Pioneer*, 21 Dec. 2001, FBIS-NES-2001-1221.
89. Windrem, 'Bin Laden's Name Raised Again' (note 53).
90. *Statement for the Record by Lt. General Michael V. Hayden, USAF, Director NSA/CSS* (note 1) p.3.
91. CM 5542, Intelligence and Security Committee, *Annual Report 2001-2002* (note 24) p.20.
92. NSA Declassification Guidance 003-96, 25 Oct. 1996, via Dr Jeffrey T. Richelson.
93. US Department of Defense, DoD Directive No. 2000.12, *DoD Antiterrorism/Force Protection (AT/FP) Program*, 13 April 1999, Enclosure 5, National Security Agency Responsibilities, <http://wcb7.whs.osd.mil/text/d200012p.text>.
94. Report of the US Senate Select Committee and US House Permanent Select Committee on Intelligence, *Joint Inquiry Into Intelligence Community Activities Before and After the Terrorist Attacks of September 11, 2001*(note 2) p.377.
95. On 13 Feb. 2002, al-Hada, age 25, blew himself up with a grenade in downtown Sana'a when cornered by Yemeni security forces. He was the brother-in-law of one of the 9/11 hijackers, Khalid Almihdar.
96. A recently declassified congressional report notes the Sigint value of this target during the years 1998–2000, but for reasons not known all references to al-Hada were deleted from the report. Instead, al-Hada's telephone is referred to as 'a suspected terrorist facility in the Middle East'. Report of the US Senate Select Committee and US House Permanent Select Committee on Intelligence (note 2) pp.155-7. For a detailed examination of the role played by al-Hada, see Michael Isikoff and Daniel Klaidman, 'The Hijackers We Let Escape', *Newsweek*, 10 June 2002.
97. Barton Gellman, 'Broad Effort Launched After '98 Attacks', *New York Times*, 19 Dec. 1991, p.A1.
98. 'Taliban Ready to Discuss US Demands to Hand Over Osama', *The Daily Star*, 8 Feb. 1999, <www.dailystarnews.com/199902/n9020813.htm>.
99. 'Citing Threats, Britain Joins U.S. in Closing Embassies in Africa', CNN, 25 June 1999, <www.cnn.com/WORLD/africa/9906/25/africa.embassies.03/>; David Phinney, 'Fund-Raising for Terrorism', *ABCNEWS.com*, 9 July 1999.
100. John McWethy, 'U.S. Tries to Get Bin Laden', *ABCNEWS.com*, 9 July 1999.
101. Barbara Starr, 'Bin Laden's Plans', *ABCNEWS.com*, 16 July 1999.
102. Bill Gertz, 'NSA's Warning Arrived Too Late to Save the Cole', *Washington Times*, 25 Oct. 2000, p.A1.
103. Jonathan D. Austin, 'U.S. Reports Increase in Terrorist Threats', *CNN.com*, 25 Oct. 2000, <www.cnn.com/2000/US/10/24/mideast.alert.02/>.
104. CM 5542, Intelligence and Security Committee, *Annual Report 2001-2002* (note 24) pp.19–20.
105. Leo Sisti and Maud Beelman, 'Arrested Italian Cell Sheds Light on Bin Laden's European Network', *The Public I*, 3 Oct. 2001, Center for Public Integrity, <www.public-i.org/story_01_100401.htm>.
106. James Risen and Stephen Engelberg, 'Failure to Heed Signs of Change in Terror Goals', *New York Times*, 14 Oct. 2001, p.A1.
107. Report of the US Senate Select Committee and US House Permanent Select Committee on Intelligence (note 2) p.203; Joint Inquiry Staff, House Permanent Select Committee on Intelligence and Senate Permanent Select Committee on Intelligence, Eleanor Hill, Staff Director, Joint Inquiry Staff, *Joint Inquiry Staff Statement, Part I* (note 34) p.20; *Statement for the Record by Lt. General Michael V. Hayden* (note 1) p.4.
108. James Risen, 'In Hindsight, CIA Sees Flaws that Hindered Efforts on Terrorism', *New York Times*, 7 Oct. 2001, p.1.
109. Pincus (note 81) p.A29.

110. Mary Dejevsky, 'US Forces on High Alert After Threat of Attack', *The Independent*, 23 June 2001, p.15.

111. Pincus, 'CIA Touts Successes in Fighting Terrorism' (note 81) p.A29.

112. 'The Proof They Did Not Reveal', *Sunday Times*, 7 Oct. 2001, p.2; 'Early Warnings: Pre-Sept. 11 Cautions Went Unheeded', *ABCNews.com*, 18 Feb. 2002.

113. Raymond Bonner and John Tagliabue, 'Eavesdropping, U.S. Allies See New Terror Attack', *New York Times*, 21 Oct. 2001, p.A1; Neil A. Lewis and David Johnston, 'Jubilant Calls on Sept. 11 Led to FBI Arrests', *New York Times*, 28 Oct. 2001, p.A1.

114. The existence of these intercepts was first disclosed in Rowan Scarborough, 'Intercepts Foretold of "Big Attack"', *Washinigton Times*, 22 Sept. 2001. Details of these messages are contained in James Risen and David Johnston, 'Agency is Under Scrutiny for Overlooked Messages', *New York Times*, 20 June 2002, p.A1; Walter Pincus and Dana Priest, 'NSA Intercepts on Eve of 9/11 Sent a Warning', *Washington Post*, 20 June 2002, p.A1; Scott Shane and Ariel Sabar, 'Coded Warnings Became Clear Only in Light of Sept. 11 Attacks', *Baltimore Sun*, 20 June 2002.

115. Joint Inquiry Staff, House Permanent Select Committee on Intelligence and Senate Permanent Select Committee on Intelligence, Eleanor Hill, Staff Director, Joint Inquiry Staff, *Joint Inquiry Staff Statement, Part I* (note 34) p.22. See also Senate Report No. 107-351 and House Report No. 107-792, Report of the US Senate Select Committee and US House Permanent Select Committee on Intelligence(note 2) p.375.

116. Press briefing by Rep. Saxby Chambliss and Rep. Jane Harman, 12 July 2002.

117. CM 5542, Intelligence and Security Committee, *Annual Report 2001-2002* (note 24) p.21.

118. Report of the US Senate Select Committee and US House Permanent Select Committee on Intelligence (note 2) p.374.

119. Gertz (note 57) p.135.

120. Douglas Waller, 'The NSA Draws Fire', *Time*, 20 July 2002, <www.time.com/time/nation/article/0,8599,322587,00.html>.

121. *Statement for the Record by Lt. General Michael V. Hayden* (note 1) p.3.

122. John Diamond, 'Terror Group's Messengers Steer Clear of NSA Ears', *USA Today*, 18 Oct. 2002, p.12A.

123. Arieh O'Sullivan, 'Mossad Head: We Need Spies, Not Just Electronics', *Jerusalem Post*, 25 Sept. 2001, <www.jpost.com/Editions/2001/09/25/News/News.35300.html>.

124. See Shmuel L. Gordon, *The Vulture and the Snake: Counter-Guerrilla Air Warfare: The War in Southern Lebanon* (Jerusalem: Begin-Sadat Center for Strategic Studies Bar-Ilan University, July 1998).

125. US Senate, Committee on the Judiciary, Subcommittee on Technology, Terrorism, and Government Information, *Crime, Terror and War: National Security and Public Safety in the Information Age*, Nov. 1998.

126. US House of Representatives, Permanent Select Committee on Intelligence, *IC21: Intelligence Community in the 21st Century*, 104th Congress, 1996, p.186.

127. Prepared statement of Dr John J. Hamre, President and CEO, Center for Strategic and International Studies, Washington DC, *Defining Terrorism and Responding to the Terrorist Threat*, Hearing Before the US House of Representatives, House Permanent Select Committee on Intelligence, 26 Sept. 2001.

128. *Congressional Record*, US House of Representatives, 7 May 1998, p.H2950; Neil King, Jr, 'U.S. Security Agency Defends Eavesdrop Use', *Wall Street Journal*, 13 April 2000.

129. National Commission on Terrorism, *Countering the Changing Threat of International Terrorism*, June 2000, <www.fas.org/irp/threat/commission.html>.

130. Confidential interview.

131. Confidential interview.

132. David A. Fulghum, 'Computer Combat Rules Frustrate the Pentagon', *Aviation Week & Space Technology*, 15 Sept. 1997, p.68.

133. Confidential interview.

134. Confidential interviews.

135. Joint Inquiry Staff, House Permanent Select Committee on Intelligence and Senate Permanent Select Committee on Intelligence, Eleanor Hill, Staff Director, Joint Inquiry Staff, *Joint Inquiry Staff Statement*, 8 Oct. 2002.
136. Confidential interview.
137. Confidential interview for conflicting tasking on NSA. For number of federal agencies involved in counter-terrorism, see US General Accounting Office, GAO/T-NSIAD-98-164, *Combating Terrorism: Observations on Crosscutting Issues*, 23 April 1998, p.4.
138. US House of Representatives, House Permanent Select Committee on Intelligence, Subcommittee on Terrorism and Homeland Security, *Counterterrorism Intelligence Capabilities and Performance Prior to 9-11*, 17 July 2002, p.v.
139. Confidential interviews.
140. Waller, 'The NSA Draws Fire' (note 120)..
141. *Statement for the Record by Lt. General Michael V. Hayden* (note 1) p.9.
142. Report of the US Senate Select Committee and US House Permanent Select Committee on Intelligence (note 2) p.374.
143. National Commission on Terrorism, *Countering the Changing Threat of International Terrorism*, 5 June 2000, p.iv; The United States Commission on National Security/21st Century, *Road Map for National Security: Imperative for Change: The Phase III Report of the U.S. Commission on National Security/21st Century* (hereafter 'Hart-Rudman Report), 15 Feb. 2001, p.85.
144. US House of Representatives (note 138) p.vi.
145. CM 5542, Intelligence and Security Committee, *Annual Report 2001-2002* (note 24) pp.10, 26.
146. Confidential interviews.
147. 'Global Traffic Review: TeleGeography 2000', <www.telegeography.com>.
148. Ibid.
149. Scott Shane and Tom Bowman, 'America's Fortress of Spies', *Baltimore Sun*, 3 Dec. 1995, p.12A.
150. Gregory Vistica and Evan Thomas, 'Hard of Hearing', *Newsweek*, 13 Dec. 1999; Frank Tiboni, 'Difficulty Grows for U.S. Intelligence Gathering', *Space News*, 12 June 2000, p.1.
151. Major A. Andronov, 'American Geosynchrenous Sigint Satellites', *Zarubezhnoye Voyennoye Obozreniye* 12 (1993) pp.37–43.
152. For NSA owning the largest communications system in the federal government, see 'Prestigious Roger W. Jones Award Presented', *NSA Newsletter*, Dec. 1994, p.3. For network problems, see Robert K. Ackerman, 'Security Agency Transitions From Backer to Participant', *Signal*, Oct. 1999, p.23.
153. Loch K. Johnson, *Secret Agencies: U.S. Intelligence in a Hostile World* (New Haven, CT: Yale UP 1996) p.21; Robert D. Steele, *Improving National Intelligence Support to Marine Corps Operational Forces: Forty Specific Recommendations*, 3 Sept. 1991, p.5, <www.oss.net/Papers/reform>.
154. Ackerman, 'Security Agency Transitions From Backer to Participant' (note 152).
155. US House of Representatives, Permanent Select Committee on Intelligence, *IC21: Intelligence Community in the 21st Century*, 104th Congress, 1996, p.120.
156. Ackerman (note 152); Vistica and Thomas, 'Hard of Hearing' (note 150); Jeffrey T. Richelson, 'Desperately Seeking Signals', *Bulletin of Atomic Scientists*, March/April 2000, pp.47–51.
157. *Congressional Record*, 19 July 1999, pp.S8777–S8796.
158. US House of Representatives (note 138) p.v.
159. Report of the US Senate Select Committee and US House Permanent Select Committee on Intelligence, *Joint Inquiry Into Intelligence Community Activities Before and After the Terrorist Attacks of September 11, 2001* (note 2) p.382.
160. Senator Paul Simon, 'Beef Up the Country's Foreign Language Skills', *Washington Post*, 23 Oct. 2001, p.A23.

161. As of 31 Dec. 2001, the US Army was authorized to employ 2,378 cryptologic linguists; the US Air Force employed 2,904 cryptologic linguists; and the US Navy and US Marine Corps possessed approximately 1,700 cryptologic linguists, known in Navy parlance as Cryptologic Technician Interpretive. For Army cryptologic linguist figures, see chart '98G Cryptologic Linguist' at <http://138.27.35.32/ocmi/career_maps/MI-DAPC45_jul_01/ slide0010.htm>. For the Dec. 2001 US Air Force figures, see 'Number of Personnel Assigned in the Active Duty Air Force – Enlisted', <http://usmilitary.about.com/library/ milinfo/blnumafenlisted.htm>. The figures for NSA civilian and Navy linguists were derived from confidential interviews.

162. Aid, 'The Time of Troubles (note 1) p.9.

163. Anonymous letter, 'Army Linguists', *Soldiers Magazine*, Aug. 2001.

164. Colonel Brian L. Tarbet, Utah ARNG and Lt. Colonel Ralph R. Steinke, USA, 'Linguists in the Army: Paradise Lost or Paradise Regained?', *Military Intelligence Professional Bulletin*, Oct.–Dec. 1999.

165. US General Accounting Office, GAO-02-514T, *Foreign Languages: Workforce Planning Could Help Address Staffing and Proficiency Shortfalls*, 12 March 2002, pp.5–6.

166. US House of Representatives (note 138), *Counterterrorism Intelligence Capabilities and Performance Prior to 9-11*, 17 July 2002, p.vi; US General Accounting Office, GAO-02-258R, *Foreign Languages: Staffing Shortfalls and Related Information for the National Security Agency and Federal Bureau of Investigations*, 31 Jan. 2002. A copy of this classified report is in the author's possession.

167. National Commission on Terrorism, *Countering the Changing Threat of International Terrorism*, 5 June 2000, p.14.

168. Report of the US Senate Select Committee and US House Permanent Select Committee on Intelligence (note 2) p.336.

169. Ian Bruce, 'Mistake in Translation Almost Proves Deadly', *Scotland Herald*, 24 April 2002.

170. Confidential interviews.

171. Report of the US Senate Select Committee and US House Permanent Select Committee on Intelligence (note 2) p.336.

172. Confidential interviews.

173. US House of Representatives, Permanent Select Committee on Intelligence, Report 107-219, *Intelligence Authorization Act for Fiscal Year 2002*, 107th Congress, 1st Session, 26 Sept. 2001.

174. Penelope S. Horgan, *Signals Intelligence Support to U.S. Military Commanders: Past and Present* (Carlisle Barracks, PA: US Army War College 1991) p.84.

175. Memorandum, *To Consider Possibilities of Using Deleted Information for Prosecion*, pp.1–3, attached to Memorandum, Belmont to Boardman, 1 Feb. 1956, FBI Venona Files.

176. Tom Blanton (ed.), *White House E-Mail: The Top Secret Computer Messages the Reagan/Bush White House Tried to Destroy* (NY: The New Press 1995) p.223.

177. Joint Inquiry Staff, House Permanent Select Committee on Intelligence and Senate Permanent Select Committee on Intelligence, Eleanor Hill, Staff Director, Joint Inquiry Staff, *Joint Inquiry Staff Statement*, 8 Oct. 2002.

178. *Statement for the Record by Lt. General Michael V. Hayden* (note 1) p.10.

179. Commission on the Roles and Capabilities of the United States Intelligence Community, *Preparing for the 21st Century: An Appraisal of U.S. Intelligence* (Washington, DC: Government Printing Office, 1 March 1996) pp.41–2.

180. Joint Inquiry Staff, House Permanent Select Committee on Intelligence and Senate Permanent Select Committee on Intelligence, Eleanor Hill, Staff Director, Joint Inquiry Staff, *Joint Inquiry Staff Statement*, 8 Oct. 2002.

181. Gertz (note 57) p.178.

182. National Performance Review, *Accompanying Report of the National Performance Review: The Intelligence Community* (Washington, DC: Government Printing Office, Sept. 1993) pp.35–6.

183. *Statement for the Record by Lt. General Michael V. Hayden* (note 1) p.10.

184. Report of the US Senate Select Committee and US House Permanent Select Committee on Intelligence (note 2) p.343.
185. *Statement for the Record by Lt. General Michael V. Hayden* (note 1) p.10.
186. Joint Inquiry Staff, House Permanent Select Committee on Intelligence and Senate Permanent Select Committee on Intelligence, Eleanor Hill, Staff Director, Joint Inquiry Staff, *Joint Inquiry Staff Statement*, 8 Oct.2002.
187. Confidential interview.
188. Commission on the Roles and Capabilities of the US Intelligence Community, *Preparing for the 21st Century* (note 179) p.38.
189. *Statement for the Record by Lt. General Michael V. Hayden* (note 1) p.8.
190. Karl Vick and Kamran Khan, 'Raid Netted Top Al Qaeda Leader', *Washington Post*, 2 April 2002, p.A1; Aftab Ahmad, 'Osama in Faisalabad?', *The Nation* (Lahore edn), 8 April 2002, FBIS-NEW-2002-0408; Ijaz Hashmat, 'US Intercepted Satellite Phone Message That Led to Raid in Faisalabad', *Khabrain*, 9 April 2002, FBIS-NES-2002-0409.
191. Rory McCarthy and Julian Borger, 'Secret Arrest of Leading al-Qaida Fugitive', *The Guardian*, 4 Sept. 2002.
192. Nick Fielding, 'Phone Call Gave Away Al Qaida Hideout', *Sunday Times*, 15 Sept. 2001, p.1; Rory McCarthy, 'Investigators Question Key September 11 Suspect', *The Guardian*, 16 Sept. 2002; Nick Fielding, 'War on Terror: Knocking on Al-Qaeda's Door', *Sunday Times*, 22 Sept. 2002, p.1.
193. Kevin Johnson and Jack Kelly, 'Terror Arrest Triggers Mad Scramble', *USA Today*, 2 March 2003; Rory McCarthy and Jason Burke, 'Endgame in the Desert of Death for the World's Most Wanted Man', *The Observer*, 9 March 2003; Kevin Whitelaw, 'A Tightening Noose', *U.S. News & World Report*, 17 March 2003.
194. *Worldwide Threat Assessment Brief to the Senate Select Committee on Intelligence by the Director of Central Intelligence, John M. Deutch*, 22 Feb. 1996, <www.cia.gov/cia/public_affairs/speeches/archives/1996/dci_speech_022296.html>.
195. Superseding Bill of Indictment, 28 March 2001, in Docket No. 3:00CR147-MU, *United States of America v. Mohamad Youssef Hammoud et al.*, US District Court for the Western District of North Carolina, Charlotte Division. See also Gary L. Wright, 'Hammoud Brothers Guilty on All Counts', *The Charlotte Observer*, 21 June 2002.
196. Gregory F. Treverton, 'Intelligence Crisis', *Government Executive Magazine*, 1 Nov. 2001, <www.govexec.com/features/1101/1101s1.htm>.
197. The cover name for the SCS when operating overseas is the Defense Communications Support Group.
198. Confidential interviews.
199. Colum Lynch, 'US Used UN to Spy on Iraq, Aides Say', *Boston Globe*, 6 Jan. 1999, p.A1; Barton Gellman, 'Annan Suspicious of UNSCOM Probe', *Washington Post*, 6 Jan. 1999, pp.A1, A22; Bruce W. Nelan, 'Bugging Saddam', *Time*, 18 Jan. 1999; Seymour M. Hersh, 'Saddam's Best Friend', *The New Yorker*, 5 April 1999, pp.32, 35; David Wise, 'Fall Guy', *The Washingtonian*, July 1999, pp.42–3.
200. Zorpette, 'Making Intelligence Smarter' (note 43).
201. Frank J. Cilluffo, Ronald A. Marks and George C. Salmoiraghi, 'The Use and Limits of U.S. Intelligence', *The Washington Quarterly* (Winter 2002) p.67.
202. John Deutch and Jeffrey H. Smith, 'Smarter Intelligence', *Foreign Policy*, Jan.–Feb. 2002.
203. *House of Commons Hansard Debates*, 22 June 2000, Part 30, Column 543, <www.parliament.the-stationery-office.co.uk/pa/cm199900/cmhansrd/cm000622/debtext/00622-30.htm>.
204. Treverton, 'Intelligence Crisis' (note 196).
205. An excellent description of ISA can be found in Jeffrey T. Richelson, 'Truth Conquers All Chains: The U.S. Army Intelligence Support Activity, 1981–1989', *International Journal of Intelligence and Counterintelligence* 12/2 (Summer 1999) pp.168–200.
206. Steven Emerson, *Secret Warriors* (NY: Putnam 1988) p.67.

207. Statement of the Under Secretary of Defense for Acquisition and Technology Paul G. Kaminski Before the House Permanent Select Committee on Intelligence on Enabling Intelligence Technologies for the 21st Century, 18 Oct. 1995, <www.acq.osd.mil/ousda/ testimonies/inteltech.txt>; Alan D. Campen, 'Intelligence is the Long Pole in the Information Operations Tent', 30 March 2000, *Infowar.com*, <www.infowar.com/info_ops/ 00/info_ops033000a_j.shtml>.
208. Campen, 'Intelligence is the Long Pole in the Information Operations Tent' (note 207).
209. Confidential interviews.
210. Paul Kaihla, 'Weapons of the Secret War', *Business 2.0 Magazine*, Nov. 2001, <www.business2.com/articles/mag/print/0,1643,17511,FF.html>.
211. US House of Representatives, Permanent Select Committee on Intelligence, Report 107-592, *Intelligence Authorization Act for Fiscal Year 2003*, 107th Congress, 2nd Session, 18 July 2002.
212. Ole R. Villadsen, 'Prospects for a European Common Intelligence Policy', *Studies in Intelligence*, Summer 2000, <www.cia.gov/csi/studies/summer00/art07.html>.
213. Assembly of WEU, Document A/1775, *The New Challenges Facing European Intelligence – Reply to the Annual Report of the Council*, 4 June 2002, <www.assemblee-ueo.org/en/documents/sessions_ordinaires/rpt/2002/1775.html>.
214. Commission on the Roles and Capabilities of the US Intelligence Community (note 179) p.127.
215. Richard A. Best, Jr, *The National Security Agency: Issues for Congress* (Washington DC: Congressional Research Service, Jan. 2001) p.27.
216. Shlomo Spiro, *Frameworks for European-Mediterranean Intelligence Sharing*, 2001, pp.5–6, <www.nato.int/acad/fellow/99-01/shpiro.pdf>.
217. Commission on the Roles and Capabilities of the US Intelligence Community (note 179) p.128.
218. Bob Drogin and Greg Miller, 'U.S. Strikes Back: Covert Moves', *Los Angeles Times*, 11 Oct. 2001, p.A1.
219. 'India's Defense Minister Backs US in Fight Against Terrorism', *Xinhua*, 16 Sept. 2001, FBIS-CHI-2001-0916.
220. David Rose, 'Spy Chiefs Call for New Rules and Money to Stop Terrorists', *The Observer*, 16 Sept. 2001.
221. *Congressional Record*, Senate, 7 Nov. 1991, p.S16305.
222. 'Panel Urges Improving System of Intelligence', Agence France-Presse, 6 Sept. 2002.
223. Confidential interview.

Terrorism, Intelligence and Law Enforcement: Learning the Right Lessons

GREGORY F. TREVERTON

By the mid-1970s, if the period still seemed one of high Cold War, at least the Communist threat on the home front had faded. In that context, the nation's first ever investigations of intelligence uncovered abuses of the rights of Americans, especially in a curious mixing of intelligence, or counterintelligence, and law enforcement at the Federal Bureau of Investigation (FBI) during J. Edgar Hoover's long tenure as director. The justification and ostensible target of this counterintelligence programs, (COINTELPRO) in Bureau acronym, was the operations of hostile foreign intelligence services.[1] But most of COINTELPRO's specific targets were American citizens, in civil rights and anti-war groups. People like the Reverend Martin Luther King were not only watched but harassed, and worse.

In reaction to the revelations, the nation came, haltingly but in the end firmly, to a striking of the balance between security and civil liberties. If the Communist threat at home had ever justified intrusive surveillance of Americans, it was judged to do so no longer. The domestic intelligence activities of the FBI were sharply restrained and the Chinese wall separating intelligence from law enforcement was built higher. A compromise between presidential discretion and civil liberties resulted in the creation of the Foreign Intelligence Surveillance Court (FISC), a court operating in secret to grant covert wiretap and other surveillance authority for intelligence – as opposed to law enforcement – purposes. Before FISC, presidents had claimed the right of warrantless searches without warrant for national security purposes.

Now, the nation confronts a vastly different threat from the Soviet Union, one that calls into question that striking of the balance. It also calls into question the legacy of organizations and processes that developed during the Cold War. In an important sense, it should not be surprising that cooperation between the Central Intelligence Agency (CIA) and the FBI before September 11 was ragged at best. We wanted it that way. Out of concern for our civil liberties, we decided the two agencies should not be too close. The FBI and CIA sit astride the fundamental distinctions of the

Cold War – distinctions between intelligence and law enforcement, between foreign and domestic and between public and private. The distinctions run very deep.

Those distinctions were not imposed by nature; rather, the United States (US) chose them mainly for good, practical and constitutional reasons. They did not serve us badly during the Cold War, but they set us up to fail in an era of terror. Now, reshaping intelligence and law enforcement means not just reshuffling organizations and refashioning their cultures, it means rethinking basic categories of threat and response.

ORGANIZATION 'OPPOSITIONS'

Law enforcement and intelligence are very different worlds, with different missions, operating codes and standards. Intelligence, what John Le Carré refers to as 'pure intelligence', is oriented toward the future and toward policy – that is, it seeks to inform the making of policy. Living in a blizzard of uncertainty where the 'truth' will never be known for certain, it seeks to understand new information in light of its existing understanding of complex situations. Thus, its standard is 'good enough for government work', or, as Pentagon officials might put it, good enough for 'TLAM therapy' – that is, cruise missile attacks launched on evil-doers. Because intelligence strives above all to protect sources and methods, its officials want desperately to stay out of the chain of evidence so they will not have to testify in court.

By contrast, law enforcement is oriented toward response. It is after the fact. Its business is not policy but prosecution, and its method is cases. It strives to put bad guys in jail. Its standard is high, good enough for a court of law. And law enforcement knows that if it is to make a case, it must be prepared to reveal something of how it knows what it knows; at least it is aware that it will face that choice. It has no real history of analysis; indeed, the meaning of the word 'intelligence' is different for law enforcement, where it means 'tips' to finding and convicting evil-doers more than looking for patterns to frame future decisions. Law enforcement and policing have also traditionally been defined in geographical units. These definitions are more and more mismatched to threats, like terrorism, that respects no geographical boundaries.

A second distinction, that between foreign versus domestic, magnifies the intelligence-law enforcement disconnect. American institutions and practices both during and prior to the Cold War drew a sharp distinction between home and abroad. The FBI had conducted wartime espionage and counterespionage in Latin America, and in December 1944 Hoover had proposed that the FBI run worldwide intelligence operations on the lines of its Latin American operations.[2] The proposal had some support outside the FBI, at the State Department in particular. But President Harry Truman worried openly that giving the intelligence mandate to the FBI would risk creating a 'Gestapo-like' organization, and so foreign operations went first to the Central Intelligence Group, CIA's predecessor, and then to the CIA. Both, however, were barred from law enforcement and domestic operations.

The congressional intelligence investigations of the 1970s were touched off by allegations during the Watergate scandal that intelligence agencies had committed abuses of the rights of Americans. Because most of the abuses the investigations found had emerged from COINTELPRO, those investigations ended up *raising* the walls between intelligence and law enforcement.

In the 1970s, it was literally true that the directors of the CIA and FBI did not speak to one another. That state of affairs has improved – it could hardly have gotten worse – but still relations between the two, in handing off spies from one agency to the other, have been ragged. The National Security Agency (NSA) too is barred from law enforcement and from domestic spying, so if the trail of conversations or signals it is monitoring becomes 'domestic' – that is, involves a US person, corporation or even resident alien – then the trail must end.

A third distinction is public versus private. During the Cold War, national security was a government – federal government – monopoly. To be sure, private companies and citizens played a role, but for most citizens, fighting the Cold War simply meant paying their taxes. That does not seem likely to be so for the campaign against terrorism and for homeland security. Civilians' lives will be affected – ranging from the inconvenience of waiting in long lines at airports, to harder questions about how much security will make use of pre-screening, national databanks and biometrics. Across the country, there are three times as many 'police' in the private sector as in governments.

All three of these distinctions were all too vividly on display before September 11. According to the joint Senate-House investigation of September 11, the CIA's procedures for informing other agencies – FBI, State, NSA and the Immigration and Naturalization Service (INS) – of suspected terrorists were both restricted and haphazard.[3] By its own guidelines and later by a January 2001 memorandum of understanding, the CIA was supposed to notify at least the FBI and NSA of all people it suspected as terrorists. In fact, it seems only to have put people on the watch list if it also had information that they were about to travel to the US – a much more restrictive criterion. Moreover, in the investigation's words, the CIA 'apparently neither trained nor encouraged its employees to follow its own rules on watchlisting'. The number of names the CIA put on the watch list soared after September 11, from 1,761 during the three months before September 11 to 4,251 in the three months afterwards.

The ragged connections between the CIA and FBI were all too graphically illustrated by their misdealings over the Al-Qaeda-affiliated terrorists Khalid al-Mihdhar and Nawaf al-Hazmi. Needless to say, the saga of what the two agencies told each other and when was played out in leaks and counter-leaks during 2002.[4] The two men attended a terrorist meeting in Kuala Lumpur, Malaysia, in early January 2000. This meeting was known to – and put under surveillance by – the CIA, which already knew that al-Mihdhar possessed a multiple-entry visa permitting him to travel to the US. NSA had independent information that linked al-Hazmi to Al-Qaeda. Neither the CIA nor NSA, however, saw fit to provide their names to the main watch list, the so-called TIPOFF database.

There is apparently some confusion over whether the CIA told the FBI anything about al-Mihdhar and al-Hazmi. CIA email traffic reviewed by the joint congressional investigation, however, suggests that the CIA did brief the FBI in general terms. The CIA, however, still did not bother to tell the FBI that al-Mihdhar had a multiple-entry visa that would allow him to enter the US.

In early March 2000, the CIA learned that al-Hazmi had arrived in Los Angeles on 15 January. Despite having just learned of the presence in this country of an Al-Qaeda terrorist, the CIA apparently did not inform other agencies. Indeed, the internal cable transmitting this information contained the notation: 'Action Required: None, FYI.' This information came hard on the heels of the intelligence community's alarm over possible 'millennium plots' by Al-Qaeda. Al-Hazmi arrived, moreover, at about the same time the CIA knew that Al-Qaeda terrorist Ahmed Ressam was also supposed to have arrived in Los Angeles to conduct terrorism operations. Still, however, the CIA refused to notify anyone of al-Hazmi's presence in the country.

By this point, both al-Mihdhar and al-Hazmi – both terrorists known to the CIA – were living in San Diego under their true names. They signed these names on their rental agreement, both used their real names in taking flight school training in May 2000, and al-Mihdhar even used his real name in obtaining a motor vehicle identification card from the State of California. In July 2000, al-Hazmi even applied to the INS for an extension of his visa, sending in this application using both his real name and his current address in San Diego (where he would remain until December 2000). INS, of course, had no reason to be concerned, since the CIA had withheld the two terrorists' names from TIPOFF. Nor did the FBI have any reason to look for them – for instance, by conducting a basic Internet search for their names or by querying its informants in Southern California – since the last it had heard from the CIA was that these two terrorists were overseas.

The CIA's failure to put al-Mihdhar and al-Hazmi on the watch list became even more inexplicable in January 2001, when the CIA discovered that a suspect in the USS *Cole* bombing also had attended the Malaysia meeting. This might have been taken as some confirmation that the two terrorists had links to Al-Qaeda operational cells, thus making them still more of concern – but the CIA still did not bother to inform TIPOFF. This failure was particularly damaging because al-Mihdhar was overseas at the time: putting his name on the watch list would have enabled INS agents to stop him at the border.

Even when given the opportunity to tell the FBI – in face-to-face meetings – about the presence of these two terrorists in the US, the CIA refused. At a meeting in June 2001 with FBI officials from the New York Field Office who were working on the USS *Cole* case, a CIA official refused to tell them that al-Mihdhar and al-Hazmi had come to the US.

Meanwhile, Khalid al-Mihdhar, in Jeddah, Saudi Arabia, applied for a new US visa in June 2001. But since neither man was on the TIPOFF list, his name did not appear when the State Department officials who took this application checked his name against their database, which incorporates TIPOFF watch list information. And so al-Mihdhar was given a visa and returned to the US unmolested in July.

The CIA finally put al-Hazmi and al-Mihdhar on the watch list in late August 2001, by which point they were already in the US and in the final stages of preparing for the September 11 attacks, and it also added the names of two others who were expected to try to enter the US. Apparently, the FBI did little with the information, and also failed to share it with the INS until the INS had already admitted the other two into the country. Questioned about its failure to follow up on this cable, one FBI official said, 'If the cable says, "Don't let them in the country, and they were already in the country, what's the point of bringing this up now?"' In any event, the FBI failed to locate Khalid al-Mihdhar and Nawaf al-Hazmi, who hijacked the jet that crashed into the Pentagon on September 11.[5]

The FBI did try to find the two but was hampered by some combination of its own regulations and the prevailing view that terrorism was a second-order mission, especially in the US. The Bureau did not shift agents to counterterrorism from its primary law enforcement mission. Nor did it search the Web for information that would have revealed al-Hazmi and al-Mihdhar living under their true names in San Diego. On 18 October 2001 the *Los Angeles Times* reported that a simple check of public records and addresses through the California Department of Motor Vehicles would have disclosed the correct location of the two hijackers. A check with credit card companies would have shown air ticket purchases and given their correct addresses.[6] (According to testimony before the congressional investigation from an FBI agent in New York who also conducted such a search after the September 11 attacks, finding al-Mihdhar's address could have been done 'within hours'.) The Bureau also did not ask for help from Treasury officials in tracking down al-Mihdhar and al-Hazmi through their credit card or banking transactions.

A State Department official testified that the FBI had refused for a decade to provide the INS with access to its National Crime Information Center Database, on the grounds that the INS is not a 'law enforcement' organization. Nevertheless, an internal FBI review concluded that 'everything was done that could have been done'.[7] Before September 11, the 'standard FBI line', according to one source who spoke to *New Yorker* writer Joe Klein, was that 'Osama bin Laden wasn't a serious domestic security threat', presumably because his earlier attacks had been abroad, not at home.[8]

No agency told the Federal Aviation Administration (FAA) to be on the lookout for the four men, apparently because it, too, was not in the law enforcement business. And the airlines were not informed because they were private, not public. A European official testified to the effect of these oppositions on the sharing of information with the US: '[T]hose we have been arresting are people we knew about before [September 11] but never thought were particularly dangerous to us inside our national boundaries'.[9] And so the two hijackers flew their plane into the Pentagon on September 11.

This sad tale is often taken as one of fights over bureaucratic turf for the control of information as power (or, perhaps, simple incompetence). Both turf and secretiveness played roles, but from my interviews and experience, the story really is one of very different cultures that were not used to cooperating closely and were not sure how much they should.[10] Cautious interpretations of the wall between intelligence and law enforcement had let that wall become very high. For instance, former Counter Terrorism Center (CTC) chief Cofer Black later testified before Congress that the CIA's refusal to tell the FBI about the two terrorists loose in the US had been entirely consistent with 'rules against contaminating criminal investigators with intelligence information'.[11] Apparently, part of the reason the FBI did not shift law enforcement investigators to the search for the two was its interpretation of the wall: information could be passed from intelligence to law enforcement only if it contained strong indications that a law had been broken.

Very different cultures compounded the effect of the wall. For instance, FBI agents have Top Secret clearance, but few are cleared into the Special

Compartmentalized Information (SCI) that is the weft and warp of intelligence. So, when faced by unfamiliar FBI counterparts in meetings, CIA officers would be sincerely uncertain how much they could say, and vice versa for different reasons for the FBI agents. The safest course was to say nothing. If the conversation turned to matters domestic, then the CIA officials would also be uncertain how much they should *hear.*

Cooperation between the two was probably best in the DCI's CTC, and the limits even there were suggested by the handling of the terrorist watch list. Because CTC was an intelligence organization, it was and is oriented abroad. It was also heavily operational, seeking to disrupt terrorist networks, again abroad. To the extent that law enforcement was a tool in that foreign task, that, too, was welcome – though CIA agents would be careful to stay out of the chain of evidence. The CTC was terrain on which cooperation between the two agencies was easier that it was in following terrorists in and out of the US.

THE FBI AND THE PRIMACY OF LAW ENFORCEMENT

If the story of the two Pentagon hijackers is testimony to the limited cooperation across intelligence and law enforcement, and across foreign and domestic, the Phoenix memorandum and the Moussaoui case speak to other aspects of the Cold War legacy, in particular the mission and practices of the FBI. The Bureau was – and is yet – preeminently a law enforcement organization, not a prevention or intelligence organization. It was and is dominated by special agents, and those agents naturally were attracted to where there were 'collars' to be made, and that was not terrorism, for terrorists ultimately might commit but one crime. Accordingly, the FBI viewed the world through the lens of the *case* and *case file.* If information was not relevant to making a case, it was not of much account.

An FBI special agent in the Phoenix field office sent the electronic communication, or EC in FBI parlance, to FBI headquarters on 10 July 2001.[12] The EC warned about potential dangers from Al-Qaeda-affiliated individuals training at US flight schools. The memo was sent to the Usama bin Laden Unit (UBLU) and the Radical Fundamentalist Unit (RFU) within the Bureau's counterterrorist organization. Headquarters personnel, however, decided that no follow-up was needed, and no managers actually took part in this decision or even saw the memorandum before the September 11 attacks. The CIA was made aware of the Phoenix special agent's concerns about flight schools, but it offered no feedback despite the information the CIA possessed about terrorists' interest in using aircraft as weapons.

Nor did the new FBI officials who saw the Phoenix EC at headquarters ever connect these concerns with the body of information already in the

FBI's possession about terrorists' interest in obtaining training at US flight schools. The full contents of the 'Phoenix Memo' have yet to be made public, but it is stunning that so little was made of it, especially since it drew attention to certain information *already in the FBI's possession* suggesting a very specific reason to be alarmed about one particular foreign student at an aviation school in the US.

That student was Zaccarias Moussaoui, the suspected '20th hijacker', who was arrested on 16 August 2001 in Minneapolis for a visa violation. FBI agents at the field office suspected him of terrorism and sought, with increasing desperation, to search his laptop computer but were denied permission by FBI headquarters. To get permission for a Foreign Intelligence Surveillance Act (FISA) search or wiretap, FBI field offices request them through headquarters and the Department of Justice's Office of Intelligence Policy and Review (OIPR), with formal requests approved in secret by the FISC. Reportedly, the FISC has turned down just one Justice Department request for authority, out of 12,000.[13] All of the 1,228 requests submitted in 2002 were eventually approved.[14]

That raises the concern that the FISA bar may be too low. The Moussaoui case, however, suggested that in practice, if not in law, the Bureau and Justice Department may have set the bar too high. In the event, headquarters and FBI lawyers briefed orally by the agent handling the case felt there was not enough evidence for a FISA search.[15] In the process, the standard apparently applied was that there had to be 'probable cause' that Moussaoui was an 'agent of a foreign power', which in turn was interpreted to mean linked to an already 'recognized' terrorist organization – which Moussaoui was not because his link to Al-Qaeda was as yet unknown.

In fact, the standard applied was more demanding than the law, which required probable cause (that is, substantial basis) that the targeted person be an 'agent of a foreign power', which in turn was defined as 'any person who...knowingly aids or abets any person in the conduct of [certain] activities'. Those activities include 'international terrorism', and one definition of 'foreign power' includes groups that engage in 'international terrorism'.[16] Moreover, those making decisions on the Moussaoui case never saw the now-famous electronic communication from the Phoenix field office, which arrived at headquarters in late July. The warnings in that communication about suspicious activity at US flying schools would have buttressed concerns about Moussaoui's own flying lessons.

The Moussaoui case can be seen as a testament to sloppy procedures, poor information technology, tensions between FBI field offices and headquarters, excessive caution or simple ignorance about complicated points of law, or all of those in some combination. It also may be that previous tensions between the FBI and the FISC had a 'chilling effect' and made for more caution. So it was alleged in the letter from Special Agent Coleen Rowley to FBI Director Robert Mueller dated 21 May 2002.[17] In any event, the case surely bespeaks considerable, perhaps excessive, caution on the part of the FBI and Justice in venturing FISA requests onto new terrain. Foreign spies were one thing; foreign 'students', even ones with worrying connections, were quite another.

The Moussaoui case underscores what Senator Richard Shelby labels the 'tyranny of the case file'.[18] That culture, if not tyranny, can hardly be overstated. Because the FBI was and still is a law enforcement organization, its agents are trained and acculturated, rewarded and promoted within an institutional culture whose primary purpose is to catch and prosecute criminals. Within the Bureau, information is stored, retrieved and simply *understood* principally through the conceptual prism of a 'case' – a discrete bundle of information that is constructed to prove elements of crimes against specific potential defendants in a court of law.

That culture is powerful and it pervades the entire organization. It is reflected at every level and in every area. It contributes to the autonomous, decentralized authority and traditions of the field offices, which is sharper in the FBI than in any government organization I have known. It is that way for a good reason: the criminals to be caught are in the field, not at headquarters. Money is allocated and careers are made through criminal investigations, not long-term analysis or other work. 'Intelligence' in the Bureau's practice is tips to finding and catching evil-doers; it is not the assembling of a broad mosaic of understanding. Producing clear, evidence-based narratives that will indict criminals is prized; drawing 'iffy' inferences based on fragmentary information in order to support decision-making is not. Given a choice between more agents on the street and better technology, the culture opted for the former, resulting in the FBI's famously backward technology. It is, in the words of one investigator, 'where the [IBM] 360s went to die', or as an FBI agent put it to me, 'we took the dirt road alternative to the information superhighway a generation ago'.

Given the tyranny of the case file, suppose, as a senior FBI counterterrorism agent put it to me, the FBI had done better at connecting the dots about flying lessons in the summer of 2001. His account is self-serving but with merit. What could the FBI have done? No crime had yet been committed, for taking flying lessons is not a crime, not even for Middle Easterners and not even if they are uninterested in landings and take-offs. Suppose then that the FBI had started knocking on doors of flying schools asking to interview Middle Eastern students – all without a crime or case. How far would it have gotten, at a time when Justice was suing local police departments over racial profiling? The question is a haunting reminder of the force of the Cold War distinctions and the law enforcement mission of the FBI.

In addition, while the distinctions have softened over time, still the gap at the FBI between special agents and 'support' is a yawning one. Activities not primarily performed by agents have been given less priority and resources, never mind whether those other activities are filing, or doing science or analyzing intelligence. Put more crudely, if you do not carry a gun at the Bureau, as agents do, you are a second-class citizen. The agents are a 'band of brothers', now including many sisters. That band makes for powerful capacity. As one agent put it to me: 'when you go out the door on an operation, you don't have to look over your shoulder to see if anyone is with you. They are.'

As with most powerful cultures, however, the pluses and minuses of the FBI culture are the same attributes. Agents shared information easily within the band – perhaps too easily, as is suggested by the case of agent Robert Hanssen, who spied for the Soviet Union and Russia. However, FBI agents were not distinguished before September 11 by their willingness to share *outside* the band. The Bureau brought, and brings, state and local police officers to work with it but does so very much on its terms, as members of FBI task forces, with clearances to match.

The culture and case file mindset meant that information the FBI collected either was or was not relevant to the case it hand. If it was, it often disappeared into federal grand juries. Before the USA Patriot Act of November 2001, it took a court order to share that information with anyone, including CIA analysts (who of course usually would not know what information was there and thus might be requested). If the information collected was not relevant to the case at hand, it often was simply discarded.

For instance, the FBI knew that convicted terrorist Abdul Hakim Murad had been involved in an extremist Islamic plot to blow up 12 US-owned airliners over the Pacific Ocean and crash an aircraft into CIA Headquarters.[19] Murad was not charged with a crime in connection with the CIA crash plot, apparently because that plot was merely at the 'discussion' stage when he was apprehended. Because the CIA crash plot did not appear in the indictment, however, the FBI effectively forgot all about it, and Murad's case file essentially ignored it. FBI agents interviewed by the joint congressional investigation confirmed that Murad's only significance to them was in connection specifically with the crimes for which he was charged: 'the other aspects of the plot were not part of the criminal case and therefore not considered relevant'.[20]

Convinced that the only information that really matters was information directly related to the criminal investigation at hand, the FBI thus ignored this early warning sign that terrorists had begun planning to crash aircraft into symbols of US power. Thus, rather than being stored in a form that would have permitted information to be assessed and re-assessed in light of a much broader set of information about terrorist plans and intentions over time, the Murad data-point was simply forgotten. Like all the other tidbits of information that might have alerted a sophisticated analyst to terrorists' interest in using airplanes to attack building targets in the US, the episode disappeared into the depths of an old case file and slipped out of the FBI's usable institutional memory.

RESTRIKING THE BALANCE

The nation is just beginning the process of striking anew the balance between liberty and security. As one observer put it: the war on terrorism put 'two vital, deeply grounded principles of American government on a collision course':

> On the one hand, the president has an unquestioned responsibility to protect the nation against foreign attack and to prevent hostile foreign powers from conducting covert intelligence activity within our borders. On the other hand, law enforcement power, always potentially dangerous to a free society, may operate only within boundaries established by the Bill of Rights.[21]

So far, the debate over the cost, in civil liberties, of fighting the war on terror sometimes has been shrill but almost always has been unfocused. For some, the country is already far down the slippery slope to losing cherished liberties. Others, looking at the same evidence, see mistakes and overreactions but conclude that, overall, the nation has done pretty well at not trampling on those liberties. In part, the difference reflects differing interpretations of particular events: what for some is a mistake of the sort inherent in large organizations looks to others like the tip of a sinister iceberg.

The civil liberties issues of concern after September 11 and the USA Patriot Act of October 2001 cover a range:[22]

- Detaining foreign nationals. In the immediate aftermath of the attack, some 1,200 foreign nationals living in the US were arrested and detained in considerable secrecy. Some 460 were still in detention in January 2002, their identities and locations undisclosed. Only 93 who were charged with a crime were ever identified. The Justice Department's own internal report, released in June 2003, was critical of the process: bureaucratic inertia left a number of innocent people languishing in jails for months while systematic understaffing left them with little chance to prove their innocence. Often no distinction was made between serious suspects and immigrants who had no connection to suspect groups.[23]

- Detaining and confining American citizens without judicial review. This small sub-set of the detentions is of particular concern. One, Yasser Esam Hamdi, had left the US with his Saudi parents when he was less than a year old and so may have lost his American citizenship, but the citizenship of the other, Abdullah al Muhajir (born José Padilla) was undisputed.

- Restricting access to counsel. When al Muhajir was transferred to military detention, one of the justifications for doing so was to prevent him from communicating with his lawyer lest he advance terrorist activity. A 31 October 2001 order by the attorney general established that restriction more widely.

- Enhancing surveillance. Because this set of concerns has the potential to touch the lives of so many Americans, it is the core concern. It, too, covers a range:

- Expanding FISA. Modern presidents had claimed, but the courts had called into question, warrantless searches for national security, as opposed to law enforcement, purposes. The Foreign Intelligence Surveillance Act (FISA) was a compromise, establishing a special secret court to review applications for national security search and wiretaps, of both citizens and non-citizens. The Patriot Act widened the scope for FISA warrants.

FISA and its court, the FISC, are the prominent tools the FBI and other federal agents have for pursuing the war against terrorism *in the absence of probable cause that a crime has been committed.* They or something like them probably are necessary because by the time terrorists commit a crime, it is too late. Ideally, the US would prevent all terrorist acts, and there never would be a crime to prosecute. By contrast, drug traffickers commit a stream of crimes.

In any case, the handling of the Moussaoui case spurred action to loosen FISA, which the Patriot Act put into effect. FISA taps always were permitted to be longer than law enforcement counterparts – 90 days rather than 30, with extensions easier to obtain. The Patriot Act extended them further, to 120 days, and it doubled, from 45 to 90 days, the period in which foreign agents, including US citizens, can be subject to clandestine physical searches.

Perhaps of greater concern, the Act made an apparently small change that is feared will have large consequences. Before September 11, obtaining foreign intelligence information had to be '*the* purpose' of FISA surveillance.[24] If evidence of crime was uncovered in the course of the tap, that evidence was admissible in court, but the foreign intelligence purpose was paramount. The Patriot Act loosened the requirement to '*a significant purpose*'.[25] Because FISA taps do not require probable cause of a crime, and are longer, more flexible and less controlled by judges than are law enforcement taps, there is concern that FISA taps will be used to troll for law enforcement purpose. That has led to tensions between the FBI and the FISC over who can approve the sharing of FISA data with FBI law enforcement agents.

- Monitoring the source and destination of email and Internet traffic. These so-called pen, and trap and trace techniques, were previously limited to telephones but were extended by the Patriot Act. They do not record content but can be put in place by a court order short of a showing of probable cause.

- Expanding clandestine searches. The Patriot Act also extended the scope of these 'sneak and peak' searches, which have little to do with terrorism since FISA confers much broader powers.

- Enlarging access to financial, education and other records. Before September 11, the FBI was permitted, for national security purposes, access to bank accounts without the holders' knowledge and without a court order. The Patriot Act expanded that access beyond banks and loosened the criterion to any foreign intelligence or counterterrorism purpose.[26] Before September 11, the letter of request had to certify that the information was for foreign intelligence purposes and that there were facts showing that the targeted customer was a foreign agent. Under the Patriot Act, it is sufficient that the request has a foreign intelligence or counterterrorism purposes.[27] A parallel change opened access to telephone records on the same basis.[28] And yet another change opened up access to educational records on roughly the same basis.[29]

- Allowing more discretion to officers in the field. Here, Moussaoui is the celebrated case and argument for more discretion in the field. On the other hand, critics see the shadows of COINTELPRO in the prospect of giving more discretion to field officers who already have a great deal. On 30 May 2002, the attorney general relaxed the prevailing guidelines to permit FBI agents to search the Internet, mine open data and attend public meetings, including those of political and religious groups.[30]

- 'Connecting the dots' about individuals. Here, the cause célèbre has been the Pentagon's program for Total Information Awareness. It was a public relations nightmare, seen by much of the public as 'Big Brother' while still in its infancy. Its director, John Poindexter, was a lightning rod for critics, for he was convicted (later overturned) for lying to Congress during the Iran-Contra affair of the 1980s. A research project, not an operation, it builds on previous artificial intelligence and data mining research sponsored by the Defense Advanced Research Projects Agency.[31] It would use modern computer power to scan public and private databases against templates of terrorist attack scenarios.[32]

Yet if the concerns are visible, so, too, the need for domestic information is plain. The September 11 terrorists not only trained in Afghanistan, they also used European cities like Hamburg and London (Brixton) as 'staging' areas where they could live, train and recruit in a protective environment. Similarly, they mixed easily in some areas of the US, 'hiding in plain sight' in south Florida and southern California, and perhaps also in Lackawanna. The need for information extends beyond simply following individuals, it also requires knowledge of what is being said on the streets and in the mosques of Brixton or Boston – it is doing 'foreign intelligence' domestically.

In March 2003, for instance, a prominent Yemeni cleric was apprehended in Germany on charges of financing terrorism, using a Brooklyn mosque to help funnel millions of dollars to Al-Qaeda and boasted that he had personally delivered $20 million to Osama bin Laden, according to federal officials. The cleric, Sheikh Muhammad Ali Hassan al-Mouyad, told an FBI informant that he was a spiritual adviser to bin Laden and had worked for years to provide money and weapons for a terrorist jihad. Sheik Mouyad boasted that jihad was his field and said he received money for jihad from collections at the Al Farooq mosque in Brooklyn. As New York Police Commissioner Raymond W. Kelly put it, 'Al-Qaeda operatives did their fund-raising right here in our own backyard in Brooklyn'.[33]

The collision of values runs through the war on terrorism. For instance, stories abound of people continually harassed when they try to fly because they are on one of the watch lists.[34] At the same time, Congress's General Accounting Office criticized the various agencies for not sharing their watch lists. Nine federal agencies maintain lists to spot terrorist suspects trying to get a visa, board a plane, cross a border or engage in similar activities – the FBI, the Immigration and Naturalization Service, the Department of Homeland Security, the Pentagon, the State Department and other agencies.

All keep such lists and share information from them with other federal officials as well as local and state police officials as needed. But the congressional study found that some agencies did not even have policies for sharing watch list information with other agencies, and that those that did often required complex, labor-intensive methods to cull information. Agencies often have different types of databases and software that make sharing information next to impossible. As a result, sharing of information is often fractured, 'inconsistent and limited', the study reported.[35]

LEARNING THE RIGHT LESSONS

In this case, both efficiency *and* citizens' rights might be served by more effective and more connected systems. The first lesson, then, is to assess any proposed measure for indications that it might be pain for no gain. That is, will it cause citizens inconvenience if not damage to their privacy for scant or no gain in the war on terrorism?

Most of the financial reporting requirements expanded under the Patriot Act fall into that category. Before September 11, financial institutions had been required to submit a Currency Transaction Report (CTR) for any cash transaction over $10,000 and a Suspicious Activity Report (SAR) when they 'had reason to suspect' that a transaction was 'not the sort in which the particular consumer would be expected to engage'.[36] Already before September 11 there were concerns over the sheer volume of such reports. However, the Patriot Act has increased that flow by expanding the requirements – from financial institutions to securities brokers and dealers in the case of SARs, and from financial institutions to any business or trade in the case of CTRs.

Those financial reporting requirements may have value for other threats, like drug trafficking. But they are pain for no gain in the war on terrorism because, alas, terrorism is not expensive. Estimates for the total cost of the September 11 attacks are in the thousands of dollars, not millions.

So, too, if we are honest, many of the airport safety measures are in the pain-for-little-gain category. In any case, it is not obvious that airport security is worth the $12bn or so the nation is now spending on it. Indeed, one of the real failures is that while the strategic warning that existed well before September 11 pointed to one fairly cheap fix – reinforced airplane cockpit doors – even that was judged too expensive before September 11. To be sure, the real purpose of many airport security measures is public confidence as much as real security but, in the end, measures that do not add much to security will not build confidence either.

Second, part of the reason for the striking cleavage in the public debate is the absence of any *compared to what? And for what gain?* It is imperative to begin to develop a systematic framework for assessing the value of particular intelligence-gathering measures, the civil liberties involved in them and costs that arise from the measures. That hard-headed assessment is all the more necessary the sharper is the clash of values; the assessment will not settle the argument over values but can at least put it in a clearer focus.

Take the issue of profiling, for instance. On the one hand, it is offensive to our values. On the other, it seems common sense. So far – though surely not forever – the terrorists of most threat to the nation have come from or had roots in one part of the world. Not to give special concern to people (so far men) who fit that description seems plain silly. Worse than silly, it seems to impose gratuitous costs on all those light-skinned grandmothers who are searched as potential terrorists. There is a considerable cost, including privacy if not liberty, to *not* profiling.

The first need is to be more open about costs and benefits. The civil liberties costs are usually argued in terms of individual cases, and those are provocative. But any system will make mistakes, and while it is a shame that those will fall disproportionately on one set of people, that shame does not eliminate the need to assess the overall costs carefully. The same is true of benefits. As with watch lists, more sophisticated profiling can be better than less. Searching every dark-skinned young male airline traveler is both offensive and wasteful. Making watch lists more discriminating by noting those who bought one-way tickets, or paid in cash or other relevant indicators can reduce the numbers who are singled out.

To be sure, collecting the information to make still more discriminating watch lists – for instance, by identifying people who had been associated with one another before but had made entirely separate arrangements to travel on the same flight – can itself invoke privacy concerns. Yet if the information is public in any case – as is true of most business and other associations – the value of permitting watch lists to assemble it probably outweighs the cost.

A third lesson is the possible value of a separate domestic intelligence agency, separately overseen. As US Senator Bob Graham (Democrat-FL) recently observed: 'I think [it is time] to look seriously at an alternative [to the FBI approach], which is to do as…many other nations have done, and that is to put their domestic intelligence in a non-law enforcement agency'.[37] Indeed, the joint congressional investigation into the September 11 attacks recommended that the administration 'consider promptly …whether the FBI should continue to perform the domestic intelligence functions of the United States Government or whether legislation is necessary to remedy this problem, including the possibility of creating a new agency to perform those functions'.[38]

The arguments for a separate domestic intelligence agency are two. The first is that the FBI is likely to remain – and perhaps should remain –

primarily a case-based law enforcement organization. It is good at that. Yet pursuing cases the way the FBI does simply is contrary to building a comprehensive intelligence picture. If the FBI identified a suspected terrorist in connection with a Hamas investigation, for example, the suspect would be labeled a Hamas terrorist with relevant information kept in a separate 'Hamas' file that would be easily accessible to and routinely used only by Hamas-focused FBI investigators and analysts. The Usama bin Laden unit would be unlikely to know about the FBI's interest in that individual. In the case of Moussaoui, when agents from the local field office began, in August 2001, looking into his flying lessons at a Norman, Oklahoma, school, they did so in ignorance of the fact that the same field office had been interested in the same flight school two years earlier because a man thought to be bin Laden's pilot had trained there.

Second, while domestic intelligence services in other countries have been willfully misused for political purposes – Italy and Peru are two cases in point – the lesson of COINTELPRO is that dangers to democracy can arise from mixing domestic intelligence with law enforcement. For similar reasons, Canada took its Royal Canadian Mounted Police (RCMP) out of the domestic intelligence business, replacing it with a separate service, the Canadian Security Intelligence Service (CSIS). Other states have been successful in creating domestic intelligence bodies that have operated effectively within the constraints of liberal democracy, including Britain (Security Service, MI5), France (*Direction de la Surveillance du Territoire*, DST), Germany (*Bundesamt für Verfassungsschutz*, BfV) and Australia (Australian Security Intelligence Organization, ASIO).

In all of these democracies, the intelligence function remains subject to legislative oversight and supervision yet retains the latitude to aid government crisis decision-making through covert and, often, unorthodox means. They, along with the COINTELPRO history, suggest that domestic intelligence might be both better and safer for democracy if it is separate, not the tail of a law enforcement dog. The US is probably not ready yet to create such a service, but it is time to begin discussing it. The new Department of Homeland Security (DHS) would be the logical place for such a homeland security intelligence service. The experiences of other countries also can provide useful ideas about how relationships among federal, state and local law enforcement agencies can be strengthened. In Canada, for example, CSIS has established a network of regional liaison officers, who help facilitate the flow of information between local and provincial police agencies and the federal authorities.

The fourth lesson is that some caution, and some slowness, is no bad thing as the nation rethinks the 'oppositions' on which Cold War institutions and processes were based. The values at stake are powerful. And we have yet to calibrate the terrorist threat. Indeed, we still do not understand what happened to the nation on September 11. We are learning, but there are still large unknowns about the terrorists' logistics, their own intelligence and so on. We sense, but do not yet know, that terrorism against the homeland will be, for the US, serious but not in a class with the threat faced by Israel. Thus, we suspect but do not yet know that the nation will not be forced to shift the balance as far toward security as Israel has had to do.[39]

Because of the controversy surrounding them, many (but not all) provisions of the USA Patriot Act are 'sunset' powers that will expire in 2005 if not specifically re-authorized. That seems wise, given that the terrorist threat is yet to be calibrated and serious assessment of the costs and benefits of particular measures is yet to be done. It seems all the wiser given that, with the benefit of some hindsight, some of the Act's provisions seem only tangentially connected to the war on terrorism.

Moreover, building domestic intelligence is a formidable task. In the first place, while local authorities collect a lot of information, they, like the FBI, mostly do so in response to crimes, not threats. That information then becomes part of cases, and may then disappear into grand juries. (It is rumored that the information about the domestic Al-Qaeda cells did not come from law enforcement at all but rather from CIA officials assigned to FBI Joint Terrorism Task Forces.) Only the several largest police departments, New York and Los Angeles, have intelligence components. For the rest, intelligence means tips to catching criminals, not assembling patterns of threat. None of the other departments has capacity for intelligence *analysis*.

At the federal level, much is in motion but not much is settled. For instance, FBI Director Robert Mueller is determined to turn the mission of the Bureau from law enforcement to prevention and intelligence, but doing so runs against the powerful grain of organizational culture that has run through this essay. The new DHS was to have an intelligence unit, but that has been very slow to emerge.[40] A Terrorist Threat Integration Center (TTIC) was created earlier in 2003 as the place to 'put the dots together'. But it will be housed at the CIA, under the Director of Central Intelligence, so, quite apart from its composition, its domestic reach will be limited, including by law. It is yet to be seen how much more it will or can be than a 'super' CTC.

Perhaps the slowly turning wheels of bureaucracy can provide time for reflection on the threats and values at stake. The 'oppositions' are not to be discarded lightly. We do not yet have consensus on where to strike the balance between security and liberty. And so we are at the beginning of a decade of rethinking and reshaping as we calibrate the terrorist threat against the homeland. As with fighting the Cold War, we probably will

come to settled new arrangements for fighting terrorism – just as the threat
has moved to something else!

NOTES

1. See *Final Report of the Select Committee to Study Governmental Operations with Respect to
   Intelligence Activities of the United States Senate*, 94th Congress, 2nd Session, 1976, Book
   II, *Intelligence Activities and the Rights of Americans*, and Book III, *Supplementary Detailed
   Staff Reports on Intelligence Activities and the Rights of Americans*. For links to these
   reports, as well as to a rich range of other documents, both historical and contemporary, see
   <www.icdc.com/~paulwolf/cointelpro/cointel.htm>.
2. See my *Reshaping National Intelligence for an Age of Information* (Cambridge: CUP 2001)
   p.139ff.
3. The findings of the joint House-Senate investigation of September 11 outline the basic story.
   It is *Final Report*, Part I, The Joint Inquiry, The Context, Part I, Findings and Conclusions,
   10 Dec. 2002. A fuller account is contained in Senator Richard Shelby's long supplementary
   document, *September 11 and the Imperative of Reform in the Intelligence Community*,
   Additional Views, 10 Dec. 2002. Both are available at <www.fas.org/irp/congress/
   2002_rpt/index.html>. See, in particular, Shelby's report, p.15ff., from which this account is
   drawn, unless otherwise indicated.
4. See Walter Pincus and Don Eggen, 'CIA Gave FBI Warning on Hijacker', *Washington Post*,
   4 June 2002, p.A1.
5. Ibid.
6. Bob Drogin, Eric Lichtblau and Greg Krikorian, 'CIA, FBI Disagree on Urgency of
   Warning', *Los Angeles Times*, 18 Oct. 2001.
7. Ibid.
8. Joe Klein, 'Closework: Why We Couldn't See What Was Right in Front of Us', *The New
   Yorker*, 1 Oct. 2001, pp.44–9.
9. See<http://specials.ft.com/attackonterrorism/index.html>.
10. This discussion and this essay are enriched by a RAND project I led for the Security Division
    of the FBI. The final report of that project, *Reinforcing Security at the FBI*, DRR-2930-FBI
    (Santa Monica, CA: RAND Jan. 2003) has been briefed to the FBI and to Congress but is not
    yet publicly released.
11. Quoted in Shelby, 'Additional Views' (note 3) p.30.
12. This episode is also discussed in the joint congressional investigation, *Final Report* (note 3)
    and in Shelby's 'Additional Views' (note 3) p.18.
13. See <http://fly.hiwaay.net/~pspoole/fiscshort.html>. See also Ronald Kessler, *The Bureau:
    The Secret History of the FBI* (NY: St Martin's Press 2002) pp.438–43.
14. The attorney general's letter-report is at <www.fas.org/irp/agency/doj/fisa/2002rept.html>.
15. This account derives from *Interim Report on FBI Oversight in the 107th Congress by the
    Senate Judiciary Committee: FISA Implementation Failures* (Feb. 2003) p.14ff,
    <www.fas.org/irp/congress/2003_rpt/fisa.html>.
16. 50 U.S.C. Section 1805 and Section 1824, and 50 U.S.C. App. Section 1801 (b).
17. A sanitized version of the letter was released to the Senate Judiciary Committee by the
    Justice Department on 6 June 2002. The quote is from pp.7–8, fn.7.
18. See Shelby's 'Additional Views' (note 3) p.36.
19. Ibid., p.37.
20. Ibid.
21. See Stephen J. Schulhofer, *The Enemy Within: Intelligence Gathering, Law Enforcement
    and Civil Liberties in the Wake of September 11* (NY: The Century Foundation 2002) p.46.
22. Ibid. This provides a very good, readable discussion of many of these categories.
23. Department of Justice Inspector General, 'The September 11 Detainees: A Review of the
    Treatment of Aliens Held on Immigration Charges in Connection with the Investigation of
    the September 11 Attacks, April 2003, <www.usdoc.gov/oig/special/0603/full.pdf>.

24. 50 U.S.C., section 1804 (a) (7) (b), emphasis added.
25. Ibid., as amended by Patriot Act, section 218, emphasis added.
26. See Dan Eggen and Robert O'Harrow Jr, 'U.S. Steps Up Secret Surveillance', *Washington Post,* 23 March 2003, <www.washingtonpost.com/wp-dyn/articles/A16287-2003Mar23. html>.
27. 12 U.S.C., section 3414(a)(1)(C); 3414(a)(5)(A) (2001).
28. 18 U.S.C., section 2709 (b) (2001), as amended by Patriot Act, section 505 (a) (2001).
29. 20 U.S.C., section11232g (j) (1)&(2) (2001)), as amended by Patriot Act, section 507 (2001).
30. Officially, the 'Attorney General's Guidelines on General Crimes, Racketeering Enterprise and Terrorism Enterprise Investigations' (30 May 2002). A sanitized version of the partly-classified 'Attorney General's Guidelines for FBI Foreign Intelligence Collection and Foreign Counterintelligence Investigations' is available at <www.usdoj.gov/ag/readingroom/terrorismintel12.pdf>.
31. See Shane Harris, 'Total Information Awareness Official Responds to Criticism', *Government Executive,* Daily Briefing, 31 Jan. 2003, <http://goveexec.com/daily/fed/0103/013103h.1.htm>.
32. For a summary of the privacy issues involved by TIA, see Gina Marie Stevens, *Privacy: Total Information Awareness Programs and Related Information Access, Collection and Protection Laws* (Washington DC: Congressional Research Service, 21 March 2003).
33. Eric Lichtblau and William Glaberson, 'Millions Raised for Qaeda in Brooklyn, U.S. Says', *New York Times,* 5 March 2003, <www.nytimes.com/2003/03/05/international/europe/05TERR.html?ex=1047>.
34. See, e.g., 'The System That Doesn't Safeguard Travel', *Business Week Online,* <http://uk.biz.yahoo.com/030417/244/dxz9z.html>.
35. General Accounting Office, *Information Technology: Terrorist Watch Lists Should Be Consolidated to Promote Better Integration and Sharing,* GAO-03-322 (Washington, DC: 15 April 2003), <www.nytimes.com/2003/04/30/international/worldspecial/30TERR.html>.
36. *Annunzio-Wylie Act of 1992,* P.L. 91-508, 32 U.S.C., section 531 (g); 31C.F.R, section 103.18(a)(2) and 108.19(a) (2) (ii).
37. As quoted in Thomas Frank, 'Push Is on to Overhaul FBI', *Newsday,* 29 Dec. 2002.
38. See *Final Report* (note 3) Recommendations.
39. Extrapolating from the Israeli experience in the first years of this century, an 'Israel-sized' terrorist threat to the US would imply about 10,000 deaths and 100,000 casualties per year.
40. For an argument for such a capability, along with the formidable obstacles to creating it, see my 'Intelligence, Law Enforcement and Homeland Security', Twentieth Century Fund, Aug. 2002, <www.homelandsec.org>.

Bombing at the Speed of Thought:
Intelligence in the Coming Age of Cyberwar

NICK CULLATHER

In December 2001, the US Army rolled out two technology-enhanced initial brigade combat teams (IBCTs) at Fort Lewis, Washington state, the first fruits of an Army transformation based on lessons from an experimental formation known as Force XXI. The units are lighter and have more wheeled vehicles than standard infantry brigades, but their armaments are strictly Cold War: they use the same M1A1s, Bradleys, Humvees, artillery and M-16 rifles that television viewers saw American soldiers using in the 1991 Gulf War. What makes these units different is that they are *wired*. 'We can share information vertically and horizontally, and we will be able to respond to near real-time intelligence as no army has in the past', Lieutenant Colonel Ralph Baker explained.[1] The unit will be able to control more territory and inflict more punishment on an adversary because its soldiers will have access to a tactical Internet known as 'battlespace'.

Modern wars have been defined and shaped by their visual representations. The 'map rooms' beneath the White House and 10 Downing Street during World War II, the U-2 photographs that triggered the Cuban Missile Crisis, Robert McNamara's computerized indices of progress, and the black and white videos taken by smart weapons each provided a distinct optic which set the limits of leaders' sights and determined what strategy and victory would look like. Battlespace is a 3-D terrain image that identifies friends and foes and is carried into battle in laptops, mobile theaters and individual eyepieces. Its promoters claim it will dissipate the fog of war, giving American commanders 'an omniscient view of the battlefield in real time, by day and night', allowing 'vital maneuver and devastating firepower to deliver the *coup de grâce* in a single blow'.[2]

Battlespace differs from earlier representations of war in four ways.

It operates in real time, meaning that targets are selected in battlespace and simultaneously attacked in real space. Older optics, even the grainy missile-cam images of the 1991 Gulf War, represented actions after they occurred. In battlespace, the synthetic battlefield and the real battlefield are one. The US Army describes the monocular eyepiece used by the digitized Land Warriors of Force XXI as a 'vision intensifier'. It allows soldiers to see across distance, through walls and at night.[3] Anything not shown on its flat-panel display is presumptively not worth seeing. The separations between intelligence, civilian decision-making and military command, carefully guarded during the Cold War, are breached by the fluid perception-decision-execution loops of cyber-warfare.

Second, it is omnipresent. Maps and their vital information were once hoarded at headquarters, but battlespace is an egalitarian management tool. Soldiers and generals have access to the same information, which can be visualized from all angles, from individual rifle-cams to orbital platforms. By combining information from satellites, unpiloted aerial vehicles (UAVs), terrain-scanning JSTARS aircraft, portable radars and airdropped electronic sensors into a single network, US forces will be able to throw a 'multi-sensor information grid' over an arena as large as North Korea or Iraq, enfolding the entire area in a single perceptual field.[4]

Third, it is autonomous. Battlespace will scan the theater, identify high-value targets and direct weapons to destroy them in the most economical way. 'It's just like Nintendo', First Sergeant Jon Clark of Force XXI explains. 'He can scroll over to the target he wants, and then the system swings the turret around to put a missile on that target. All he has to do is punch a button.'[5] The software acts as a force multiplier by allowing each soldier to control more space. Choosing the appropriate projectile and placing it precisely on target, it automates steps one and two of the find, fix and finish sequence, letting commanders strike the first and final blow at the moment of their choosing. And by optimizing the movement of forces and supplies, it allows strikes to be mounted directly from the United States (US).[6]

Finally, in the vision of its designers, Battlespace is completely coordinated. The maps, logs and after-action reports that represented each unit's version of previous wars will be instantaneously integrated into a single master narrative by a multi-service 'C4ISR backbone'.[7] Tolstoy painstakingly reconstructed battles from the fragments of memory and paper left by participants, but the Army Historical Program plans to 'provide commanders with "real time" historical products'.[8] Battlespace will record a single, undisputed version of events, visible at all echelons, live or in reruns. The fragmentary truths of previous wars will be replaced by one truth, one history.

The virtual battlespace is part of what Clinton administration officials called the Revolution in Military Affairs (RMA) and Donald Rumsfeld calls Force Transformation, a clean sweep of outdated doctrine and strategy by information age technology. RMA enthusiasts argue that just as e-commerce created a new economy, the tactical Internet will radically alter the nature of warfare. In June 1999, Pentagon spokesman Kenneth Bacon explained that 'battlespace awareness' was what distinguished Kosovo from earlier wars. 'That's the reason we're making the progress we're making without forces on the ground. That's the revolution in military affairs.'[9] George W. Bush has promised to deliver 'a revolution in the technology of war'.[10]

RMA proponents felt their day had finally arrived when Rumsfeld placed Andrew W. Marshall, a techno-enthusiast, in charge of a comprehensive review of Pentagon planning, but military futurists have been honing their arguments since the early 1990s. Theorists compare the RMA to past revolutions in tactics and technology: the invention of the stirrup, or the Romans' use of checkerboard formations to break the Macedonians' phalanx, each of which led to the rise of a new hegemon.[11] Unlike past revolutions, however, RMA will reinforce the military superiority of the power already dominant in the old technology, the US Defense Secretary William Cohen, watching the Force XXI exercises at Fort Hood in 1997, observed that 'dominance of the information world will put us in a position to maintain superiority over any other force for the foreseeable future'.[12] Military planners believe they are on a historical cusp between modern and postmodern war, or between second and third wave warfare.

Their vision of future war also contains a vision of future intelligence that might be described as counter-revolutionary. The virtual battlespace fulfills predictions made by theoreticians of intelligence in the mid-twentieth century, but it also makes claims to perfect or near-perfect objectivity, integrity and coordination that they would have found difficult to accept. Battlespace also embraces ideas, interpretations and methods of assessment from outside of the intelligence discipline, from the literatures on business and computers and from futurists Alvin and Heidi Toffler.

From this mixed inheritance of ideas a few genetic strands are discernible, one of which is the dream of central intelligence as it was first articulated in the 1940s. Cyber-warriors' anticipation of a system offering visibility, predictability and full coordination echo the predictions of Sherman Kent, William Langer and other intelligence modernists, who foresaw that in an ideal future 'intelligence might come to be revered by its users as a superior brain'.[13] Centralized intelligence would provide decision-makers with an agreed-upon set of facts, a single sheet music to harmonize policy. In 1947, Brigadier General Hayes Kroner, the War Department's deputy G-2, told Congress that the new Central Intelligence Agency (CIA) should be charged with 'laying before the national planners years before the war takes place that evaluated information, the very essence of which will dictate the answer to what our government should do'.[14] Centralized intelligence would eliminate misperception as well as ideological and political disagreement; it would set the parameters of discussion and separate 'policy planning' from politics. With the facts settled by neutral experts, planners would concern themselves only with choosing a course of action.[15]

The designers of central intelligence spoke of their ability to present a high-fidelity image of the world as confidently as battlespace designers speak of lifting the fog of war. Hanson W. Baldwin, in one of the first books to propose a central intelligence agency, defined strategic intelligence as 'the creation, out of disparate and localized and specific information, of an intelligible and *correct* over-all picture' (emphasis in original).[16] This optimism rested on the impressive development of the social sciences, whose continued progress appeared as certain in 1947 as the future of the Internet does today.[17] The intelligence fraternity, according to Wilmoore Kendall, adopted the mental habits of the Yale History Department, emphasizing certainty over contingency and projecting observable trends into the indefinite future. 'The course of events is conceived not as something you try to influence', he noted, 'but as a tape all printed up inside a machine; and the job of intelligence is to tell the planners how it reads.'[18]

As the utopian prospects of social science faded, the first line of defense grew more comfortable with fragmentary truths and dispersed authority. Intelligence officials continued to aspire to perfect vision and perfect coordination, but they talked less and less about attaining it. A dispute unresolved by the creation of the CIA concerned whether the agency ought to seek the unitary, coordinated perspective Kroner described, or to allow policymakers to choose from viewpoints provided by several agencies.[19] The structure of the intelligence community, with semi-autonomous services collected under a central authority, institutionalized this postmodern ambiguity. Kent conceded that decision-makers should be free to discuss the sources and slant of intelligence, which could never be more than a 'semi-finished good'.[20]

Casting aside these hard-earned doubts, battlespace resurrects the dream of total clarity, total coordination, along with the founders' promise of an end to bureaucratic conflict. 'If it improves enough', Martin Libicki ventures, 'even perfect situational awareness may *understate* what US forces can see.'[21] Admiral Bill Owens argues that inter-service rivalry will disappear when immersed in a unified, multi-service pool of synchronized information. Battlespace will end decades of contention between Army, Navy and Air Force and bring 'cultural harmony' to the Pentagon.[22] And military futurist Jeffrey Cooper concurs that 'integration cannot work without defeating the friction inherent in operations conducted by diverse forces'.[23] Some theorists claim the same reasoning applies to international rivalries, that in a coming age of 'neocortical warfare' images will defeat adversaries before violence becomes necessary. Shown to potential enemies, the virtual battlespace would act as a cyber-deterrent, exposing their vulnerability on the transparent battlefield.[24] One has to look to the years before 1914 to find similar expressions of faith in the power of reason and rapid communications to render war obsolete.

The US military has systematically applied science to warfare for the past 50 years, and battlespace contains inheritances from that effort. Britain pioneered operational research during World War II but the Pentagon grafted it onto an American military and scientific culture. Whereas British scientists concentrated on inventing devices and techniques of military use (radar, ship degaussing, codebreaking), the American Office of Scientific Research and Development (OSRD) took a Taylorist approach, sending scientists into the field to 'optimize' operations from reconnaissance search patterns to the placement of anti-aircraft guns. From the beginning there was an emphasis on statistical measures of performance coupled with pressure to improve efficiency per unit.[25]

The success of this approach made OSRD the model for postwar 'R & D' in universities, corporations, government and hybrids like the RAND Corporation. Robert McNamara, a Harvard business professor and operations analyst for the 20th Air Force during the war, World War II taught the method at Harvard, applied it to manufacturing automobiles at Ford, and then brought it back to the Pentagon as secretary of defense. His 'systems analysis' took statistical modeling techniques from economics and applied them to war with the help of a battery of IBM 360/65s.[26] He built an Eisenhower-era science office, the Advance Research Projects Agency (ARPA), into a laboratory for computerized warfighting. University of California scientists under ARPA contract invented the Internet (first known as the Arpanet) and ARPA designed the first sensor-driven, real-time, animated targeting map: Operation 'Igloo White'.[27]

Computers at Nakhom Phanom air base in Thailand read signals from sensors planted along the Ho Chi Minh Trail and plotted them on a map grid display as a 'worm' whose movement indicated the progress of a truck convoy. By 1968 the computers could transmit coordinates to computers aboard attack aircraft, automatically guiding them to the target box. Foreshadowing Sergeant Clark's Nintendo analogy, a technician boasted that 'Igloo White' 'wired the Ho Chi Minh Trail like a drugstore pinball machine, and we plug it in every night'.[28] The North Vietnamese showed their own pinball wizardry, using water buffalo urine, tape-recorded noise and truck-mounted electromagnets to generate phantom worms. 'Igloo White' was targeting its own sensors.

Systems analysis conditioned military planners to translate the lessons
of combat into requisitions for new technologies. Vietnam led to
investments in sensors and precision weapons. The 1991 Gulf War, seen as
a technological triumph outside the Pentagon, was regarded as a near failure
inside it. No future adversary (certainly not North Korea) would permit the
luxury of a four-month buildup during which US forces could familiarize
themselves with the terrain and devise a strategy. Once 'Desert Storm' was
underway, operations moved with unprecedented speed but battle damage
assessment advanced at the deliberate pace of satellite tasking and photo
interpretation. Commanders demanded the ability to observe the battlefield
in real time, to plan and train in simulated environments, and the capability
to transport troops and supplies from the continental USA to combat, all key
elements of the RMA.[29]

Under McNamara, the Pentagon's culture had taken fewer cues from West
Point and more from the Harvard Business School, as the blood-and-guts
generals were replaced by professional 'officer-managers'. The new
generation of military MBAs, now holding the senior ranks, have left
distinguishing marks on the Defense Department's 'imagineering' of future
war. One of the pillars of RMA, 'focused logistics', is Wal-Mart's just-in-
time-inventory scheme applied to warfare.[30] Descriptions of the RMA are
replete with references to 'synergies', 'thinking outside the box', and
'teaming', along with footnotes to business futurist texts with titles like
Mastering the Dynamics of Innovation and *Only the Paranoid Survive*.
Among these, the works of Alvin and Heidi Toffler are prominent. The
Tofflers, authors of *Future Shock* and *War and Anti-War*, are known for their
'wave theory' of human history that divides the past into periods –
agricultural, manufacturing, and now information – in which the dynamics of
business and war are determined by the way wealth is created. We are now in
the middle of the third wave in which 'intangible assets...ideas, innovation,
values, imagination, symbols, and imagery' set the pace of change.[31]

Military theorists rewrote history to fit the Tofflerian model, showing
that Lee won at Chancellorsville because of an information edge, and that
the Allies' mastery of intangibles such as codebreaking tipped the balance
in World War II. In the 1980s, social history began to move from the
academe into command and staff colleges. Michael Doubler and other
social/military historians told the history of World War II from the bottom
up, arguing that it was the American army's ability to listen to the men from
the lower ranks ('ideas, values, imagination') that allowed it to devise
tactics to defeat the Wehrmacht.[32] Merging with the message of pop business
books such as Thomas Peters' *In Search of Excellence*, this interpretation
provided a rationale for using information technology to bring bottom-up
management to the armed forces.[33]

Given its intellectual lineage, it is unsurprising that the RMA's force modernization bears such a strong resemblance to 1990s-style corporate restructuring: It involves a downsized labor force in which each soldier is expected to do more with a technology assist. It incorporates management techniques that appear to be based on information-sharing and egalitarianism, but which can seem to the soldier like deskilling and surveillance.[34] The 1997 Quadrennial Defense Review and Joint Vision 2010 (1997) placed emphasis on 'quality people', but the desired qualities were not leadership, instincts or coolness under fire but the qualities required to serve networked machines.

Like the virtual corporation, the RMA makes investments based on conjectural capabilities and gains, much to the dismay of the US General Accounting Office (GAO). Just as Enron and Worldcom stock rose despite the absence of actual profits, battlespace technology captured the future before it could translate information dominance into observable effects on the practice battlefield. At two large-scale exercises, at Fort Irwin, California, in 1994 and Fort Hood, Texas, in 1997, Force XXI lost handily to the undigitized defenders. RMA theorists charge that evaluating cyber-warfare by the old yardstick of attrition – ground taken, tanks killed, troops routed – is to gravitate 'to the most inane levels of inquiry, as water seeks the lowest point'. Such measures fail to recognize that cyber-warfare 'is more important and far-reaching than the invention of the wheel, gunpowder, or the internal combustion engine'.[35] The GAO was unconvinced. The federal government's accountants point to the potentially unlimited cost of digitization and the Pentagon's failure to set *any* baseline or criteria against which to measure success.[36]

Predictably, most of the resistance to the RMA came from the bottom up. Already, the Army has scrapped the original vision of Land Warrior, its digitized system, because of soldiers' complaints about its weight (65lb), two-hour battery life and inability to withstand the damp. At the Texas and California exercises, Force XXI foot soldiers expressed their disdain by dedigitizing themselves – leaving the suit on the truck – and by using the system's capability to send pornographic videos up the chain of command.[37] The exercises revealed that local knowledge – the defender's understanding of the terrain and the likely answers to tactical questions – could neutralize an attacker's information advantage. They also revealed some disturbing weaknesses in the system, notably a marked increase in friendly-fire accidents.

Battlespace advocates were able to use the promise of yet unattained capabilities to deflect both criticism and the lessons of experience. Colonel Bill Wheelehan, an Army spokesman, reports that: 'In 2000, we're spending $108.4 million to equip the digitized division, and we're not letting anything get in the way.'[38] The 18-hour firefight on 3–4 October 1993 in Mogadishu, Somalia, provides the best case study of the use of real-time imagery under actual battle conditions. The Army's Delta Force and Rangers, equipped with the latest in portable tactical radios with earpieces and handheld GPS systems, fought under the observation of Orion spy planes and recce helicopters relaying live and infrared video images back to command headquarters. When Somali infantry shot down a Blackhawk helicopter in a congested area of central Mogadishu, commanders used their situational awareness to direct a convoy to the crash site.

This was information dominance at work; commands were given and executed nearly simultaneously. 'Nearly', however, is an important qualifier. The slight delay (of single or split-seconds) incurred by the cycle of relaying images, issuing voice commands and executing them was enough to frustrate efforts to get the convoy to the stricken helicopter. As casualties inside the caravan mounted, the Humvees meandered through the streets of Mogadishu, passing within a block of the Blackhawk twice before giving up and returning to base. Soldiers on the ground without input from headquarters, easily located the crash site by following the trail of smoke.[39] Somalia should raise questions about the immanence of a cyberwar millennium, but to the US Army the lesson is that still more technology is required. 'The fight in Mogadishu is a study in why this program should go [forward]', affirms Colonel Hank Kinnison, the officer in charge of the Land Warrior program.[40]

Within the Pentagon the RMA is past criticism. General Gordon R. Sullivan recalls that there never was a decision to digitize, that by the early 1990s the trend was clear and the Army's only contribution was to try to make 'a virtue out of this inexorable movement'.[41] In government and foundation think tanks there is more disagreement. Military analysts are split into 'technicists' who defend the revolution and 'historicists' who believe the fundamental character of intelligence and war remains unchanged.[42] Major General Robert Scales Jr, director of the Army War College, contends that electronics are no substitute for courage and initiative on the battlefield, and that the quest for transparency fails to recognize that uncertainty may be in the fundamental nature of war.[43] Michael O'Hanlon of Brookings is concerned about technology's influence on the budget process. The RMA provides easy justifications, he suggests, for skimping on weapons, overseas deployments and support forces, the real ingredients of deterrence and readiness.[44]

The military's latest planning scenarios, Joint Vision 2020 (June 2000) and the 2001 Quadrennial Defense Review (QDR) (30 September 2001), ratify core principles of RMA doctrine while tempering some of the early enthusiasm. Information is now described as an operational environment –

like land, sea or air – in which combat takes place. RMA is expected to give US commanders 'decision dominance' in that field, allowing them to make choices at a faster tempo than their adversaries. Reflecting the downturn in the information economy, however, the new documents reveal doubts about how long the US can hold its superior position. 'In the future', the QDR observes, 'it is unlikely that the United States will be able accurately to predict how successfully other states will exploit the revolution in military affairs.'[45] Asymmetric threats and off-the-shelf software could make the American advantage disappear faster than the value of NASDAQ shares. The timing of these reports (after the Internet bust but before the Afghanistan War) indicates that doctrinal shifts respond as much to attitudes in the information industry as to combat experience, and perhaps more.

The intelligence community should share the historicists' concern that Battlespace tailors perception and decision to suit military requirements. In the mass of documentation on the RMA, there is little indication that the virtual battlespace will be visible to the president, cabinet, Congress, or indeed any civilian. A Defense Science Board report in 1999 drew a distinction between the 'dominant battlespace knowledge' in the military's purview and the 'strategic situation knowledge' belonging to civilian policymakers.[46] The 1997 QDR circumscribed policymakers' involvement in military operations to identifying 'a clear mission, the desired end state of the situation, and the exit strategy for forces committed'.[47]

Stephen J. Blank of the Army's Strategic Studies Institute complains that battlespace designers 'have factored out strategic political decision-making'. Cyber-warfare is civilian-military conflict by other means. 'This separation of strategy from operations, and political objectives from military means', he contends, 'is pervasive across both our civilian and military elites, who seem unable to talk to each other openly.'[48]

Mogadishu provided a foretaste of the surprises awaiting policymakers. Although images and reports of the fighting were relayed instantaneously to CENTCOM, the US Central Command at Tampa, Florida, President Clinton saw his first footage on CNN, when along with the rest of America he watched crowds dragging American casualties through the streets.[49] President Bush has also taken a hands-off approach to managing the war in Afghanistan. Whether elected officials shrink from their authority to direct war or military commanders bypass democratic institutions, the disengagement of policy from operations curtails the influence of civilian intelligence institutions.[50]

The RMA's hyper-confidence in the use of 'awareness' to control the material environment is matched by a converse distrust (or dismissal) of intelligence's ability to understand the social and political environment.

Confining perception and decision to the operational level and schematically representing the battlefield as an array of assets and targets, Battlespace presents a politics-free zone, a fable of antiseptic conflict. Inputs from analysts, allies, journalists, Humint, the UN and political decision-makers – even if they can be shown visually – can be dismissed as sub-optimal. If in the future, as Wesley Wark predicts, national security means the defense of 'a pluralized system of governance, across which "citizens" are likely to spread their appeals for safety and prosperity', portions of that pluralized system (refugees, international war criminals, cultural treasures, UN missions, human rights, embassies) ought to be in the military's SimCity.[51]

Technicists recognize that simulations need to build in 'some empathy and...some understanding of the cultures and of the people and of the context they're in, 'but they do this by tweaking the software, adding an overlay of "intelligent agents"'.[52] Artificial intelligence is not the same as intelligence, which involves not just visualization but comprehension.

Discrepancies between the virtual and the actual battlefields account for the high civilian death toll (over 400 at current count) from mistaken airstrikes in Afghanistan. Groups of Afghans, including a convoy of tribal elders, a wedding party and a mosque, have been targeted by American smart weapons on the basis of sensors, aerial surveillance and thin Humint support, sometimes just a phone call from an informant.[53] In each case, it took military spokesmen days to bridge the cognitive gap between battlespace and reality as they continued to insist that the targets were Taliban or Al-Qaeda concentrations despite tragic and conclusive evidence to the contrary.

Intelligence rests on an assumption, now frequently doubted, that the enemies of order and security are comprehensible, that they respond to some calculus, however twisted, of self-advantage and capability. This assumption affronts a postmodern strategic sensibility that places adversaries beyond the reach of reason or deterrence. Rogue states, terrorists and parastatal armies are often seen as representing a resurgence of primitivism, to which the only practical response is to destroy their military assets with precision strikes facilitated by information dominance.

But the conflicts of the post-Cold War era – Kosovo, Timor, Bosnia, Chechnya, Somalia, Rwanda, Haiti, Afghanistan, Iraq – have histories and trajectories that are knowable to intelligence analysts. Mary Kaldor of the London School of Economics has shown that these 'new wars' have common origins in the economic dislocations of the 1980s and 1990s and follow a similar logic. They begin with the displacement of state controls by the rules of the global market just before the market itself dissolves, either through embargoes or disrupted trade patterns. Following the creation of an underground, criminalized economy, the state outsources its monopoly on violence to 'horizontal coalitions' of armed groups – Serbian paramilitaries, anti-independence militias, Ton Ton Macoutes, Saddam Fedayeen etc. They follow a similar progression, aiming to destabilize societies and displace populations through the use of atrocity, desecration of monuments and shelling of civilians. And they end indecisively; ceasefires mark only a transition to sporadic violence. 'The new wars are rational', Kaldor explains, 'applying rational thinking to the aims of war and rejecting normative constraints.'[54] Twenty-first-century warfare continues to have a logic, but not a logic that can be understood or resolved in battlespace.

NOTES

1. Dennis Steele, 'Soldiering Outside the Box', *Army*, Sept. 2000, p.25.
2. Admiral Bill Owens, *Lifting the Fog of War* (NY: Farrar, Straus, Giroux 2000) p.14. See also Matthew DeBord, 'Battlespaces', *Feed Magazine*, 7 July 1999, <www.feedmag.com/essay/ es224lofi.html> accessed 10 July 1999; Robert L. Bateman III (ed.), *Digital War: A View From the Front Lines* (Novato, CA: Presidio 1999); Stuart E. Johnson and Martin Libicki (eds.), *Dominant Battlespace Knowledge: The Winning Edge* (Washington, DC: National Defense UP 1995).
3. Jim Garamone, 'Army Tests Land Warrior for 21st Century Soldiers', American Forces Press Service, <www.dtic.mil/ afps/news/9809117.html> accessed 19 Oct. 1999; 'The Wired Warrior', *Fortune*, 21 Dec. 1998, pp.184–5.
4. US Congress, House, Committee on National Security, *The Quadrennial Defense Review* (hereafter *QDR*), 105th Congress, 1st session, 1997, p.168; Department of the Army, *Army Vision 2010* (Washington, DC: US Army 1997) p.17.
5. William Greider, *Fortress America: The American Military and the Consequences of Peace* (NY: Public Affairs 1998) p.124.
6. Alvin H. Bernstein, 'High Tech: The Future Face of War?', *Commentary*, Jan. 1998, p.29; Michael O'Hanlon, 'Can High Technology Bring U.S. Troops Home?', *Foreign Policy* 113 (Winter 1998–99) pp.72–86.
7. Committee on National Security, *QDR* (note 4) p.168; Owens, *Lifting the Fog of War* (note 2) p.205. C4ISR stands for command, control, connectivity, computers, intelligence, surveillance and reconnaissance.
8. Army Historical Program, *Strategic Plan 2010* (Washington DC: Military History Center c.1998) p.7.
9. Joel Achenbach, 'Victory That Defies Logic; Military Strategists Maintain that the War was Lost, in Theory', *The Washington Post*, 12 June 1999, p.C1. For contrasting views on the RMA, see Norman C. Davis, 'An Information-Based Revolution in Military Affairs', in John Arquilla and David Ronfeldt (eds.), *In Athena's Camp: Preparing for Conflict in the Information Age* (Santa Monica, CA: RAND 1997) pp.79–98; and Michael O'Hanlon, *Technological Change and the Future of Warfare* (Washington, DC: Brookings 2000).
10. Bill Keller, 'The Fighting Next Time', *The New York Times Magazine*, 10 March 2002, p.34.
11. Owens, *Lifting the Fog of War* (note 2) p.16; Douglas A. Macgregor, *Breaking the Phalanx: A New Design for Landpower in the 21st Century* (Westport, CT: Praeger 1997) p.1.
12. Quoted in James Der Derian, 'The QDR, the Theater of War, and Building a Better Rat-Trap', June 1997, <www.comw.org/qdr/jderian.htm> accessed 21 Oct. 1999.

13. Sherman Kent, *Strategic Intelligence for American World Policy* (Princeton UP 1949) p.189. Kent and Langer have been called traditionalists, but modernist is a more fitting descriptor. Modernism, according to David Harvey, 'has been identified with the belief in linear progress, absolute truths, the rational planning of ideal social orders, and the standardization of knowledge and production' along with the expectation that the arts and sciences would be instrumental in achieving these ends. David Harvey, *The Condition of Postmodernity* (London: Basil Blackwell 1989) pp.9, 13.

14. House Committee on Expenditures in the Executive Departments, *National Security Act of 1947*, 80th Congress, 1st session, 27 June 1947, p.55.

15. The founders also expected that coordination and centralization would reduce the cost of intelligence. Rhodri Jeffreys-Jones, 'Why Was the CIA Established in 1947?', *Intelligence and National Security* 12/1 (Jan. 1997) p.30.

16. Hanson W. Baldwin, *The Price of Power* (NY: Harper and Bros. 1947) p.207.

17. 'Effective strategic intelligence in the future will depend on the application and development of social science...the social sciences *are* capable of most fruitful guidance on many problems, and will be capable of better performance in the future than in the past.' George S. Pettee, *The Future of American Secret Intelligence* (Washington, DC: Infantry Journal Press 1946) pp.57–8.

18. Willmoore Kendall, 'The Function of Intelligence', *World Politics* 1/4 (July 1949) p.549.

19. House Committee on Expenditures, *National Security Act* (note 14) p.50; Kevin P. Stack, 'Competitive Intelligence', *Intelligence and National Security* 13/4 (Winter 1998) pp.194–202.

20. Kent, *Strategic Intelligence* (note 13) p.171.

21. Martin C. Libicki, 'DBK and its Consequences', in Johnson and Libicki, *Dominant Battlespace Knowledge* (note 2) p.28.

22. Owens, *Lifting the Fog of War* (note 2) pp.14, 206.

23. Jeffrey Cooper, 'Dominant Battlespace Awareness and the Future of Warfare', in Johnson and Libicki, *Dominant Battlespace Knowledge* (note 2) pp.113–14.

24. Richard Szafranski, 'Neocortical Warfare? The Acme of Skill', in Arquilla and Ronfeldt , *In Athena's Camp* (note 9) pp.395–416. Martin C. Libicki recommends displaying the battlespace image during negotiations, so that 'if disputes arise, they at least do so from a common base of evidence and are that much more resolvable'. The US can avoid tipping its hand too far by revealing only the yield from sensors, and not from pattern recognition and data fusion software; 'we can show people what we can make out, but leave unsaid what we can in fact see'. Libicki, 'DBK and its Consequences' (note 21) p.48. James Der Derian speculates that this kind of cyber-theater might be used to feign strengths and cloak weaknesses. James Der Derian, 'The QDR, the Theater of War' (note 12) p.3.

25. Lincoln R. Thiesmayer and John E. Burchard, *Combat Scientists* (Boston, MA: Little, Brown 1947); Conrad H. Waddington, *O.R. in World War 2: Operational Research Against the U-Boat* (London: Elek 1973).

26. Gregory Palmer, *The McNamara Strategy and the Vietnam War: Program Budgeting in the Pentagon, 1960–68* (Westport, CT: Greenwood 1978); Deborah Shapley, *Promise and Power: The Life and Times of Robert McNamara* (Boston, MA: Little, Brown 1993) pp.228–32.

27. Barnaby J. Feder, 'A Military Agency Spends Billions on Seemingly Fantastic Projects to Ensure U.S. Battlefield Supremacy', *New York Times*, 18 Sept. 2000, p.C4.

28. Paul N. Edwards, *The Closed World: Computers and the Politics of Discourse in Cold War America* (Cambridge: MIT Press 1996) pp.3–8.

29. See discussion of the Gulf scenario in Chap. 2 of David A. Ochmanek et al. (eds.), *To Find and Not to Yield: How Advances in Information and Firepower Can Transform Theater Warfare* (Santa Monica, CA: RAND 1998), <www.rand.org/publications/MR/MR958/ MR958.pdf/#contents>; William E. Odom, *America's Military Revolution: Strategy and Structure After the Cold War* (Washington, DC: American UP 1993) pp.54–65.

30. House Committee on National Security, *QDR* (note 4) p.170.

31. Alvin and Heidi Toffler, 'Foreword: The New Intangibles', in Arquilla (ed.), *In Athena's Camp* (note 9); (note, p. xiv) [???]; also in Alvin and Heidi Toffler, *War and Anti-War* (Boston, MA: Little, Brown 1993). For critical views, see Michael O'Hanlon, 'Future Schlock?', *Foreign Policy* 113 (Winter 1998–99) p.82; and R. L. DiNardo and Daniel J. Hughes, 'Some Cautionary Thoughts on Information Warfare', <www.airpower.maxwell.af.mil/airchronicles/apj/dinardo.html> accessed 29 Oct. 1999.

32. Captain Michael D. Doubler, *Busting the Bocage: American Combined Operations in France, 6 June–31 July 1944* (Leavenworth, KS: US Army Command and General Staff College 1988; Michael D. Doubler, *Closing With the Enemy: How GIs Fought the War in Europe, 1944–1945* (Lawrence, KS: UP of Kansas 1994). This perspective was incorporated in the popular works of Steven Ambrose, especially *Citizen Soldiers* (NY: Simon & Schuster 1997).

33. Thomas J. Peters, *In Search of Excellence: Lessons from America's Best-Run Companies* (NY: Harper and Row 1982); Doubler, *Closing With the Enemy* (note 32). Stephen Ambrose's popular books on the GI's eye view of the war draw heavily on Doubler's interpretation.

34. Norman C. Davis notes that, 'the "virtual corporation" has obvious parallels for this military restructuring'. Davis, 'An Information-Based Revolution in Military Affairs' (note 9) p.93.

35. Robert R. Leonhard, 'A Culture of Velocity', in Bateman (ed.), *Digital War: A View From the Front Lines* (note 2) pp.135–6.

36. General Accounting Office, *Electronic Combat Consolidation Master Plan Does not Appear to be Cost Effective* GAO/NSIAD-97-10 (Washington DC: GAO, June 1997); GAO, *Battlefield Automation: Army's Digital Battlefield Plan Lacks Specific Measurable Goals* GAO/NSIAD-96-25 (Washington, DC: GAO, Nov. 1995).

37. Greider, *Fortress America* (note 5) p.126.

38. George I. Seffers, 'Is Digitization in Danger?', *Army Times* 59/32 (8 March 1999) p.26.

39. Mark Bowden, *Black Hawk Down: A Story of Modern War* (NY: Penguin 1999). 'All of the men had heard veterans talk about the "fog of war"', Bowden notes. 'But it was shocking nonetheless to see how hard it was to get even the simplest things done' (p.99). His account suggests that the 'fog' is not the absence of awareness but a surfeit of stimuli that overwhelms action and decision.

40. 'The Wired Warrior', *Fortune*, 21 Dec. 1998, p.185.

41. Gordon R. Sullivan, 'Introduction', in Bateman, *Digital War* (note 2) p.xvii.

42. Michael Ignatieff, 'The New American Way of War', *The New York Review of Books*, 20 July 2000, p.46.

43. Steven Lee Myers, 'On Empty Battlefields, the Shadows of Cyberwarriors', *New York Times*, 1 Jan. 2000, p.2.

44. O'Hanlon, *Technological Change and the Future of Warfare* (note 9) p.193.

45. US Department of Defense, *Quadrennial Defense Review Report*, 30 Sept. 2001, p.7, <www.defenselink.mil/pubs/qdr2001.pdf>; see also US Department of Defense, *Joint Vision 2020* (Washington, DC: US Government Printing Office, June 2000).

46. Vernon Loeb, 'NIMA: Intelligence Vision or Folly?', 9 Aug. 1999, <www.washingtonpost.com/intelligencia> accessed 20 Aug. 1999.

47. House Committee on National Security, *QDR* (note 4) p.140.

48. Paul Mann, 'Revisionists Junk Defense Revolution', *Aviation Week and Space Technology*, 27 April 1998, p.38.

49. Bowden, *Black Hawk Down* (note 39) pp.26, 304.

50. Michael Ignatieff connects virtual warfare to a politics of 'virtual consent in which lawyers, but not lawmakers, have a say'. Michael Ignatieff, *Virtual War: Kosovo and Beyond* (NY: Metropolitan Books 2000) pp.176–84, 197.

51. Wesley K. Wark, 'The Intelligence Revolution and the Future', *Studies in Intelligence* 37/5 (1994) p.14.

52. The quotation is from Michael M. Macedonia, the chief scientist at STRICOM, the Army's simulation command. J. C. Herz, 'At Play, It Takes an Army to Save a Village', *New York Times*, 3 Feb. 2000, p.D11; James Der Derian, 'War Games: The Pentagon Wants What Hollywood's Got', *The Nation*, 3 April 2000, pp.41–5.
53. Dexter Filkins, 'Flaws in U.S. Air War Left Hundreds of Civilians Dead', *New York Times*, 21 July 2002, p.1.
54. Mary Kaldor, *New and Old Wars: Organized Violence in a Global Era* (Stanford UP 1999); Mary Kaldor, 'A Cosmopolitan Response to New Wars', *Peace Review* 8/4 (Dec. 1996) pp.505–15.

A New American Way of War? C4ISR, Intelligence and Information Operations in Operation 'Iraqi Freedom': A Provisional Assessment

JOHN FERRIS

Over the past decade, the idea of a 'revolution in military affairs' (RMA) has shaped debates about military policy in the United States (US). This idea assumes that information will transform the knowledge available to armed forces, and thus their nature and the nature of war itself. Colonel John Warden, USAF planner and strategic theorist, has argued: 'Information will become a prominent, if not predominant, part of war to the extent that whole wars may well revolve around seizing or manipulating the enemy's datasphere.'[1] Strategic policy predicts the rise of forces with 'dominant battlespace awareness', better knowledge than, and 'decision superiority' over, an enemy, and unprecedented flexibility of command: the ability to combine freedom for units with power for the top'.[2]

Officials have also created new concepts about intelligence and command, including net-centric warfare (NCW), the idea that armed forces will adopt flat structures, working in nets on the net with data processing systems at home serving as staff for the sharp end through reachback; C4ISR (command, control, communications, computers, intelligence, surveillance and reconnaissance: loosely speaking, how armed forces gather, interpret and act on information); and 'IO' (Information Operations), the actions of secret agencies. These ideas shape American ideas about war. Command and Control Warfare (C2W), the main form of operations the US plans to fight, is a version of blitzkrieg which seeks 'to deny information to, influence, degrade, or destroy' the enemy's 'information-dependent process', so to shatter its ability to perceive and command.[3] Revolutionaries advocate a higher and 'knowledge-centric' mode of war, Rapid Decisive Operations (RDO), which will open with the pursuit of a 'Superior Information Position (Fight First for Information Superiority)' and then function through 'Operational Net Assessment' (ONA), with commanders constantly gathering, analyzing and synthesizing intelligence on all aspects of an enemy in real time and from all sources.[4]

Operation 'Iraqi Freedom' provides the first serious test of these ideas, but not a simple one. The struggle was so unbalanced that one must take care in extrapolating from triumph; judgments from failure are easier to make. How many lessons useful for September 1914 could have been drawn from Omdurman? How many of those could a victor have believed? Any lessons drawn from the Iraq campaign will be intended to shape military policy in 2020, and the nature of (to use the jargon) the 'objective' force – yet it was fought by 'legacy' forces, using some elements of 'interim' C4ISR. Arguably, the keys to victory were absolute air supremacy, vehicle and body armor, the incompetence and subversion of Iraqi officers and the psychological effect on Iraqi soldiers of the power and invulnerability of Coalition artillery and tanks. A Marine Colonel noted some of his tanks survived seven RPG rounds, and 'became the unkillable beast and caused them (Iraqis) nightmares'.[5] General Tommy Franks, head of Central Command, wrote that the Coalition solved the problem of irregular forces simply by moving armor into towns: 'the Fedayeen would sacrifice themselves by climbing up on the tanks. They had no tactics to deal with armor.'[6]

Yet any lessons learned from this campaign will be used to explain why 'legacy' forces must be transformed, and heavy tanks are bad. Again, our data on the role of intelligence are limited, though a surprising amount is available even on the most secret of matters – communication intelligence and deception; times have changed. This essay goes to press before the Pentagon releases any of its 'lessons learned' memoranda, while those of the US 3rd Infantry Division are available to military personnel but not the public. Much good official, demi-official and unofficial commentary is available, but the database is incomplete, and the assessments of observers vary dramatically, with their own experiences. Personnel from signals units and headquarters in Iraq and the US emphasize the power and reach of communications and intelligence. Colonel Dobbins, Base Commander of 392nd Air Expeditionary Group, thought the global positioning satellite (GPS) satellite constellation had provided a 'common and accurate picture' to all participants. The 1st Marine Division, conversely, praised GPS, but denied that it shared a 'common operating picture' with any outside authority. The director of C4 for the Joint Chiefs of Staff (JCS) said, 'We do not believe (the Iraqis) had any situational awareness of what we were doing or where we were...We could tell you, even in Washington, DC, down to 10 meters, where our troops were'.[7] That may have been true of Americans in Washington, but not always in Iraq.

Any 'lessons learned' process runs the risk of over-generalizing from individual events, doubly so when military politics enters the fray. And this event will be politicized. Already, slogans like 'lazerkrieg' have been coined; in a frequently cited and almost officially sanctioned phrase, General

Richard Myers, the JCS Chairman, described Operation 'Iraqi Freedom' as demonstrating 'a new American way of war'. The issues merit consideration more than cheerleading. In a study of American operations in Afghanistan during 2001–2, Stephen Biddle argued that some aspects of warfare arguably had been transformed, others certainly had not been, and both cases had to be examined in order to learn the right lessons.[8] So too, Iraq.

Far more than with most campaigns, Operation 'Iraqi Freedom' was intelligence-driven. American authorities attempted to apply their doctrine and concepts, to follow all historical best practices simultaneously and with sophistication, and to harness all these matters to C2W. They did not achieve all their aims, but their actions were able, matching those of the Western allies during 1944 in form, if not necessarily effect. Planning at Central Command, so said Franks, assumed 'that we would not gamble but we would accept prudent risk'. It focused on surprise and flexibility, allowing either land or air forces to open the attack, as chance or need required. Intelligence was intended to start the machine, of which IO was a major part. The plan included 'five fronts'. Conventional forces dominated just one of them, the central thrust from Kuwait. Such forces were intended to lead the second front, in Kurdistan, but ultimately deception and Special Forces did so. Special Forces dominated the third front, the west, while airpower and subversion did the fourth, working 'not only from the outside in, but from the inside out' to prevent the enemy from creating 'a fortress in their strategic center of gravity, which was the Baghdad-Tikrit area'. The 'fifth front was information' – subversion to weaken the regime, electronic warfare to destroy 'principal lines of communication for the purpose of giving orders' including pre-war attacks in the 'no-fly zones' against fiber-optic links, forcing the Iraqis to radio and cellphone circuits; 'Candidly, we knew we wanted to leave some other communications links up because there is benefit in understanding what orders are being given.' This front turned on a 'combination of two things. One was as much silence as we could get in terms of public knowledge of the things I previously described, and deception which we wanted to feed into the Iraqi regime to cause them to react in ways that we wanted them to react'.[9]

In Operation 'Iraqi Freedom', the success of C4ISR and IO was mixed at strategic-political levels, and overwhelming at operational ones, better at action than calculation. Authorities got Iraqi politics wrong. They overestimated their ability to topple Saddam Hussein's regime through subversion without having to smash it, and the ease of occupation. Probably these failures stemmed from policy-makers rather than specialists, but that is a condition of life; C4ISR has changed the nature neither of net assessment, nor of the politicization of intelligence.[10]

The failure of subversion weakened the American ability to stop the most dangerous strategy open to Iraq, the creation of a fortress Baghdad; fortunately, Iraqi incompetence and the USAF blocked this threat. Again, Anglo-American assessments of Iraqi weapons of mass destruction (WMD) were wrong, and their use of intelligence for public relations incompetent; their dossiers of February 2003 are classic bad examples in that genre. Even more, fears that the enemy had and would use biological or chemical weapons or Scud missiles caused Coalition forces to take counter-productive steps at all levels of war, from forcing soldiers to wear Nuclear Biological Chemical (NBC) suits to creating fears about the so-called 'red line' around Baghdad and the need for a 'western' front.[11] These strategic problems stemmed not from the falsification of intelligence, but its normal limits. As Franks noted, material on the issue came from high-level defectors, low-level human sources and 'monumental reams of intercepted information'. Yet, 'Intelligence information is much more often imprecise than it is precise...one never knows the validity of the intelligence, much like intelligence preparation of the battlefield, which says this is what we believe, now we must go confirm the existence'.[12]

With hostilities commenced a website war, posing new problems for media influence. Here, American authorities mixed success at home with failure abroad. They did not counter al-Jazeerah's influence on Arab audiences, though victory discredited it, nor manage hostile European media. This stemmed partly from IO failures: an American military newspaper conceded many American officials 'were hostile to Arab reporters in briefings and in person. And only rarely were high-level US officials offered as interview subjects.'[13] Western media gave Saddam Hussein better intelligence than most armies in history ever have had, while a new problem emerged in the form of websites focused on strategic affairs, which gather and assess information with power, often providing archives and links to other sites. The retired General Lucian Truscott IV noted, 'the book says you've got to keep the enemy ignorant of where you are, what you're going to do. And I said to my wife one day, I opened up the *New York Times*, turned it to the back page and said, "if I was an Iraqi general I could fight the war off of this map"'.[14] The problem of operational security for western military forces continues to rise. In a serious war, it might matter.

Conversely, 'embedded' journalists, attached to units so to counter Saddam, 'particularly practiced in the art of disinformation, misinformation, denial, deception, downright liar quite simply', as Deputy Assistant Secretary of State for Defense Whitman said,[15] played to the fad for reality television and provided a ballast of constant good filler for home consumption. The roughly 600 'embeds' attached to American forces and 100 more with British ones, were intended to counter Iraqi disinformation, in which their success was mixed until Baghdad fell. More significantly, the 'embeds' gave the military a chance to shape the tone of coverage; the 1st Marine Division treated them as 'an entirely winnable constituency' and told its soldiers 'media were not to be "escorted", they were to be "adopted" and made members of the Division family'. It noted that 'sharing austere living conditions, danger and loss, journalistic desires of impartiality gave way to human nature' which 'enables our story to be told in a very personal, humanistic way. To the viewers and readers, the 1st Marine Division was not an anonymous killing machine, it was an 18-year-old Marine from Anywhere, USA.[16]

That American doctrine about IO fuses in one category matters once treated as 'black' (psyops) and 'white' (public relations), presents problems for journalists, the public and the military itself. 'Embeds', after all, did follow their own professional instincts, their reports were honest, however impressionistic, while casualties were low and action fast. One may wonder how far this experience can be repeated. The greatest attrition suffered by 'embeds' came from those who preferred to avoid the reality after experiencing the training: 15 of 60 assigned to the 1st Marine Division bowed out when given the chance, and another 6 of the 27 assigned to one regimental combat team never showed up.[17] 'Embeds' on Omaha Beach in June 1944, conversely, would have transmitted pictures like the first 20 minutes of the film *Saving Private Ryan*. Contemporaries would not have taken them for entertainment.

American strategic intelligence worked better in purely military spheres, if less so on matters of quality than quantity. Its picture of the enemy order of battle, deployments and tactical characteristics was good. It appreciated fairly well the strength needed to destroy its foe, though it assumed the war would last for 125 days, as against 25, and grossly overrated the enemy's quality and rationality. In technical terms these were major errors yet perhaps unavoidable in the circumstances, and minor in practical import (far less costly than the mistakes about WMD). The Coalition could hardly have attacked with fewer forces than it did, or earlier, or with less damage inflicted on either side. Even seasoned analysts had grounds for uncertainty about the capabilities and intentions of enemy forces – would they all be bad, or would some achieve mediocrity? Would they stand in the field, or the cities? As the British Ministry of Defence noted:

> Although we knew much about the broad structure and disposition of Iraqi land and air forces, very little was known about how they planned to oppose the coalition or whether they had the will to fight. Objective analysis had to take into account Iraqi bluster and disinformation...The lack of clear information meant that the coalition

did not anticipate that Iraqi organised military resistance would collapse so quickly and completely.[18]

When V Corps commander, Lt. General William S. Wallace, said the Iraqis were 'not the enemy we wargamed', he merely expressed surprise they were foolish enough to fight in the open.[19] He would have been foolish to assume they would – that the foe would be as incompetent as possible and follow the worst strategy it could. Clearly, however, there had been no revolution in military intelligence at some basic levels, where recurred old problems in assessment, especially of Western armies about non-Western foes. The 1st Marine Division noted that American forces grasped enemy capabilities well:

> but we remained largely ignorant of the intentions of enemy commanders…This shortcoming was especially critical as much of the war plan was either based on or keyed to specific enemy responses. When the enemy 'failed' to act in accordance with common military practice, we were caught flat-footed because we failed to accurately anticipate the unconventional response. This was primarily due to a dearth of Humint on the enemy leadership. In trying to map out the opposition's reactions we were largely relegated to our Osint sources and rank speculation based on our own perceptions of the battlefield to make our assessments … Our technical dominance has made us overly reliant on technical and quantifiable intelligence collection means. There is institutional failure to account for the most critical dimension of the battlefield, the human one.[20]

American strategic intelligence was mediocre, but better by far than that of the enemy. The Iraqi regime was surprised by the time of the attack, its forces caught in normal positions, because it misread its own and the Coalition's capabilities and plans, and perhaps because of deception. According to Franks, throughout 2002, forces for war against Iraq were deployed and strengthened in as 'invisible' a fashion as possible, so not to stampede Saddam into undesirable actions and 'to achieve surprise in the event we had to go to war'. Equipment was moved secretly, in container ships, presumably to avoid detection by spies or satellites. In 2003, the Coalition very much wanted to keep the 11 regular and two Republican Guard divisions in Kurdistan from destroying the northern oilfields, attacking Kurds or moving south. Thus, the US 4th Infantry Division went to ships in the eastern Mediterranean, able to achieve that end whether it could enter Turkey or not.

> You have tactical efficiency if you are able to introduce a division from the north, but you have strategic surprise simply by having the

division positioned in the eastern Mediterranean. We believed we could through intelligence means have some influence on the regime through information warfare and deception, and we wanted the regime to believe that force would be introduced in the north, and that the timing of that introduction might be discussed with the Turks. We wanted some uncertainty in the mind of Saddam Hussein about whether the Turks were planning to permit the landing of the force, so I kept the force waiting long past the point where I knew it would not be introduced in the north.[21]

Though the US preferred to send the 4th Division through Turkey, this end was subordinate to that of freezing Iraqi forces in Kurdistan, and it always pursued a second plan – using deception to pin the Iraqis, with special forces and an airborne brigade to create a skeleton front, at the price of slowing 4th Division's move to Kuwait by several days. The equation was complex. In Franks' mind, 4th Division's role was to keep Iraqi forces in Kurdistan. If they were pinned, it mattered little whether that formation was ready for other operations; thus it was not, reducing the divisions in Kuwait on 20 March by 20 per cent, a high cost for deception. However, 4th Division and 1st Armored Division would be available some weeks into the attack, which Franks thought 'took the gamble out of the equation and placed the level at what I call prudent risk'. The option of not attacking until those forces were in Kuwait, would have strengthened the blow while losing surprise. Franks thought the alternative of deploying 4th Division in Kuwait from the start, at the risk of letting Iraqi forces move from Kurdistan, would dull the Coalition's edge.

So to cover these intentions (and, later, sites for airborne assaults), says Franks, 'we initiated deception operations to pass information to the regime that would cause either uncertainty or chaos'.[22] How this was done is uncertain, given the lack of data about American intelligence on, and means to deceive, Iraq. These means probably included disinformation through diplomatic and intelligence channels, but at present just one conduit can be assessed, the media.

The weeks before the attack witnessed classic signs of media-borne deception. Some American forces quietly slipped from the record (as the GlobalSecurity website noted) while others were advertised, especially the location of ships containing 4th Division and its equipment. As the Turkish front collapsed, press reports from Washington emphasized that would delay Coalition plans, and indicated the attack would begin later than it did, only after 4th Division reached Kuwait. Presumably the Americans pursued surprise through the classic means of encouraging an enemy to focus on the wrong indicators and to assume an attack would occur later than intended, which would suit their IO doctrine and sense of Iraqi preconceptions.[23] Later, the Defense Secretary, Donald Rumsfeld, speculated Iraq:

> ...very likely expected Gulf War II, a long air war that would give them time to do whatever they thought they wanted to do, leave or take cover and what have you, followed at some distance by a ground war, and probably a massive ground war...they did not expect a ground war to start without an air war and they did not expect a ground war to start without the 4th Infantry Division while it was still up in the Mediterranean. I also suspect that they didn't expect the first air attack that took place the day before the ground war began.[24]

That attack occurred late on 19 March when, after telling the media the war would not start that day, American authorities struck to kill Saddam when intelligence indicated his apparent location – an improvised and unsuccessful use of deception. Innocent embeds, too, supported deception. All of them were called up to training exercises in the days before the operation began, none went with the special forces used to clear the western desert just before the battle, others were sent with the 173rd Airborne Brigade as it flew from Italy to Kurdistan, to attract attention there. Between 22 and 30 March, Americans spread disinformation about airborne assaults (rather fewer occurred than were hinted) and their sites; they may have overplayed media accounts of their problems in the south so to lure Iraqi forces forward, while small but publicized actions occurred in Kurdistan. In particular, the 173rd Airborne Brigade began its ostentatious activities on 26 March, as Americans approached the Iraqi main line of resistance between Karbala and Kut, but was not fully deployed or conducting operations there until 1 April, almost a week later. Again, a feint covered the thrust through the Karbala gap during 1–3 April.

American deception was sophisticated and followed its doctrine and historical best practices. It aimed to affect enemy actions, not its ideas, and did so both by aiming to cause confusion and misdirection where its preconceptions could be fathomed (the deployment of so many forces in Kurdistan, for example, signaled an expectation of threat in that region). The evidence does not indicate how far deception shaped Iraqi errors. At the operational level, probably it achieved more through confusion than misdirection, which is the norm. Iraqi commanders seem to have been confused, probably in part because deception did further 'uncertainty or chaos', though it may not have mattered much to that effect, given the many factors at hand. Conversely, deception did not achieve its full end of pinning Iraqi forces in Kurdistan before or during the war – Saddam needed no encouragement to keep regular divisions there and the two Republican Guard divisions finally did move south, to annihilation by air, though in staying and going they served American plans.

However, given the fact Coalition forces in Kuwait were small, with big reinforcements on the way, the deceptions of 2002–3 probably contributed to Iraq being taken by surprise about the timing of the attack (and also foreign states to which it listened, multiplying the problem), and thus to shaping the politics of the outbreak of war. Some governments doubted the US was ready to attack while Saddam routinely walked to the edge of a precipice before signaling a willingness to back down. If he or they misunderstood when the attack would start, they would not have seen the immediate need to avoid it through diplomacy, and thus not have taken the slim chances to avoid catastrophe. Perhaps deception mattered more through its unintended effects than the intended ones, not for the first time. American authorities played other sorts of mind games – what the Pentagon Director of Force Transformation, Admiral Cebrowski, termed 'direct movement(s) into the cognitive domain'.[25] This approach was not novel. Political warfare is among the oldest forms of covert action or information operations, espoused by Sun Tzu and the Artashastra, practiced ably by Philip II of Macedon and more recently by Britain in two world wars. Advocates of transformation, however, regard these matters as being more central to warfare than ever before. In the 1990s one pioneer of the RMA, Colonel Richard Szafranski, argued that information warfare aimed at 'targeting epistemology'.[26]

The American practice of these principles in Iraq was among the most sophisticated and thorough on record, with some original features. Through radio and television broadcasts and 50 million leaflets, psyops was conducted against Iraqi civilians and soldiers, without apparent impact. It never reached soldiers in some units, perhaps most of them, lacking personal radios and surrounded by Ba'athist security; while the Coalition entirely failed in a key area of political warfare, to make civilians affect the war. More significantly, the Coalition launched a 'fused' IO attack on enemy epistemology, so to cripple its communication and corrupt its information. Cebrowski claimed that, knowing 'a dictator can't trust his information' and Saddam would have to 'script the whats and whens' of his war even though 'he doesn't know if people will carry them out', the US aimed to wreck his 'feedback loop', his ability to know what was happening on the battlefield.[27]

This approach involved the physical destruction of command and communication targets, and more. The air attacks on Saddam, and the claims they rested on reports from agents in Baghdad, were highly publicized, to shock his subordinates. His trust in his officers, and their mutual confidence, was sapped by announcements Americans were subverting Iraqi officers, and systematically contacting via email those with access to computers. This effort, combining psyops, bribery, deception and a human form of cyberwar, manipulated the characteristics of a Stalinist regime and a paranoid political culture, seemingly with effect. After the war, one Iraqi officer stationed on the southern Iran-Iraq frontier, Colonel Sa'ad, held psyops had little effect on his men whereas emails to officers had a 'big impact'. 'Even if officers immediately reported all such contacts to a superior, "Imagine him thinking: If the Americans are able to get into the mind of a senior commander this way, how can I protect a whole division?"'.[28]

At the operational level, the story is mixed. Military planners pursue a 'Common Operating Picture' (COP) for commanders and a 'Common Relevant Operating Picture' (CROP) for soldiers, to give everyone in any decision-making loop the same, good information. Meanwhile, the intelligence agencies seek to maximize their ability to support the operations of expeditionary force. The National Security Agency (NSA) seeks to 'anticipate warfighter intelligence needs – on time, anywhere, at the lowest possible classification' and 'expand "pull" dissemination capabilities to enable customers to initiate real time requests to improve crisis support'.[29]

The National Imagery and Mapping Agency (NIMA) aims to give 'customers direct access to targeting support and navigation data from the NIMA precise point database'.[30] NIMA and NSA exchange personnel and combine imagery, geospatial and signals intelligence at the point of first production, before it is sent to consumers.[31] These ambitions seem to have been realized tolerably well at the theater level, including component commands down to corps level, which is fairly common in the historical record, but not at lower levels. The 1st Marine Division held:

> After crossing the Line of departure, the Division received very little actionable intelligence from external intelligence organizations. The Division had to assemble a coherent picture from what it could collect with organic and DS assets alone.
>
> The nature of the battlefield, the extreme distances, high operational tempo and lack of a coherent response from a conventional enemy all made it difficult for an external agency to know what was tactically relevant and required by the GCE commander. The byzantine collections process inhibited our ability to get timely responses to combat requirements with the exception of assets organic to or DS to the Division. This made the Division almost exclusively reliant on organic or DS collection assets. The Division found the enemy by running into them, much as forces have done since the beginning of warfare...
>
> On a fluid, high tempo battlefield, a highly centralized collections bureaucracy is too slow and cumbersome to be tactically relevant. The

best possible employment option is to push more assets in DS to the lowest tactical level and increase available organic collections....

Operation 'Iraqi Freedom' presented the intelligence community with unprecedented robust collection architecture to support combat operations. Unfortunately it also presented the community and more specifically the tactical user with the equally unprecedented cumbersome collection bureaucracy.

The existing hierarchical collections architecture, particularly for imagery requirements, is wildly impractical and does not lend itself to providing timely support to combat operations.

This division confronted every standard problem of bottlenecks and overload in information, and the failure of almost every 'push' and 'pull' technique touted to manage them. National intelligence sources were 'great for developing deep targets, subject to the prioritization of high headquarters (Division and higher). Navigating the labyrinth of collection tasking processes proved too difficult in most cases to get reporting on Division targets, and certainly for Battalion-level collections'. Communications within intelligence sections were better, but 'at all levels (they) were inundated with information and data that had little bearing on their mission or Intelligence requirements'. The only exceptions to these strictures were systems organic to the division. Thus, JSTARS (the Joint Surveillance Target Attack Radar System) provided excellent intelligence on the movement and location of hostile vehicles. 'Because they were close to the point of decision, those JSTARS operators shared the sense of urgency and "can-do" attitude. They worked aggressively to find ways to answer questions instead of deflect them.'[32]

Granted, Marine technology for communication and intelligence is less sophisticated than that of the Army, while no digitalized forces fought in Iraq. Still, in 2003, divisions seem to have had no better intelligence in battle than during 1944, though that available was useful. For example, units made good and fast use of prisoners, psyops and Iraqi cellphone traffic.[33]

At a higher level, intelligence was handled well, as planned and with rare efficiency. It set the machine in motion. On 19 March, American authorities had intelligence on Saddam's location for several hours before the ultimatum ended, but did not act on it until that period ended, when they did so immediately. On 20 March, they opened the land attack 24 hours earlier than intended, when intelligence indicated Iraqi forces were moving on the southern oilfields. Over subsequent days, intelligence provided clear indications of the movement south of the Republican Guard, and guided airstrikes on them. Franks noted commanders had 'much more precise technology-based information'; at his headquarters, before receiving any reports from below, he detected the 'thunder run' (armored thrusts with close air support) from the Karbala Gap to the Saddam Hussein International Airport via GPS and channel-surfing through to the reports of a CNN 'embed' with the 3/7th Cavalry. 'The combination of these technologies was very, very powerful, and at the same time as we had this advantage, we knew for a certain fact the regime was unable to communicate with its subordinate Republican Guard forces to give them instructions to respond, to react.'[34] Franks' Deputy Commander, John Abizaid, held:

> Never before have we had such a complete picture of enemy tactical dispositions and intentions. I think largely the speed of the campaign was incredibly enabled by the complete picture we had of the enemy on the battlefield.' Intelligence was the most accurate I've ever seen on the tactical level, probably the best I've ever seen on the operational level and perplexingly incomplete on the tactical level in regards to weapons of mass destruction...Operationally we came up with a remarkably clear picture. We expected to fight the main battle between the line of Karbala, Kut and Baghdad, we expected it to be fought against the four Iraqi Republican Guard divisions and we expected their exact positions on the battlefield.
>
> Both C4ISR and IO had worked well and with unprecedented quality, though we found it difficult at times to assess and measure (IO's) effects during the operation while our ability to strike rapidly sometimes exceeded our ability to sense and assess the effects as quickly as we would have liked.[35]

At the operational level, Special Forces and agents with cellphones provided news and stopped demolitions of oil wells or dams which might have flooded the approaches to Baghdad, or the possibility of Iraqi Scud attacks against Israel. The Coalition appears to have gained little from agents about strategic matters before the war, but more on tactical issues during it. How, how far and how usefully, cryptanalysis or traffic analysis was conducted remains unclear. Apparently, however, plain language traffic often was intercepted in real time and used effectively at operational and tactical levels, implying the presence of interpreters (probably defectors) at formation staffs and units down to battalion levels, able quickly and accurately to translate colloquial Arabic to usable English. Other reports suggest that lack of interrogators was a critical problem for interrogation of prisoners, one reason why Iraqi soldiers were left to melt back into the population (which magnified subsequent security problems). The American military had just 70 qualified Arabic translators in its ranks, many of whose knowledge of Arabic or Arabs was sketchy. According to one American interrogator, 'British interrogators are hands-down better than we are...First, they are officers, and the only thing they do is study interrogation and study language. Most of the guys can speak the target language at a nearly native level. You cannot say that about U.S. military or DIA [Defense Intelligence Agency] linguists.'[36]

The Coalition used imagery, from satellites and Predators, and GPS with unprecedented power; for the first time, GPS was the leading source of tactical intelligence. Information surged across the system without swamping it, carried, one journalist wrote, by 'an unsung corps of geeks improvising as they went, cobbling together a remarkable system from a hodgepodge of military-built networking technology, off-the-shelf gear, miles of Ethernet cable, and commercial software', and Microsoft Premier online help for trouble-shooting.[37] Reachback, push and pull techniques and a 'Warfighting Web' linked national intelligence agencies to theater commands and rear headquarters, like Air Force Space Command, to ground forces, equipped with 100,000 portable GPS receivers, one each to most squads of nine soldiers or five Marines.

Commands shared a common picture of operations, as did the members of any unit, though little of this passed either way through the interface of divisional and corps headquarters, while national boundaries also proved problematical. Perhaps 3,000 commanders from corps to section level shared a tactical intranet with a map overlay, which always let everyone know where everybody was, and one text-messaging system, which allowed instant contact with some others at adjacent levels of command (anyone whose screen name one knew). Chat rooms on SIPRnet (the classified military intranet system) joined Tactical Operations Centers (TOC) at brigade level to the world – by sending a question to a TOC; in theory a soldier on the front was one interface from an expert, though the number of chat rooms (perhaps 50 for the Army and 500 for the Navy) and people yearning to participate threatened information overload.[38]

This danger and those of micromanagement and the pursuit of certainty seem to have been avoided, but others were not. It is unclear whether chat rooms gave front line soldiers much useful advice, or created problems. One observer noted: 'Rumour spreading was rife in particular over the most secure means the SIPRNET. People were using it as a chat room and making unsubstantiated allegations and claims on this means. Commanders lost faith in the SIPR and chose direct voice comms as the best means. It also created confusion and fear amongst Marines that was unnecessary.'[39]

The greatest change appears to have come in airpower. Traditionally, in air warfare, the need to build and distribute daily Air Tasking Orders (ATOs), sometimes the size of a telephone book, caused strangulation and overload in information, and confusion and friction for command. In Iraq during 2003, conversely, web-based ATOs let commanders change many missions at will; carrier-borne aircraft striking Baghdad received their target orders just as they got to the city's edge. Fleeting news or chances which once would have been lost in the shuffle led to precise strikes – in Iraq, as in Afghanistan and Yemen, American forces could bomb a ten by ten foot box within 20 minutes of its detection by any source. A soldier using a laser rangefinder linked to GPS could send via satellite the coordinates of a target to a command site hundreds of miles away, which fed those coordinates onto the GPS-enabled bombs of an aircraft in another locale – and even change them in flight. Much of this success stemmed, however, not from transformation but, as one senior officer said, from 'having lots of airplanes in the air constantly with numerous types of munitions' – what others called 'racked and stacked' aircraft in a 'racetrack' pattern.[40] As with the 'cab rank' system of 1944 for air support, the flexibility, speed and range of air strike expanded not simply because of improvements in command and intelligence, but also because of the presence of large numbers of aircraft and the absence of air opposition.

How far this situation reflects a permanent transformation of C4ISR in airpower is uncertain. Perhaps this operation occurred somewhere above a margin for the optimum use of airpower, below which performance rapidly begins to spiral down. In the Kosovo campaign, against an enemy with good camouflage and useful air defenses, and a high degree of influence from political factors, over-centralization, bureaucracy, confusion between levels of command and the fruitless search for certainty crippled the use of airpower. Similarly, during March 2002 in Afghanistan, officers in superior headquarters at home and abroad bombarded operational commanders with questions and advice based on live pictures transmitted from Predators in flight during operations.[41] In one case of friendly fire in Afghanistan, information overload, friction between layers of command and inexperienced personnel, swamped exactly those air forces and commands which fought in Iraq a year later. Data was so plentiful that USAF squadron commanders could not or did not circulate much of it from ATOs to their pilots, while staff officers would not change their procedures, thus ensuring confusion between all layers of command.[42]

The system processed and circulated far more information faster than ever before, but in this high tempo environment, the need to spend just 30 seconds in checking or retrieving data could produce error or tragedy. This system is so fast moving, fragile and complex that system errors are inevitable even in the absence of an enemy; the only questions are how often and at what cost, and how much the presence of an enemy will multiply them.

C4ISR seems to have changed little below the corps level in land warfare. Within 3rd Infantry and 1st Marine Divisions, the speed of reaction between calls for fire support to the moment batteries received their orders was 180 to 200 seconds – if anything, the system was less speedy and sophisticated than that for Allied artillery in the Battle of Normandy, though the guns themselves could deliver a more accurate and devastating weight of fire (an improvement much less marked than with airpower). Personnel in both divisions criticized their inability to call for or receive tactical air support.[43]

C4ISR increased the powers of aircraft in interdiction, but not close support. Much communication equipment was incompatible or clumsy, producing unexpected failures in significant links of the chain which might have mattered against a real foe; planning cycles within Marine (and probably Army) corps and divisions were so slow that formations could not really coordinate and control their forces – the performance of 2003 fell well below the absolute standard of 1944. Below the corps level, the officially promoted COP failed; there was no ONA – indeed, there seems to have been little operational intelligence in the classic sense. Though advocates of the RMA often claim that the operational level of war will vanish, one doubts they had this in mind!

One also may question the assumption that ground operations in Iraq were a matter of transformed command, inspired leadership and the conscious use of 'swarm' tactics. The real picture seems to be one of a big country with few enemy forces, which attackers entered in a dispersed fashion and continued forward, propelled by their own momentum, determined junior leaders and the principle of 'point me toward the enemy'. This war could be won by divisional or regimental commanders, and precisely they took the key operational decisions – the 'thunder runs' from Karbala to Saddam Hussein International Airport, and from there into Baghdad – without access to intelligence. This in part was for a good reason – Franks' 'experience in Vietnam was that we did not want the guy we used to call Snowball 6 orbiting overhead and telling our platoons what to do. I made sure I never did that.' He avoided over-centralization at the price of dividing intelligence from operations. Intelligence was good, it guided the use of airpower and gave senior commanders a good grip on events, but it did not influence the key actions on the ground.[44]

Franks' instincts were sound, and should be remembered by his successors, but this approach could not have worked so well against a better enemy. In that case, command might have had to be more centralized, initiative curtailed and intelligence perhaps more useful. What journalists call swarms look rather like the use of columns in nineteenth-century imperial warfare, less an innovation than a standard procedure. Again, in

2003 signals were not necessarily better than in 1944, nor were all improvements in communications good for command. Major General James Mattis led 1st Marine Division as though in the Western Desert during 1941, through plain language radio transmissions and a personal vehicle that let him easily and quickly visit his forces in action. One grizzled Marine sergeant noted, 'NCOs run the fight no matter how much you get on the radio. Sit back and listen to them. You might just learn something from them.'[45]

Operation 'Iraqi Freedom' demonstrates a new standard for conventional war. Cebrowski proclaimed 'the discovery of a new "sweet-spot" in the relationship between land and air warfare and a tighter integration of the two. The things that compel are good sensors networked with good intelligence disseminated through a robust networking system, which then yields speed. Speed turns out to be a very, very important factor.'[46]

C2W, C4ISR, IO and NCW worked as planned, because Coalition forces had the initiative and followed their plan, while the enemy was passive, overwhelmed, unable to strike their forces or C4ISR, or even to take the obvious step of forcing the enemy to fight hard in urban areas. Had the Iraqis jammed GPS or tactical communication, they would have broken most of the Coalition's enhanced power in intelligence and precision of attack; had they harmed satellites, strategic signals or computers, they would have crippled the enemy's command; American satellite communications capacity came close to the limit even in this easy campaign, especially for forces 'on the move'.[47]

The sources of one's strength are one's vulnerability. How far this success can be repeated is uncertain – NCW, C4ISR and IO worked less well in Kosovo; turkey shoots offer few lessons in tactics. C2W worked here, as it sometimes has in the past; but sometimes it has not. So one-sided was this war that intelligence served primarily for target acquisition rather than ONA. Insofar as ONA was attempted, it failed, which raises serious questions about the concept of RDO. Dust and heat in rooms housing SIPRnet servers and routers endangered C4ISR more than did the Iraqis. Sometimes, the tactical intranet broke down, or signals went in plain language via civilian cellphones.[48]

Once again, as in the Gulf War of 1991, American soldiers preferred to buy commercial GPS and radio sets rather than rely on those officially issued. Could this near-NCW system work in complex operations against an able and aggressive enemy? In Afghanistan and Iraq, precise strikes often have failed, showing they work only when the machine performs without friction. Any friction yields failure; no system can always be perfect. An enemy which fights by its own rules, like light infantry willing to die, or else silently to steal away, has caught American forces at a disadvantage. One enemy can learn from another's successes and failures, or the nature of American tactics. They follow their playbook; they do what their doctrine says, and they test the ideas they are discussing. They are more formulaic than they think. Uncertainty remained.

C4ISR multiplied some forms of combat power more than others. The gains were most notable and remarkable in links between theater and component commands, in their ability to direct centralized firepower, and for aircraft to learn of targets of opportunity and to conduct interdiction missions. On occasion, airpower was directed with unprecedented speed, power, precision and reach. Yet one should not take the most spectacular rises in performance for their norm, nor over-generalize from particulars – by assuming Iraq in 2003 represents the future for war as a whole, or that land forces suddenly can behave as if they have wings.

Since 1933, air forces have been able to apply NCW to some aspects of air combat, as have navies since 1955, while armies have not. Technology enables transformation; the fact that in 2003 it multiplied the interdiction power of aircraft far more than it did land tactics is suggestive. It points to one of the key factors in any attempt to learn lessons – the difference between problems and conditions. Problems can be solved; conditions must be endured. If the aim simply is for national intelligence services to meet quickly and effectively the intelligence needs of each of five divisions in an expeditionary force, this can be done. One cannot eliminate uncertainty forever from war as a whole. Judgments are even harder to make because one needs so many of them. One can easily say that the enthusiasts for RMA are wrong, because their system would fail against a serious enemy or a real war. Yet if the latter cannot occur in the next 20 years, why does that objection matter? The real point is less the transformation of forces, or of their quality, than of their quantity, of one's power relative to one's enemy. When Americans draw lessons from Iraq, they can apply them to a special case of conflict, of giant against dwarf, rather than to war as a whole. Any other states drawing lessons from this conflict must adopt a broader perspective.

Advocates of transformation appreciate the limits to C4ISR and NCW in Operation 'Iraqi Freedom'. John Osterholtz, of the DOD's chief information officer's office, notes 'there were pockets of net-centric operations, but it was not a general operating paradigm'. Cebrowski held: 'what we're seeing is essentially net-centric warfare for the joint task force commander. The next step is network-centric warfare for the warfighter – reflecting increased "jointness" at the tactical level of war'.[49] How far can their hopes be realized?

C4ISR and NCW will most affect tactics and operations where, all too often, friction at the systematic level has reduced the value of intelligence;

one actor had information another could have used but did not have in time to act, knowledge available in time could not be used with effect; failures by any one cog prevented the whole machine from working well, or at all. In conventional war, NCW and C4ISR may ensure that every cog of the machine works well at the same time, reducing friction to the lowest level possible. All national intelligence assets will focus on giving every unit every chance to exploit every fleeting opportunity; one's forces will be used to asking for or receiving such information and using it instantly, and well; and often they will be able to do so.

C4ISR and NCW will raise the bar on the best use of intelligence, and the frequency of optimum uses, in conventional war. In particular, the US owns airpower; this will cripple any conventional enemy, unless the latter can find a means to degrade or evade that strength – as did Serbia in Kosovo. Little, however, will change where equals engage, or the weaker side evades one's strength or strikes one's C4ISR, or against guerrillas. A force strong enough to crush an army may be too weak to control a people. The RMA has done many things, not everything. It has multiplied American strengths without reducing its weaknesses. It has increased the value of high technology and firepower in conventional war, but for little else; where these things matter, they do more than ever; where they do not, nothing has changed. Iraq shows that the US will aim to practice intelligence, command and war at a higher level than ever achieved before. When it can play to its strengths, it will succeed.

NOTES

1. Colonel John A. Warden III, 'Air Theory for the Twenty-first Century', *Aerospace Power Chronicles, "Battlefield of the Future: 21st Century Warfare Issues"*, 1995.
2. 'Joint Vision 2010' and 'Joint Vision 2020', <www.dtic.mil/doctrine>.
3. Joint Pub 3-13.1, *Joint Doctrine for Command and Control Warfare (C2W)*, Joint Chiefs of Staff, 7 Feb. 1996.
4. Department of Defense, *Transformation Planning Guidance*, April 2003, APP 4, 'Joint Concept Guidance', <www.oft.osd.mil/>; US Joint Forces Command, *A Concept for Rapid Decisive Operations, RDO White Paper*, J9 Joint Futures Lab, 2.3, 4.1, 4.3.1.3.
5. Marine Corps Colonel and First Sergeant, Task Force Tarawa, April 2003, <www.urbanoperations.com/ifaar2.ht>.
6. Joseph L. Galloway, 'General Tommy Franks Discusses Conducting the War in Iraq', 19 June 2003, Knight Ridder Washington Bureau, <www.realcities.com/mld/krwashington/6124738.h>.
7. 'What Went Right?', *Jane's Defence Weekly*, 30 April 2003; 'Operation Iraqi Freedom, 1st Marine Division, Lessons Learned, 28 May 2003'; accessible from the website of The Urban Operations Journal, Operation Iraq Freedom, AARs, Observations, Analyses and Comments; for one interview with rear area personnel, see Dan Caterinicchia, 'Command Keeps Troops Connected', *Federal Computer Weekly*, 1 April 2003; and Dawn S. Olney, 'Network-centric Operations Score Big in Iraq, DOD's Frankel Says', *Government Computer News*, 26 May 2003.

8. Stephen Biddle, 'Afghanistan and the Future of Warfare: Implications for Army and Defense Policy', Strategic Studies Institute, US Army War College, 11 Feb. 2002; Antony Cordesman, *The Lessons of Afghanistan, Warfighting, Intelligence, Force Transformation, Counterproliferation, and Arms Control* (Washington, DC: Center for Strategic and International Studies, 12 Aug. 2002) pp.39–71, draws similar conclusions.

9. Galloway, 'General Tommy Franks Discusses Conducting the War in Iraq' (note 6).

10. Anthony H. Cordesman, *Intelligence and Iraqi Weapons of Mass Destruction: The Lessons from the Iraq War* (Washington DC: Center for Strategic and International Studies, 1 July 2003).

11. Ibid.

12. Galloway (note 6).

13. Lisa Burgess, 'Iraq War: Swift, Lethal Battle Shot Down Many Cold War Theories', *European and Pacific Stars & Stripes*, 'Freedom in Iraq' special section, 27 May 2003.

14. Online Newshour, 'Lessons of War', 1 May 2003, <www.pbs.org/newsho..ddle_east/jan-june03/lessons_05-01/ht>.

15. Transcript, 'BBC Interview, Deputy Assistant Secretary Whitman on Media Operations During Operation Iraq Freedom', <www.urbanoperations.com/whitman.ht>.

16. 'Operation Iraqi Freedom, 1st Marine Division, Lessons Learned, 28 May 2003' (note 7).

17. Ross W. Simpson, 'Operation Iraqi Freedom, Going to War', *Leatherneck, Magazine of the Marines*, July 2003.

18. *Operations in Iraq, 2003: First Reflections*, UK Ministry of Defence, July 2003, p.15, <www.mod.uk>.

19. Kamal Ahmed, 'Blair "Expected War to Last Four Months"', *The Observer*, 6 July 2003; 'Fifth Corps Commander, Live Briefing from Baghdad, 7 May 2003', <www.urbanoperations.com/ifaar4.ht>.

20. 'Operation Iraqi Freedom' (note 7).

21. Galloway (note 6).

22. Ibid.

23. Joint Chiefs of Staff, Joint Pub 3-58, *Joint Doctrine for Military Deception*, 31 May 1996 (under revision as of time of writing, June 2003); John Ferris, 'The Roots of Fortitude: The Evolution of British Deception in the Second World War', in T.G. Mahnken (ed.), *The Paradox of Intelligence: Essays in Honour of Michael Handel* (London & Portland, OR: Frank Cass forthcoming, 2003).

24. Anthony Cordesman, *The 'Instant Lessons' of the Iraq War, Main Report, Seventh Working Draft* (Washington, DC: Center for Strategic and International Studies, 28 April 2003) p.186.

25. Arthur Cebrowski, 'Speech to the Heritage Foundation', 13 May 2003, *Transformation Trends*, 27 May 2003, <www.oft.osd.mil/>.

26. Colonel Szafranski, 'Information Warfare', *Airpower Journal*, Spring 1995.

27. David A. Fulghum, 'The Pentagon's Force-transformation Director Takes an Early Swipe at What Worked and What Didn't in Iraq', *Aviation Week and Space Technology*, 28 April 2003, p.34.

28. Scott Peterson and Peter Ford, 'From Iraqi Officers, Three Tales of Shock and Defeat', *Christian Science Monitor*, 18 April 2003.

29. NCS-21 (*National Cryptological Strategy for the 21st Century*), <www.nsa.goc/programs/ncs21/index>.

30. Vector 21 website, *Defense Intelligence Agency Strategic Plan, 1999-2000*; NCS-21 (note 29); Director of Central Intelligence, *The 2002 Annual Report of the United States Intelligence Community*, 1 March 2003, <www.cia.gov/cia/publications/Ann_Rpt_2002/index>; 'Statement for the Record by Lieutenant General Michael V. Hayden, USAF, Director, National Security Agency/Chief, Central Security Service, Before the Joint Inquiry of the Senate Select Committee on Intelligence and the House Permanent Select Committee on Intelligence, 17 October 2002', <www.nsa.gov/releases/speeches>.

31. Dan Caterinicchia, 'NIMA, NSA Increasing Collaboration', *Federal Computer Weekly*, 30 Jan. 2003.

32. 'Operation Iraqi Freedom' (note 7).

33. Marine Corps Colonel and First Sergeant, Task Force Tarawa, April 2003',
    <www.urbanoperations.com/ifaar2.ht>.
34. Galloway (note 6).
35. Jim Garamone, 'Abizaid: U.S. Displaying "Offensive Spirit" in Iraq', AFIS, 25 June 2003,
    <www.defenselink.mil/news/Jun2003/nO6252003_200306251> ; United States Senate
    Armed Services Committee, 25 June 2003, 'LTG Abizaid Senate Confirmation Hearing,
    Questions and Answers (24 June 2003)', <www.senate.gov/^armed_services/testimony/
    cfm?wit_id=2312&id=8>.
36. Joseph Farah and Jon Dougherty, 'Iraq Theater's Tower of Babel', *WorldNetDaily*, 18 Oct.
    2002; Paul Sperry, 'U.S. Miscalculations Left Troops Vulnerable', *WorldNetDaily*, 10 July
    2003.
37. Joshua Davis, 'If We Run Out of Batteries, This War is Screwed', *Wired*, 21 May 2003.
38 Ibid; for the Navy's 500 chat rooms, cf. Dan Caterinicchia, 'Defence IT Leaders Outline
    Challenges', *Federal Computer Weekly*, 8 May 2003.
39. 'Notes Based on a Briefing by an Observer of 1st Marine Division OIF Operations',
    accessible from the web site of The Urban Operations Journal, Operation 'Iraq Freedom',
    AARs, Observations, Analyses and Comments.
40. 'What Went Right?', *Jane's Defence Weekly* (note 7).
41. Cordesman, *The Lessons of Afghanistan, Warfighting, Intelligence, Force Transformation,
    Counterproliferation, and Arms Control* (note 8) pp.63–4.
42. 'Verbatim Testimony of Colonel David. C. Nichols and Colonel Laurence A. Stutzreim,
    Tarnack Farms Enquiry', 1 March 2003, <www.barksdale.af.mil/tarnackfarms/ rosenow>.
43. 'Operation Iraqi Freedom' (note 7); 'With the "Marne 500" in Iraq, U.S. Army Officer, 3rd
    Infantry Division, March 2003', <www.urbanoperations.com/ifaar7>.
44. Galloway (note 6).
45. 'Operation Iraqi Freedom, Quick-Look Tactical Observations, Marine Corps 1st Sergeant, 24
    Marine Expeditionary Unit, "The Warlords", May 2003', <www.urbanoperations.com/
    ifaar5>; 'Operation Iraqi Freedom' (note 7); 'Notes Based on a Briefing by an Observer of
    1st Marine Division OIF Operations' (note 39).
46. 'What Went Right?', *Jane's Defence Weekly* (note 7).
47. 'LTG Abizaid Hearing' (note 35).
48. Davis, 'If We Run Out of Batteries, This War is Screwed' (note 37).
49. Dan Caternicchia, 'Network-centric Warfare: Not There Yet', *Federal Computer Weekly*, 9
    June 2003.

Deep Probe:
The Evolution of Network Intelligence

RONALD J. DEIBERT

Intelligence has been defined as the collection and analysis of information so that informed decisions can be made on strategic issues. It is a practice with roots reaching back to ancient times.[1] It has been during the modern era and particularly during the Cold War, however, that intelligence has acquired its most identifiable characteristics. Modern intelligence evokes the realm of 'high politics', covert action and intense secrecy.[2] It is also a practice that is typically associated with states or state-like units, as opposed to other international actors. Not surprisingly, much of the attention accorded to the future of intelligence, whether focusing on new technologies or changing world political contexts, carries with it a state-centric bias.[3]

In this essay, I focus on a different type of intelligence practice that is emerging not among states but among non-state actors and in particular among citizen groups with computer networking capabilities – a distributed, transnational form of intelligence that I refer to as 'network intelligence'. There are a variety of good reasons to monitor network intelligence.

First, the social forces that are propelling network intelligence – namely citizen groups and non-governmental organizations (NGOs) around the world – are formidable and continue to grow.[4] The tentacles of these groups now permeate nearly every issue-area in world politics and have had a tangible influence on international negotiations and treaties in a variety of fora. While they do not determine the rules of the game in the way that powerful states do, these groups are increasingly important players in world politics. It is time that theorists of world politics begin to take seriously how these groups operate and what sets them apart from states and corporations.

Although it is generally recognized that one of the principal reasons for the rapid ascent and proliferation of these networks is new information and communication technologies, very rarely does such recognition extend beyond the usual platitudes about speed and organization.[5] As I show below, one of the novel ways that citizen networks are employing information and communication technologies is best understood, I argue, as a new specimen of 'intelligence' gathering and analysis with several distinct characteristics. Working through the Internet, network intelligence has emerged out of the blending of the activities of two hitherto largely discrete social forces: NGOs and activists on the one hand, and computer hackers on the other.

While still largely nascent in form and structure, several clear illustrations of this expanding set of distributed practices can now clearly be identified. What merging has occurred to date, however, provides only a hint of what will likely occur in the future as these two social forces capitalize on their respective strengths to create a potent combination. This new formation on the world political landscape will alter the environment in which traditional state-based intelligence agencies operate and may, in fact, be the most important long-term consequence for the 'future of intelligence'.

TRACING THE ROOTS OF NETWORK INTELLIGENCE

To properly discern the future trajectory and potential force of network intelligence we need to first trace its distinct history and roots. Citizen network intelligence is today a prominent species in the global ecology. But its potency derives from its unique history. It is a hybrid of two distinct social forces that have had relatively long and separate histories: civil society groups and NGOs, on the one hand, and computing and technology hackers on the other. The trajectories that they have respectively taken, separate until recently, have now begun to converge. Through symbiosis, they have complemented and reinforced each other, each bringing strengths that the other has traditionally lacked. Together, they are expanding and diversifying, filling niches in and around the traditional structures of international political processes.[6]

While the topic of global citizen networks is a relatively novel one among those who study world politics, it is by no means a recent phenomenon. The rise and gradual spread of democracy in the nineteenth and twentieth centuries helped to generate social movements organized around specific issue-areas or social causes. For example, the British and Foreign Anti-Slavery Society, founded by Quakers in 1839, employed many of the same strategies and organizational models as contemporary NGOs to push for the abolition of slavery around the world. It was, additionally, a *transnational* movement, having links among units in Britain, France, Africa, South America and the United States (US).[7] Several other late nineteenth and early twentieth century examples of transnational NGOs can be found as well.[8] It is during the twentieth century, however, and in particular following World War II, that movements such as these have begun to flourish and spread.[9]

It is difficult to determine precisely the exact number of NGOs that operate around the world given their widely divergent characteristics. NGOs range extensively in size, duration, sophistication and presence. One clear trend that can be discerned, however, is their rapid expansion around the world. For example, human rights NGOs alone increased from 38 in 1950, to 72 in 1960, to 103 in 1970, to 138 in 1980, and to 275 by 1990.[10] In all, 5,000 NGOs work on developing literacy in the Third World.[11] The Union of International Associations (UIA) now recognizes some 17,000 international NGOs.[12] Thousands of other more informal groups not recognized by the UIA exist as well – as many as 29,000 by other counts.[13] Their visibility in a wide variety of international fora and conventions, and their growing influence on both international and domestic policy, make them hard to ignore.[14] As an illustration of the growing importance of some of these groups, NGOs provided $8.3 billion in aid to developing countries in 1992 – 13 per cent of development assistance worldwide.[15]

It is also clear that the number of issue-areas around which NGOs have formed has broadened. Today, citizen networks orbit around nearly every major issue-area in world politics, such as environment, labor, peace and security, trade, health, development and human rights, among others. Many of the largest, such as Greenpeace or Worldwide Fund for Nature, have a program or interest in several.[16] As a consequence of both the size and diversity of NGOs, no international meeting of significance on any issue can take place today without seemingly scores of NGOs orbiting around the venue, either in protest in the streets or in a more formal consultative or participatory capacity.[17]

Given the importance of strategy, knowledge and political acumen to their activities, it is not surprising that these groups have typically engaged in what might be called a rudimentary form of 'intelligence' analogous to that undertaken on behalf of state decision-makers. For example, in a survey of the transnational NGOs that attended the 1972 Stockholm conference on the environment, Anne Feraru found that many attended with the intention of:

> ...getting information about the global environment to transmit to the organization's members or to the wider public. Almost half of the organizations sent delegates to Stockholm to 'observe', to 'find out what's going on', and more than a third say that they will be active in providing information about, and mobilizing public support for, the UN Environment Program.[18]

Similar sentiments would likely be expressed among NGOs attending conferences or meetings in virtually any other issue-area today. Performing an educational or consciousness-raising role, through information gathering and analysis, has long been recognized as one important function of NGOs.[19]

The character of the intelligence has tended to differ in fundamental ways from traditional forms of state intelligence. NGO intelligence operations have tended to be less formal and hierarchical, lacking the typical command and control chains of bureaucracy common to state intelligence organizations.[20] As I will argue below, in combination with networked communications such a characteristic has become one of the strengths of citizen networks. But prior to the Internet, NGO intelligence tended to be as a consequence more disconnected and sluggish with the intelligence operations compartmentalized among NGOs spread across the world over multiple state jurisdictions.[21]

What intelligence sharing occurred was sporadic and uneven and typically centered on occasional face-to-face meetings supplemented with postal traffic, faxes and intermittent telephone exchanges. The relatively large expenses associated with the last meant that the slower and less interactive modes of the former were more common. NGO intelligence gathering and analysis operated within a similar set of constraints. Prior to the Internet, acquisition of government or international organization documents and reports had to take place through formal postal requisitions, library searches or trips to departments and ministries, all of which reduced the pace and analytical capacities of individual NGOs, most of whom typically operated (and still do) with very modest budgets.[22]

Computer hacking has almost as long a history as do NGOs.[23] From the first prototypes employed in encryption cracking during World War II, computer technology has attracted devoted enthusiasts and programmers.[24] The term 'hacking' today conjures up images of criminality and terrorist activity, largely due to the use of the term by law enforcement, defense and intelligence agencies. But it did not always have such felonious associations. The term likely has its origins in the Massachusetts Institute of Technology's Artificial Intelligence laboratory, where a large group of technically proficient programmers and engineers coalesced in the 1960s.[25] A hacker culture began to flourish widely with the development of ARPANET and the connection to the early Internet of computer science departments and other academic nodes around the world. As the Internet expanded, so too did the numbers and sophistication of hackers. Many informal hacker groups sprouted, occasionally meeting at large international conferences. DefCON, an annual meeting of defense contractors held in Las Vegas, Nevada, has become the most visible and arguably the largest conference of hackers, though others exist as well.[26]

Hacker culture has tended to be almost purely apolitical. There has been no distinct politics of hacking per se.[27] In part, this can be explained by the apolitical biases of the computing and engineering professions. In part, it can be explained by the age of typical hackers, who have tended to be teenagers who lack worldly sophistication and strong political beliefs. At best, a kind of unrefined libertarianism has pervaded hacker culture – a legacy of the West Coast-Californian roots of a large portion of early Internet development.[28] Until recently, this ideological outlook has rarely translated into concerted political action beyond support for unencumbered networks, strong encryption and freedom of speech. These activities are often coupled to the highly contested notion that the Internet cannot be controlled or regulated – that it is an anarchic environment – and that its development will, as a consequence, act as a positive force for global society as a whole.

THE EMERGENCE OF NETWORK INTELLIGENCE

The Canadian economic historian Harold Innis once described the contingent effect of social forces and technology environments coming together fortuitously to complement and reinforce each other in what he described as a kind of *cyclonic* interaction.[29] Separately, or in different contexts, the social forces would have less of an impact. But in particular contexts and circumstances in which they are linked, they come together and erupt onto the political landscape having a force combined beyond their separate strengths. Such *cyclonic* interaction is now occurring among civil society groups and hackers. Civil society groups are becoming more technologically sophisticated with an increasing reliance on computer networks. Hackers, on the other hand, are becoming increasingly politicized. I will refer to this combined social force as a whole as 'citizen networks', and their activities as 'hacktivism'.[30]

It is important to note that the groups that make up citizen networks are not homogenous. They are so diverse, in fact, that grouping them together under a single label may be misleading. Groups comprising citizen networks include everything from anarchists to Marxists and virtually everything in between. In spite of their ideological differences, however, these groups share enough normative and practical commonality to make coordination worthwhile. Among the shared interests is a sense that global capital markets and planet-roaming corporations have too much power and unaccountable authority – that, in effect, globalization has gone too far. There is also a deep mistrust of states and international organizations. This mistrust can manifest itself at times in a paranoid 'us versus them' mentality, with all traditional structures of political power lumped together as a single amorphous global unit or Empire, and resistance to any cooperation with formal authorities ruled out altogether. Others among citizen networks take a much more conciliatory approach to states and international organizations and even work together with them on projects and meetings.

The origins of network intelligence can be traced back to the early 1980s when social change and activist groups began to employ computer networks as a mode of information-dissemination. These early networks were, quite literally, basement operations in most cases with individuals donating their time and computing equipment to assist in the NGO activities of which they were a part.[31] By the late 1980s, more formal links had been established among networks in England (GreenNet) and the US (PeaceNet and EcoNet), and then later Sweden (NordNet), Canada (Web), Brazil (IBASE), Nicaragua (Nicarao) and Australia (Pegasus).[32]

In 1990, these networks jointly founded the Association for Progressive Communications (APC), an umbrella network that still exists as a coordinating system among NGO networks worldwide. Its mission statement outlines its intelligence-gathering and dissemination function:

> ...to empower and support organisations, social movements and individuals in and through the use of information and communication technologies to build strategic communities and initiatives for the purpose of making meaningful contributions to equitable human development, social justice, participatory political processes and environmental sustainability.[33]

One of the earliest examples of network intelligence involving the APC was the 1992 UN Earth Summit in Rio de Janeiro. The Earth Summit was to be a unique event in that it would involve the extensive and official participation of numerous NGOs from around the world. Leading up to the summit, the UN and the APC began to coordinate the establishment of a network that would facilitate communications among NGOs and disseminate official summit information.[34] As O'Brien and Clement note: '[b]ackgrounders to the issues, draft policies, country briefings, and logistical bulletins were posted by the UN to a set of computer conferences shared internationally on all APC networks. This allowed several thousand civil society groups around the world to be kept informed at very little cost to the UN.'[35]

The global, distributed nature of the NGO participation – in other words, the fact that groups not physically present at Rio nonetheless had a hand in participating – was instrumental in particular in the formulation of the several 'alternative treaties' that were put forth from the parallel NGO summit, called 'the Global Forum', held simultaneously with the Earth Summit.

One of the more remarkable aspects of the network intelligence that occurred leading up to and during the Rio summit was that provided by *The*

Bulletin. *The Bulletin* began as a two-page electronic summary on the status of UNCED PrepCom negotiations, written by three NGO representatives who attended the meetings in New York and distributed through the APC networks. Once the summit began, *The Bulletin* continued to serve the same purpose, providing 'a vital news source for those who could not attend the conference and for attendees attempting to keep abreast of the substance of the Summit, which was often complicated and negotiated behind closed doors'.[36] Significantly, the APC activities at the summit generated a sustained network of communications among the participating NGOs that did not end once the summit was officially over. Several email lists generated during the summit continue to operate to this day, circulating intelligence on government policy, international negotiations, academic reports, and upcoming meetings and events among the environmental NGO community.

Another case that illustrates well network intelligence is the International Campaign to Ban Landmines (ICBL) –a campaign begun in 1992 and involving over 1,000 NGOs in both developed and developing countries. Although the campaign did not employ computer networks in any substantial sense until about 1995, from that point onwards computer networks were vital to collecting and disseminating information and forming strategy in the ICBL across its membership in more than 70 countries. The networks were, according to participants, crucial in lowering organizational costs and integrating into decision-making structures members from poorer, developing countries.[37]

More importantly, it dramatically augmented the intellectual capacity of the ICBL member NGOs, who were able to bring analytically and empirically informed analyses to the table when meeting with states on the landmines issue. It also knit the diverse participants together into a relatively coherent unit, particularly with regard to the ICBL strategy. As some prominent leaders of the ICBL noted, the 'the ease and speed of communication within the ICBL provided by e-mail clearly had a great impact on the ability of civil society organizations from diverse cultures to exchange information and develop integrated political strategies'.[38]

The network intelligence dimension of the ICBL was, perhaps, best illustrated during the 1997 treaty signing conference in Oslo. Groups involved in the ICBL closely monitored state policies and statements during the conference, and then communicated back to their respective national members what their governments were doing and saying so that pressure could be applied to policymakers in their domestic arenas.[39] Such a swift relay of intelligence among a globally diverse alliance of thousands of NGOs in dozens of states could not have occurred without the speed and interactivity of computer networks.

While peace, environmental and other NGOs have tended to employ network intelligence separately in their respective issue-areas, there has been an increasing merging and blending of information networks in recent years. Additionally, since 1995 the media through which network intelligence takes place has broadened with the development of the World Wide Web. In recent campaigns, NGOs have supplemented their traditional email and news group information exchanges with the posting/publishing and multi-media capacities of websites. Perhaps no better illustration of the power of this combined set of capacities exists than the campaign against the proposed Multilateral Agreement on Investments (MAI), a treaty on investment rules that was being negotiated at the Organization for Economic Cooperation and Development (OECD) from 1995 to 1998.

The MAI negotiations were a watershed event in that what traditionally had been publicly-ignored and highly arcane negotiations, in the case of rules of investment, were suddenly the object of a concerted citizen network campaign involving thousands of NGOs of all varieties from both developed and developing countries. As I have argued elsewhere, the Internet played a vital role in the anti-MAI campaign, helping citizen networks to pressure politicians, publicize their views and – most importantly for the topic of this paper – to coordinate strategically the exchange of intelligence.[40] In an analogous manner to the ICBL, the anti-MAI activists who were 'on site' of the OECD negotiations in Paris relayed information to national activists around the world who then put pressure on their national representatives. As Maude Barlow of the Council of Canadians noted in the midst of the campaign: 'We are in constant contact with our allies in other countries...If a negotiator says something to someone over a glass of wine, we'll have it on the Internet within an hour, all over the world...If we know something that is sensitive to one government, we get it to our ally in that country instantly.'[41] In fact, in the case of both Australia and Canada many national members of parliament were not even aware of the MAI negotiations until being informed of them by anti-MAI activists.

At the center of the anti-MAI infrastructure was and remain several electronic mailing lists that distribute information among participants worldwide. These lists are the material nerves linking the global anti-MAI campaign. Information from any one of the participants is immediately forwarded to anyone else on the list. In this way, members of the anti-MAI lobby are kept apprised of negotiations, meetings, protests, letter campaigns, editorials, news items, websites of interests and general information.[42] On a typical day during the campaign, the traffic on each of the main MAI lists ran at about 30–40 postings a day, with the volume increasing on some days relative to current events.⁴³ This volume of postings continues to this day. A typical posting might have a notice of an upcoming event or demonstration, contact information for politicians or other activists and background information. By providing a form of distributed intelligence, the lists help augment the knowledge, capacity and responsiveness of the anti-MAI network in a way that telephones or faxes alone cannot.⁴⁴

While the lists were employed in a concerted fashion not unlike the way in which they were employed in previous campaigns, the anti-MAI network helped introduce the web as a formidable new dimension of network intelligence. Hundreds of sites from around the world formed links in the distributed anti-MAI campaign. Many anti-MAI sites provided the email addresses of MPs and state representatives.⁴⁵ Many included form letters to employ to voice concern about its approval, letters that could be sent with a click of a button.⁴⁶

One site provided a series of sample city and county resolutions against the MAI, how to go about lobbying local councils to have them adopted and stories from MAI activists who were successful in doing so.⁴⁷ Significantly, many of the resolutions that were successfully passed – through the Berkeley City Council and the Corporation of the City of Mississauga, to give just two examples – contained identical texts supplied by a World Wide Website based in Washington DC. Other municipalities passed resolutions with only minor modifications to the text. On the lists and websites, the times and locations of where important MAI-related meetings were taking place were announced beforehand so that protests could be coordinated strategically. Even the times and locations of where prominent politicians were meeting on topics unrelated directly to the MAI would be announced so that activists could have the chance to protest. In combination with the email lists, the numerous websites formed the foundation of anti-MAI network intelligence.

Following the defeat of the MAI negotiations, the networked infrastructure that was created by anti-MAI networks was sustained, broadened and improved in significant ways. From the Seattle World Trade Organization ministerial meeting in November 1999 to the Washington DC, World Bank/IMF meeting in April 2000 and beyond, the anti-MAI network has continued to bristle with the exchange of strategic information. One of the more noteworthy examples of network intelligence along these lines was the website, <www.a16.org/>. The site was created as an organizing and intelligence-sharing forum for activists planning to attend the April 2000 meetings of the World Bank and IMF. Among the information provided on the site was details on where and when to catch buses and other modes of transportation from cities across North America heading to

Washington; where to sleep and where to rally in Washington; 'talking points' for addressing the media; and precautionary steps to be taken against the use of pepper spray. Remarkably, the site has evolved following the April meetings to become yet another clearinghouse of information for anti-globalization activists, with links to independent radio and video news, information on upcoming meetings, as well as the usual links to related organizations and information all of which is organized around user contributions, giving the site a distributed format.

Significantly, much of the improvement and capacity-building of network intelligence that has recently occurred has focused on better use of computer networks themselves – an indication of the influence and fusing of more technologically-minded activists and politically-oriented computer hackers. Increasingly, citizen network websites provide detailed information on the technology itself in addition to the substantive issue-area concerned.

One of the best examples is the Federation of American Scientists' (FAS) 'CyberStrategy' website, on which a header reads 'Empowering Citizens through the Web'.[48] The site provides links to hardware and software tools to exploit the full potential of the Internet. It has detailed information on how to author information on the Web – a crucial component of the distributed nature of network intelligence. One of the most remarkable aspects of the site is the detail that is given to privacy and security, including encryption and firewalls, and links to sites that provide security information. The FAS site is not unusual in this respect. Many citizen network websites provide information on and links to publicly available encryption technologies to secure private or sensitive exchanges.[49] Such a concern for security suggests a deepening and solidifying of transnational citizen intelligence networks.

Encryption tools and software to secure network intelligence are but one example of the way in which new technologies are being employed to advance citizen intelligence networks. Some sites are being created using 'slash-code' software, which allows for much greater website interactivity, particularly in the area of information posting of multimedia. The IndyMedia organization offers one remarkable example. IndyMedia is a collective network of 28 independent media organizations from three continents all of which encourage and rely on users to upload or 'publish' text, audio and video of their own making to their site directly from their browser.[50]

In other words, maintenance of the website itself, including its content, is a distributed activity. IndyMedia sites have, as a consequence, not only multimedia information but also 'newswires' that are comprised of up-to-the-minute members' information. Another form of advanced Internet media increasingly being employed by citizen networks is Internet Relay Chat (IRC), where simultaneous exchanges of information take place. For example, IRCs were and are employed by street activists to engage in 'real-time' strategic organization of protests. The use of IRC adds a subterranean layer to network intelligence, in a deeper realm of the Internet, beyond the more familiar and 'user-friendly' World Wide Web. Such burrowed networks amid the thousands of roaming IRC sites on the Internet provide a hermetic – yet flexible and global – domain for tactical, 'real-time' citizen intelligence.

While most of the examples above portray the increasing technological sophistication of NGOs, the story could be told from a different angle as well: hackers have, for their part, become increasingly politicized. Several years ago, most of the more prominent hacking activities – the defacement of web pages or the probing of network security systems – would be categorized as largely apolitical. In recent years, however, dedicated hacker networks have become more political, with their activities having clearly defined political goals.[51] One of the most illustrative in this respect has been the activity of the Electronic Disturbance Theatre (EDT).[52] In a series of innovative 'web sit-ins', the EDT has organized and engaged in several acts of electronic civil disobedience. The most successful of these was the virtual sit-in of Mexican President Ernesto Zedillo's website in opposition to the Mexican government's treatment of the Chiapan people. Using software called 'Floodnet, the EDT encouraged sympathetic hactivists to flood the president's website with access requests that overwhelmed the system. Many of the requests asked for files with names such as 'human rights' or the names of Chiapan dead, so that network administrators would later find responses indicating 'human rights not found on this network'.[53] The EDT has organized other sit-ins as well. Such sit-ins could not occur, however, without the exchange and circulation of intelligence, which for hacktivists like the EDT occur mostly through email lists and IRC.

OPEN SOURCE AND NETWORK INTELLIGENCE

One can contrast the network from the traditional state intelligence cycle.[54] Unlike in the state intelligence cycle, *direction* is much more loosely configured because of the lack of hierarchy and hence clearly articulated goals. In the network intelligence cycle, direction is obtained rather by broadly-defined values and interests of the network which are inferred by the participants themselves. This means that the net is often cast widely. Both collection and processing are typically done in a decentralized and distributed fashion with dissemination towards the unfiltered and open end of the spectrum, as opposed to restricted and compartmentalized.[55] Network intelligence is non-hierarchical, open and distributed rather than hierarchical, secretive and compartmentalized.

It is important not to confuse citizen network intelligence with another emerging forms of non-state intelligence: commercial open/source intelligence.[56] Numerous private intelligence agencies have sprouted in the wake of the Cold War with both the relaxation of prior secrecy policies and the utilization of the Internet as a mode of dissemination. While this form of non-state intelligence is significant and certainly worthy of analysis, it differs in fundamental respects from the type of network intelligence described here.

First, with citizen network intelligence profit motivations are rarely, if ever, involved. Most NGOs are non-profit organizations. Their interests are political, rather than commercial, value-driven rather than market-oriented.

Second, the nature of the 'open source' in each case is somewhat different. 'Open source' in the case of private intelligence refers to the private or commercial nature of the service, a reference drawn in contrast to the closed sources of public or state intelligence agencies. 'Open source', when used in conjunction with citizen network intelligence, refers to a specific type of Internet technology – open source software.[57] Websites like IndyMedia and others depend on open source software as a crucial means of underpinning their distributed communications and information postings. Some go so far as to link the development of open source (or 'free' as it is also known) software with the protection of free speech on the Internet, an obviously critical component of network intelligence.[58]

IMPLICATIONS FOR TRADITIONAL STATE INTELLIGENCE

Citizen intelligence networks have already begun to transform the activities of international organizations and international negotiations, as mentioned above. But they will also increasingly impinge on the activities of traditional state intelligence agencies changing the environment in which they have operated until now. Most importantly, network intelligence puts an unprecedented bright spotlight on the activities of states and state intelligence agencies. Because of the activities and interests of network intelligence, states are caught in an increasingly intense and dispersed surveillance grid. The activities of FAS, alluded to earlier with respect to Internet tools, are a prime example. The FAS website provides a virtual compendium of resources on state weapons sales and manufacturing, intelligence operations and secrecy policy. One of the more remarkable aspects of the FAS site is the use of commercial satellite imagery of intelligence headquarters around the world, as well as weapons testing facilities and weapons systems. Another part of the site provides a point-and-click map of the US detailing weapons production by state.

Because of the activities of groups such as FAS, the secrecy of state intelligence may be increasingly difficult to support and sustain. Unlike the informal collusion often maintained by superpower intelligence agencies, citizen networks share no operating norms. On the contrary, citizen networks 'blow the lid' at every opportunity. The spread of information regarding the so-called 'Echelon' state surveillance network is a good example. However inaccurate or not the information may be, many citizen networks have thrived on the circulation of information concerning the signals intelligence capabilities and intelligence sharing arrangements among the US, UK, Canada, Australia and New Zealand. The hacktivist mailing list organized a 'jam Echelon day' on 21 October 1999 during which participants flooded the Internet with keywords meant to overwhelm the Echelon system.[59]

While it is unlikely the protest achieved anything beyond symbolism, the event certainly contributed to a greater public awareness of what had otherwise been a highly secretive system. Nor has the activity dissipated. In fact, dozens of sites now exist that provide information on the Echelon system, as well as its counterparts in other state intelligence agencies. At the American Civil Liberties Union Echelon Watch site, for example, there is detailed information on the surveillance networks operated by Russia, the People's Republic of China, Germany, Israel, France and India. There is also information about domestic surveillance networks, such as the US's Carnivore, the European Union's Enfopol system and others. There are resources with links to other like-minded organizations, and sections with prepared form letters to send to congressional representatives in the US to express concern about electronic eavesdropping.[60] What this suggests is that citizen network intelligence will make it difficult for states to operate in secrecy. It also suggests that a great deal of time and energy will be spent by intelligence agencies fighting public relations fires and enquiries from the media, politicians and concerned citizens. Far from omniscient high-tech machines, the 'future of intelligence' from this perspective makes states look more like naked emperors.

Because of their adversarial relationship, and because of the way in which many citizen activists are disruptive of the status quo, traditional state intelligence agencies will increasingly focus on citizen networks, as they have already to date.[61] For example, in a 2000 public report entitled, 'Anti-Globalization – A Spreading Phenomenon', the Canadian Security Intelligence Service (CSIS) warned of the growing threat of anti-capitalist and anti-corporate activism, a significant portion of which had demonstrated a potential for violence. The CSIS report went further to state that:

The Internet will continue to play a large role in the success or failure of globalization protests and demonstrations.Groups will use the Internet to identify and publicize targets, solicit and encourage support, organize and communicate information and instructions, recruit, raise funds, and as a means of promoting their various individual and collective aims. The Internet remains a major source of protest motivation and planning; it will require careful monitoring by conference planners to determine the intentions and goals of demonstrators, and to forestall unexpected incidents.[62]

One might surmise from the report that 'conference planners' are not the only ones who have a keen interest in monitoring citizen networks on the Internet. Yet penetrating and monitoring citizen networks is no simple matter. On the one hand, the way in which a great deal of information-sharing takes place over the open Internet puts citizen networks in a transparent light. Intelligence officers assigned to monitoring their planning and activities have actually benefited by their move to the Internet in this respect. On the other hand, however, there are reasons why citizen networks will present problems for state intelligence as an object of analysis. Monitoring the activities of citizen networks is not just a simple matter of turning Kremlinologists into Linux-ologists. Unlike the Soviet Union, the citizen network arena is a fast-paced one of constant change and technological innovation. More importantly, it is also one in which a concern for information security, hitherto largely ignored, is fast growing as outlined above. Paradoxically, the more that citizen networks are targeted by traditional state intelligence agencies the more the security of their information flows will harden, pushing citizen networks deeper into the subterranean layers of the Internet. So while the technology is making some of what citizen networks do increasingly transparent, it is also facilitating an avenue for more secure and impenetrable communications should citizen networks desire it.

There are additional constraints that have less to do with technology than regulations. Network intelligence is, by definition, multinational. Yet most state intelligence agencies operate within regulatory frameworks that prohibit collecting intelligence on their own citizens. How the information flows of citizen networks can be properly disaggregated and unbundled to respect such regulations is unclear given the boundary-less character of Internet websites, mailing lists and IRCs. There is a contradiction, in other words, between the operating procedures and the object of state intelligence – in this case, of citizen networks. Together these two constraints will make the job of monitoring citizen networks by state intelligence agencies an increasingly formidable task.

CONCLUSION

The explosion of new information and communication technologies has altered the environment of world politics in a myriad of ways over the past 20 years. Among the most important of these transformations is certainly the rise of transnational citizen networks. Although some theorists of world politics may remain skeptical about the significance of these movements as powerful or important actors, the evidence presented here suggests that they are only going to continue to expand and proliferate. Citizen networks are intensifying their linkages, burrowing deeper into the Internet to develop transnational webs of communication and organization. Fuelling this intensification has been the conjunction of forces that has occurred between NGOs and hackers – a cyclonic interaction that has propelled citizen networks from relatively marginal groups to sophisticated actors. Indicative of their increasing sophistication, citizen networks have employed the Internet to augment their intelligence capacity in a variety of innovative ways. This augmented capacity has provided the basis for the success and increasing power of citizen networks in a variety of world political arenas – success and power that seem destined to grow and expand.

Such a new form of non-state intelligence not only presents challenges for traditional state intelligence activities by putting their activities under an intense and distributed form of surveillance. More fundamentally, it begins to transform the very basis of the Westphalian state-system upon which the activities of state intelligence agencies rest. Dense, transnational networks of citizen activists weaving in and around the traditional structures of state interaction are part of a very different world from that with which most theorist practitioners of world politics are accustomed. It is a world in which states, while still theoretically sovereign, are in practice digitally embalmed and fiber-optically enshrouded. More than new threats or disintegrating states, it is this transformation of world order that presents the most important challenge for the future of intelligence.

NOTES

1. See, e.g., Rose Mary Sheldon, 'The Ancient Imperative: Clandestine Operations and Covert Action', *International Journal of Intelligence and Counterintelligence* 10/3 (Fall 1997) pp.299–315; Rose Mary Sheldon, 'Spying in Mesopotamia', *Studies in Intelligence* 33/1 (Spring 1989) pp.7–12; and Francis Dvornik, *Origins of Intelligence Services: The Ancient Near East, Persia, Greece, Rome, Byzantium, the Arab Muslim Empires, the Mongol Empire, China, Muscovy* (New Brunswick, NJ: Rutgers UP 1974).
2. For an analysis that explores these characteristics with a special focus on satellite reconnaissance, see William E. Burrows, *Deep Black: Space Espionage and National Security* (NY: Random House 1986). For a more general account focusing on the US, see Daniel Moynihan and Richard Gid Powers, *Secrecy: The American Experience* (New Haven, CT: Yale UP 1998).

3. This is not to say that studies of the future of intelligence ignore non-state actors. Contrarily, terrorist groups and criminal organizations are now considered primary foci of intelligence operations. But it is the intelligence organizations of *states* that are under consideration, rather than those of non-state actors.

4. In this essay, I use the term 'citizen networks' to cover those groups that are also known in the literature on world politics as non-governmental organizations, civil society networks and transnational social movements. For general studies and definitional discussions of these phenomenon, see Ronnie Lipschutz, 'Reconstructing World Politics: The Emergence of Global Civil Society', *Millennium: Journal of International Studies* 21/3 (1992) pp.398–420; Leslie Paul Thiele, 'Making Democracy Safe for the World: Social Movements and Global Politics', *Alternatives: Social Transformation and Humane Governance* 18/3 (Summer 1993); Robert Cox, 'Civil Society at the Turn of the Millennium: Prospects for an Alternative World Order', *Review of International Studies* 25/1 (Jan. 1999) pp.3–28; Jessica Matthews, 'Power Shift', *Foreign Affairs* 76/1 (Jan./Feb. 1997) pp.50–66; Daniele Archibugi, David Held and Martin Kohler (eds.), *Re-Imaging Political Community* (Stanford UP 1998); and David Rieff and Michael Clough, 'Civil Society and the Future of the Nation-State: Two Views', *The Nation*, 22 Feb. 1999.

5. In my *Parchment, Printing, and Hypermedia: Communication in World Order Transformation* (NY: Columbia UP 1997), I explore some of the ways in which citizen networks are flourishing because of new information and communication technologies.

6. Although beyond the scope of this paper, the language of 'symbiosis', 'niche' and 'ecology' is evocative of an evolutionary theoretical approach to social change – what I have elsewhere referred to as an 'ecologist holist' approach. See Ronald J. Deibert, 'Harold Innis and the Empire of Speed', *Review of International Studies* 25/2 (April 1999) for an extended discussion. See also P. A. Corning, *The Synergism Hypothesis: A Theory of Progressive Evolution* (NY: McGraw Hill 1983).

7. See Ethan A. Nadelman, 'Global Prohibition Regimes: The Evolution of Norms in International Society', *International Organization* 44/4 (Autumn 1990) pp.479–526. As Nadelman points out, 'The British and Foreign Anti-Slavery Society thus represented perhaps the first transnational moral entrepreneur – religious movements aside – to play a significant role in world politics generally and in the evolution of a global prohibition regime specifically' (p.495).

8. The Red Cross was formed after the Battle of Solferino in 1859. See 'Sins of the Secular Missionairies', *The Economist*, 29 Jan. 2000.

9. For a good historical overview of the rise of NGOs, see Lipshutz, 'Reconstructing World Politics' (note 4). The term 'non-governmental organization' was first applied to citizen groups during the creation of the UN. NGOs have been involved with the UN ever since.

10. Kathryn Sikkink, 'Human Rights, Principled Issue-networks, and Sovereignty in Latin America', *International Organization* 47 (Summer 1993) p.418.

11. C. Gerard Fraser, 'Taking NGOs and Activists Seriously', *Earth Times*, 24 Aug. 2000.

12. See the statistics collected at the Union of International Associations website, <www.uia.org/uiastats/stybv296.htm#1909>.

13. Fraser, 'Taking NGOs and Activists Seriously' (note 11).

14. See Paul Wapner, 'Politics Beyond the State: Environmental Activism and World Civic Politics', *World Politics* 47/3 (April 1995) pp.311–40, for a good overview of the growing importance of these movements and of the way they have exploited the hypermedia environment to further their interests.

15. Peter Spiro, 'New Global Communities: NGO Organizations in International Decision-Making Institutions', *Washington Quarterly* 18/1 (Winter 1999) p.49 of pp.45–56.

16. Of course many are 'single issue' interest groups – a characteristic that brings NGOs some criticism. For discussion, see Michael Bond, 'The Backlash Against NGOs', *Prospect Magazine*, April 2000.

17. Consultations with NGOs have become more common as the pressure from citizen networks increases. Some 2,500 NGOs participated in the 52nd annual DPI-NGO Conference at the UN, a grand consultation of sorts that featured NGOs, states and corporations. See the website, <www.un.org/MoreInfo/ngolink/52conf.htm>.

18. Anne Thompson Feraru, 'Transnational Political Interest: Global Environment', *International Organization* 28/1 (Winter 1974) p.39.

19. To give just one illustration, Greenpeace Canada notes on its website that 'Greenpeace is an independent not-for-profit campaigning organization that uses nonviolent, creative confrontation to expose global environmental problems...Working with international experts, we conduct scientific, economic and political research, publicize environmentally sound solutions and lobby for change.' Greenpeace's self-description would be one that most other NGOs around the world share.

20. For a good detailed overview of the character of citizen networks, see Margaret Keck and Kathryn Sikkink, *Activists Beyond Borders: Advocacy Networks in International Politics* (Ithaca, NY: Cornell UP 1998).

21. Feraru, "Transnational Political Interest: Global Enviroment' (note 18) provides a good historical perspective on these constraints.

22. The forming of transnational citizen networks is no simple matter. Even though the Internet and cheaper transportation has greatly facilitated their activities, as the topic of this essay exemplifies, there are still numerous constraints. For a good overview of these many constraints, see Sidney Tarrow, 'Beyond Globalization: Why Creating Transnational Social Movements is So Hard and When is it Most Likely to Happen', <www.antenna.nl/ ~waterman/tarrow.html>.

23. For a good historical overview, see S. Levy, *Hackers: Heroes of the Computer Revolution* (NY:Anchor Press/Doubleday 1984).

24. A good history of computer technology enthusiasts with a focus on the early development of the Internet is found in Katie Hafner and Matthew Lyon, *Where Wizards Stay Up Late: The Origins of the Internet* (NY: Simon & Schuster 1996).

25. See Eric Raymond, *The Cathedral and the Bazaar*, <www.tuxedo.org/~esr/writings/ cathedral-bazaar/>.

26. See <www.defcon.org/>.

27. For discussion, see Douglas Thomas, 'The Politics of Hacking', *Online Journalism Review*, 16 Sept. 1998, <http://ojr.usc.edu/content/story.cfm?request=70>.

28. The entry for 'politics' in the popular *New Hacker's Dictionary* describes hacker politics as being: 'Vaguely liberal-moderate, except for the strong libertarian contingent which rejects conventional left-right politics entirely. The only safe generalization is that hackers tend to be rather anti-authoritarian; thus, both conventional conservatism and "hard" leftism are rare. Hackers are far more likely than most non-hackers to either (a) be aggressively apolitical or (b) entertain peculiar or idiosyncratic political ideas and actually try to live by them day-to-day'. Found online at <www.logophilia.com/jargon/jargon_59.html>.

29. See Harold Innis, *Empire and Communication* (Univ. of Toronto Press 1950).

30. For a different interpretation of hacktivism, see Dorothy Denning, 'Activism, Hacktivism, and Cyberterrorism', paper prepared for the Nautilus Institute, Dec. 1999, <www. nautilus.org;/info-policy/workshop/papers/denning.html>. While I find the empirical portion of Denning's article illuminating, her definition of 'hacktivism' is misleading, employing the typical law enforcement practice of associating hacking with criminal activities – an association that not only ignores the history of hacking but the positive potential of hacking as a tool for legitimate citizen activism. I prefer the term 'cracking' for criminal activities directed at or through computer networks.

31. A good history of the member networks that formed the APC can be found in Susanne Sallin 'A Case Study Prepared' of the Harvard-CIESN Project on Global Environmental Change Information Policy, 14 Feb. 1994. The Association for Progressive Communications: A Cooperative Effort to Meet the Information Needs of Non-Governmental Organizations, at: <www://ftp.ciesin.org/kiosk/publications/94-0010.txt>.

32. See a brief history of the APC at <www.apc.org/english/about/history/index.htm>.

33. The APC mission statement is at <www.apc.org/english/about/mission/index.htm>.

34. Rory O'Brien and Andrew Clement, 'The Association for Progressive Communications and the Networking of Global Civil Society: APC at the 1992 Earth Summit', <www.apc.org/english/about/history/rio_92.htm>.

35. Ibid.

36. Shelley Preston, 'Electronic Global Networking and the NGO Movement: the 1992 Rio Summit and Beyond', *Swords and Ploughshares: A Chronicle of International Affairs* 3/2 (Spring 1994), <www.stile.lut.ac.uk/%7Egyedb/STILE/Email0002089/m12.html>.
37. Developing countries of course suffer most from indiscriminate landmining.
38. Jody Williams and Stephen Goose, 'The International Campaign to Ban Landmines', in Maxwell A. Cameron, Robert J. Lawson and Brian W. Tomlin (eds.), *To Walk Without Fear: The Global Movement to Ban Landmines* (Toronto: OUP 1998).
39. Richard Price, 'Reversing the Insights: Civil Society Targets Landmines', *International Organization* 52/3 (Summer 1998) pp.613–44.
40. See Ronald J. Deibert, 'International Plug n' Play? Citizen Activism, the Internet, and Global Public Policy', *International Studies Perspectives* 1 (2000) pp.255–72.
41. As cited in Madeline Drohan, 'How the Net Killed the MAI', *Global Mail*, 29 April 1998.
42. World Wide Web pages serve the same notification function as do listserves. For a good example from the Australian context, see 'The International Week of Action Against the MAI' and other notices at <www.avid.net.au/stopmai/>.
43. For example, on the MAI-NOT listserv from Wednesday 5 May 1999 to Friday 9 April 1999, there were 597 postings by 57 people. The MAI-NOT listserv statistics were available on <http://mai.flora.org/>.
44. The Australian STOP MAI coalition set up a list that attracted 400 subscribers. Richard Sanders, who headed the coalition, said that the list worked as a 'network of networks'. In other words, the elite of the groups involved in the STOP MAI coalition would pass on information from the list to their own individual grassroots memberships. Interview, 17 Aug. 1999.
45. See, e.g., the detailed list of Members of the House of Commons of the 36th Parliament, at <**http://mai.flora.org/mai-info/mps-list.htm**>, and the mailing addresses of the members of the US House of Representatives at <http://mai.flora.org/mai-info/hor-mems.htm>.
46. For an example of a sample letter opposing the MAI to be sent to a Representative or Senator, see <www.citizen.org/pctrade/mai/What%20you/congrs.html>. For an example of a letter opposing the MAI that could be sent by email to the Australian Parliament directly from the website, see <www.avid.net.au/stopmai/letter/>. For a sample of Canadian letters to MPs, see <http://mai.flora.org/mai-info/letters.htm#1>.
47. See <www.citizen.org/pctrade/mai/What%20you/city.htm>.
48. Found at <www.fas.org/cp/>.
49. See, e.g., the TAO website on Internet security at <http://security.tao.ca/>.
50. The main website is at <http://global.indymedia.org.au/>, but there one can find links to the 28 independent organizations located around the world.
51. Brendan Koener, 'To Heck with Hacktivism', *Salon.com*, 20 July 2000, <http://salon.com/tech/feature/2000/07/20/hacktivism/index.html>.
52. See <www.thing.net/~rdom/ecd/ecd.html>.
53. Denning, 'Activism, Hacktivism, and Cyberterrorism' (note 30). Denning sees the work of the EDT as illegitimate and probably criminal. I see it in a more charitable light, obviously.
54. The Central Intelligence Agency website provides an overview of its view of the 'intelligence cycle'. See <www.odci.gov/cia/publications/facttell/intcycle.htm>.
55. Some citizen network email lists are moderated and even IndyMedia sites have requirements to screen publications.
56. For discussion, see Robert Steele and Mark M. Lowenthal, 'Open Source Intelligence: Private Sector Capabilities to Support DoD Policy, Acquisitions, and Operations', <www.fas.org/irp/eprint/ oss980501.htm>.
57. See <www.opensource.org/>.
58. See, e.g., Richard Stallman, 'Why Software Should be Free', <www.gnu.org/philosophy/ shouldbefree.html>. See also the OpenCode project, organized by the Harvard Berkman Center for Internet and Society, <http://cyber.law.harvard.edu/projects/opencode.html>.
59. For details, see <www.echelon.wiretapped.net/>.
60. See <www.aclu.org/echelonwatch/highlights.html>.

61. A Danish newspaper, *Ekstra Bladet*, reported that the Red Cross was targeted for surveillance by the Echelon network and in particular by US Air Force intelligence, a charge that was neither confirmed nor denied by the US Air Force. For discussion, see <http://abcnews.go.com/sections/world/DailyNews/spying000331.html>.

62. 'Anti-Globalization – A Spreading Phenomenon', Canadian Security Intelligence Service Report #2000/08, 22 Aug. 2000, <www.csis-scrs.gc.ca/eng/miscdocs/200008e.html>.

INDEX

Lightning Source UK Ltd.
Milton Keynes UK
09 September 2009

143517UK00001B/61/A